EASTERN FRONT
COMBAT

The Stackpole Military History Series

THE AMERICAN CIVIL WAR
Cavalry Raids of the Civil War
Ghost, Thunderbolt, and Wizard
Pickett's Charge
Witness to Gettysburg

WORLD WAR II
Armor Battles of the Waffen-SS, 1943–45
Army of the West
Australian Commandos
The B-24 in China
Backwater War
The Battle of Sicily
Beyond the Beachhead
The Brandenburger Commandos
The Brigade
Bringing the Thunder
Coast Watching in World War II
Colossal Cracks
A Dangerous Assignment
D-Day to Berlin
Dive Bomber!
A Drop Too Many
Eagles of the Third Reich
Eastern Front Combat
Exit Rommel
Fist from the Sky
Flying American Combat Aircraft
  of World War II
Forging the Thunderbolt
Fortress France
The German Defeat in the East, 1944–45
German Order of Battle, Vol. 1
German Order of Battle, Vol. 2
German Order of Battle, Vol. 3
The Germans in Normandy
Germany's Panzer Arm in World War II
GI Ingenuity
The Great Ships
Grenadiers
Infantry Aces
Iron Arm
Iron Knights
Kampfgruppe Peiper at the Battle
  of the Bulge
Kursk
Luftwaffe Aces

Massacre at Tobruk
Mechanized Juggernaut or Military
  Anachronism?
Messerschmitts over Sicily
Michael Wittmann, Vol. 1
Michael Wittmann, Vol. 2
Mountain Warriors
The Nazi Rocketeers
On the Canal
Operation Mercury
Packs On!
Panzer Aces
Panzer Aces II
Panzer Commanders of the Western Front
The Panzer Legions
Panzers in Winter
The Path to Blitzkrieg
Retreat to the Reich
Rommel's Desert Commanders
Rommel's Desert War
The Savage Sky
A Soldier in the Cockpit
Soviet Blitzkrieg
Stalin's Keys to Victory
Surviving Bataan and Beyond
T-34 in Action
Tigers in the Mud
The 12th SS, Vol. 1
The 12th SS, Vol. 2
The War against Rommel's Supply Lines
War in the Aegean

THE COLD WAR / VIETNAM
Cyclops in the Jungle
Flying American Combat Aircraft:
  The Cold War
Here There Are Tigers
Land with No Sun
Street without Joy
Through the Valley

WARS OF THE MIDDLE EAST
Never-Ending Conflict

GENERAL MILITARY HISTORY
Carriers in Combat
Desert Battles
Guerrilla Warfare

EASTERN FRONT COMBAT

The German Soldier in Battle from Stalingrad to Berlin

Edited by Hans Wijers

STACKPOLE
BOOKS

Published by
STACKPOLE BOOKS
5067 Ritter Road
Mechanicsburg, PA 17055
www.stackpolebooks.com

Cover design by Tracy Patterson

Printed in the United States of America

10 9 8 7 6 5 4 3 2 1

FIRST EDITION

Library of Congress Cataloging-in-Publication Data

Eastern Front combat : the German soldier in battle from Stalingrad to Berlin / edited by Hans Wijers. — 1st ed.
p. cm. — (Stackpole military history series)
Includes index.
ISBN 978-0-8117-3442-4
1. World War, 1939–1945—Campaigns—Eastern Front. 2. World War, 1939–1945—Personal narratives, German. I. Wijers, Hans J.

D764.E23 2008
940.54'13430922—dc22

2008017303

This book is dedicated to the one person in my life
who gave me the strength to do this. Thanks, SP.

Table of Contents

Introduction

This book of combat narratives contains accounts from German soldiers who fought on the Eastern Front against Russia between 1941 and 1945 in World War II. The stories have been put together to give you, the reader, a sense of what it was like to live, fight, and die in the war's greatest battles.

I've been interviewing German veterans for years and compiling their accounts covering nearly all the battles of World War II. These veterans, some aged close to ninety now, are still willing to talk about the past. The soldiers telling their stories here are just a few of the lucky ones that survived the war when millions of their countrymen did not.

From the Battle of Stalingrad to the bitter end in Berlin in 1945, these men tell their story as they experienced it. What they have to say is not about glory and heroism, but of life and death, and how they survived. I knew each of these veterans personally, and knowing that their accounts will live on in this book is important. The war on the Eastern Front was a different battle from the one fought in the West, and the harshness of the last battles became more than simply stopping the enemy, but defending their homeland, the soil they were born on, the house they lived in, their parents, and their families.

One of these veterans is Joachim Stempel, a survivor of Stalingrad and many long years in Russian captivity. There is also the story of Ernst Panse, another Stalingrad veteran, providing his perspective on the desperate fighting from inside the Stalingrad pocket. The account of Alfred Regeniter of the 276th Assault Gun Brigade gives more details about how fierce the fighting on the Eastern Front could be, even when protected in an armored assault gun firing high explosives. Gerd Döhler describes the futile defense on the Oder River in 1945 in the face of a massive Russian attack, holding out with a handful of sixteen-year-olds—*Luftwaffen Helfer*—knowing that any victory would be only a temporary one. There are also accounts from the final days in Berlin, the German capital, where some soldiers still believed that the *Wunderwaffen*—Wonder Weapons— promised by Hitler would help them turn the tide. It was a vain hope.

This book is about the Eastern Front. When you read these stories, you'll learn again that war is humanity's most terrible affliction. For those that were there, the memories remain, even to this day.

Hans J. Wijers

CHAPTER 1

The 24th Panzer Division at Stalingrad

Ernst Panse

In this report, I'd like to explain how my unit—the 9th Company, 3rd Battalion, 24th Panzer Division (field post number 11468)—was ordered to intervene in the encirclement battle of Stalingrad in the area of Kalach on the Don and how we experienced the bitter end on February 2, 1943, with the surrender of Stalingrad.

With my memoir of the Stalingrad cauldron, whose end had major repercussions for the remainder of the Second World War, I wanted to make clear how horrible war becomes when the orders are to hold on and hold out to the last breath. As a simple soldier, a private first class and radioman in the tank of the commander of 9th Company, I experienced what men can survive in 20 to 30 degrees of frost and an icy steppe wind—for two and a half months with daily rations of only 100 grams of bread, 60 grams of meat or fat, six cigarettes, half a liter of tea or coffee, and, if it was available, half a liter of horse meat soup. I want to explain the horrors of war, in which thousands of men are killed, frozen to death, starved, or devoured by lice.

My personal experiences in the war made me very philosophical in life because I asked myself, "What is the purpose of this horrible shedding of blood? What is the purpose of these horrors the survivors had to experience before they found peace at home after the war?" I did not see one soldier who gave his life out of enthusiasm for Führer and country, but all of them fought for their lives until the last. Death kept hundreds

Ernst Panse.

of thousands from going home. Their bones fill mass graves in and around Stalingrad. Even today, thousands of people are still listed as missing. Even today, family members mourn their dead.

LOOKING BACK ON THE STALINGRAD "CAULDRON"

On November 22, 1942, the "cauldron" began. Our unit, the 9th Company of the 24th Panzer Division, was pulled out of the battles in Stalingrad to be refreshed ninety kilometers to the west in the rear areas. The big losses of men and materiel made this necessary. We were billeted at the State Sovchoze Krepp on a small hill in the Don Steppe. Certainly, there wasn't much produced here except oats, barley, and grain. But there was water in the shape of a small lake and several sources in the village, which consisted of about thirty houses that had been scattered about the area. Furthermore, there was a first-aid post and a big, beautiful school in which the 3rd Platoon was billeted. For the first time in a long time, we had the chance to make ourselves a bit comfortable. Apart from a daily company roll call and guard duties, we had no jobs to do. We used this opportunity to get a thorough clean-up and to catch up on our letter writing.

The local population consisted of Kolchoz farmers, but even more of refugees, which had come from the area of the Ukraine. The houses were billeted to capacity, even more as some houses had to be evacuated for our soldiers. The civilians capable of work were compelled to help with the digging in of our vehicles by our unit. In the hard steppe soil, this was no easy task. For this they got a warm midday meal and cold ration everyday. Why dig in the vehicles? For starters it was a protection against bombing, and second, we wanted to spend the winter here. At that time we did not know things would turn out differently. We made a lively use of the sauna and the shower, and our dirty laundry was washed, ironed, and repaired by women and girls from the village. In exchange for that, from time to time we would give them a tin of conserved goods, bread, or chocolate, whatever we still had at this time. In political discussions all Russians, however, clung to their views that Stalin would win the war instead of Hitler. The presence of our Servicing Company on the Kolchoz was very valuable. Day by day we worked diligently to prepare the tanks for battle. Here we received some new reinforcements in combat techniques and men.

Days and weeks passed by. We felt good and would have preferred to wait here for the end of the war. The tanks were combat-ready again. In this time, there were some transfers within the tank crew. As radioman of the platoon commander, I bade farewell to Lieutenant Höfel and had to mount up with company commander Capt. Cuno von Meyer. I was not pleased with this higher assignment, but it was an order. But until the end, we got along well together.

At a roll call on November 15, all technical equipment was checked for readiness. I had the job of checking all the radios, aligning the frequencies, and subsequently reporting about their readiness. Four days passed.

On November 21, seventeen operational tanks were allotted to their crews. They were given full loads of ammunition and gas. A radio check was carried out, and everything was aligned. We now started to grow tense because we suspected a new battle. Everyone had to take care of their private effects, like laundry or mail. Extra rations were received; the iron rations were renewed. So something was definitely in the wind.

We were informed at a company briefing that we were to leave Krepp the next day at 8:00 A.M. In the afternoon, the company commander returned from the regimental staff. In a subsequent briefing—which I attended as main radioman—we were sworn to silence and informed that the Russians had assembled heavy forces, including armor, in the Kalmuck steppe and were about to threaten our left flank. Our objective for the next day's march would be Kalach on the Don, about eighty kilometers away. From there, other orders came. Everyone split up in silence. In the evening, I collected my laundry from the laundry maid, who was saddened by our sudden departure. I had brought her a few tins of bread and chocolate. I slept very badly during this last night; the days to come would be similarly insecure.

At 6:00 A.M. on the dot the next morning, we were awakened, drank our coffee, and quickly ate a few slices of bread. At 7:00, we were ordered to dismiss, and we mounted the vehicles, which had already been warmed up. All the tank commanders were called to see the company commander one last time. I ordered radio tests; everything worked. Then the call came to mount up. "Company march!" At 8:00, we left our beautiful quarters. The dawn was foggy and murky; it was five degrees, and there was a little snow. The majority of our workshop company remained as several tanks and trucks were in need of repairs. These men were placed under Lieutenant Höfel with orders to follow as soon as possible.

In our column, there were seventeen tanks: ten Panzer IIs with 5cm short-barreled and long-barreled guns; five Panzer IVs, of which four had 75mm short-barreled guns and one had a 75mm long-barreled gun (our most penetrating one); and two 5cm short-barreled guns, which were company commander's vehicles with additional radio equipment. I was in one of these with the company commander. In addition to this operational combat unit, there were also the necessary supply vehicles.

We made good progress in the beginning, but the snowdrifts became more and more dense. In the Rachels or Balkas, which are ravines that are often found in the Don steppe, dangerous skidding occurred. Some of these ravines were so big that we could not drive around them but had to cross these seemingly insurmountable obstacles in one way or another. With a delay of two hours, we reached our objective, Kalach. In a briefing, we learned that the first Russian armored units had reached the outskirts of Kalach but had withdrawn after a short firefight.

Our unit received its orders for the next day. We radiomen got new encrypted radio documents with specific orders not to let them fall into enemy hands. After a short evening meal of bread in our warm hut, we stretched out and slept without tak-

ing our clothes off. By morning, it was quite cold. Disorder set
in when some artillery shells were heard detonating outside;
tanks guns also intervened. Without food or drink, we rushed
out to the vehicles, whose engines warmed up quickly. Off we
went to the action.

Our task was to secure the southern edge of the town with
our tanks. As the company commander's tank, we looked for
a point from which we could keep an eye on all three platoons. But we soon found out that our location was very insufficient for radio communications; a big power line strongly
influenced the operations of the radio, and we had to change
position. Although the radio communications improved dra-
matically, we lost visual contact with our 1st Platoon and could
keep in touch only via the wireless. Every thirty minutes, the
platoon commanders had to report in on their position and
situation. Oberfeldwebel Frenzel of 1st Platoon had to secure a
wooden bridge that crossed a stream like the Unstrut, though
it was devoid of water. This bridge was to be secured only from
the eastern side and not crossed in a westerly direction. The
reports that came in brought nothing new for the first two
hours. Then all of a sudden, there was a message from 1st Platoon: "On the western side, large Russian cavalry units are
approaching. I'm crossing." That was his last report. For us, he
was no longer useable. Both of the other platoons could withdraw by evening without any bigger fighting.

A report from Oberfeldwebel Frenzel, which reached us
before Christmas in the cauldron, contained the following
description:

> According to my estimation of the position on the east-
> ern bank of the bridge, I could not undertake any
> viable action against the cavalry. I gave the order to
> cross and in this way I got into the flank of the cavalry,
> which had not seen us properly yet. We opened fire
> from all barrels and forced the cavalry to turn away
> with heavy losses. Suddenly eight T-34s appeared in
> front of us and opened fire immediately. This uneven

battle ended very quickly despite our defense. In about five minutes, all five of our tanks were killed and burned. Of the twenty-five men in the crews, only five managed to save themselves; all the rest were dead. The five of us each searched out a wandering horse from the cavalrymen and made ourselves scarce. At dusk, in ever increasing snowdrifts, we reached the first German infantry units. There we were debriefed and sent to the rear.

He also gave us the names of the men who had survived the ride. At the end, he added that Lieutenant Höfel also had managed to get away and reach German lines with two German tanks and several trucks after having spent the night in a Russian column. Furthermore, two days after our departure from Krepp, Russian units were reported to have entered it. That was the beginning of the Stalingrad cauldron.

BITTER TIMES

The battle of encirclement hardly had begun when we felt the mighty pressure of the Red Army. We soon found out that the Russians had planned to turn the tide and stop us once and for all. We did not like the reinforced appearances of the T-34s since we knew that these were far superior to our tanks in fighting technology. A direct hit on our Panzer IIs or Panzer IVs would enter at the front and exit at the rear. The only one that could defend against the T-34s was our Panzer IV with the 75mm long-barreled gun. But this applied only to the strength of the gun; with regard to the strength of our armor, it was still far inferior. This unequal battle now had to be waged day after day. Our only relief was that not all bullets and shells hit their mark.

We had to leave Kalach, a small steppe city on the Don, to the enemy after a few days. The Russians pressured us with far more powerful units, especially tanks with mounted infantry. From this time on, only the bald steppe was our home. Sharp icy winds blew day after day in our faces. The snow was still bearable in its amounts, but with storms and sharp winds, it became a hell. At this time, I often thought of our infantrymen, who had to endure this hell in holes dug in the snow or in the ground; because of the continuous movement of the front, there were no prepared positions. In our tanks, we still had a roof over our head. But none of us had any winter clothing. When we were moving about in the daytime, it was somewhat warm in the fighting compartment, but during the night, it was unbearably cold, although we wrapped up in any blanket available. At that time, we did not have any heating in our tanks. Our driver, Alfons Bartsch, had organized a heating lamp, which did excellent service for us five men everyday.

Our daily fighting took place as if we were the fire department. Wherever there was action at the front, we were sent into it. This inevitably cost us men and materiel. Of the seventeen tanks we carried into action, only eight were left, and these looked mightily run down. The so-called rubbage bin at the turret looked like a sieve. It contained our personal effects like blankets, overcoats, cooking utensils, and materials with which to wash and clean up. The track covers all had been damaged to some extent and hung there like rags. The water-collection tube had been shot off my bow MG, and the daily-thaw water ran into my ball mounting. Every morning, I had to thaw it out from the inside with our heat lamp in order to be able to fight. That always was very pleasing because of the heat generated, even when our nasal orifices turned black.

After only a week, the Red Army had closed the ring around Stalingrad so tightly that there was no way out. The supply of the encircled 6th Army under Colonel General von Paulus from now on was carried out by Ju52 and Ju90 airplanes. From this moment onward, the supplies of the troops changed radically. After two weeks, the entire army was put on half rations and after that on one-quarter rations. This meant that every soldier daily received only 100 grams of bread, 60 grams of meat or fat, and, if available, a soup of dehydrated vegetables or horse meat. These rations contributed to the rapid weakening of the fighting power of the troops. Icy winds, snowdrifts, no roof overhead, and an empty stomach—all of that affected strength for combat. Only the fear of the Russians and captivity sustained our fighting morale to some extent.

In the meantime, December had come. The cauldron grew smaller and smaller as the Russians pressed in from all sides. The slogan "Hold on, Manstein is coming!" became the only hope for the encircled men. But nothing came of this. There were heaps of wounded, frozen men, and dead. There were 350,000 men in the cauldron: how many will be left of them today? Then all of a sudden, there was a new variation, a new glimmer of hope. There was talk that on the road over the Don heights, heavy units, tanks, artillery, and motorized infantrymen had been assembled in order to try a breakout from within. Something moved in these directions. At the time our small group was assembled, we were in the area of Pitomnik and Karpowka. When we passed a stream with a wooden bridge in our advance toward the road over the Don heights, we noticed a sign on which was written, "Berlin 3600 km?"

When we arrived at our objective on a large plain, there were hundreds of vehicles standing around. This first day in the assembly area brought nothing. On the second day, a mighty tank battle developed in the afternoon. In the meantime, Russian tank units had reached our assembly area. At this point, we were so strong, however, that we could decide the battle in our favor. We stood about three kilometers to the west and had little influence on the outcome of the battle. Suddenly to our left, there was a series of detonations, and twenty-five pillars of smoke rose straight into the sky. A short while later, six trucks (Opel Blitz) with aircrews mounted showed up in front of our positions. The aircrews had blown up their aircraft on the German front airfield, as the Russians were overrunning it with their tank columns as well. There was no more time to take off.

The third day was quiet again, and everyone was waiting for the order to break out. This breakout hit a snag; all motorized units could and should take part in the breakout with the condition that the infantry units were to remain in the cauldron. In this large assembly area from which the breakout was to be launched, aircraft were constantly landing and taking out wounded soldiers; at the same time, they were bringing in war materiel like shells, ammunition, fuel, and food. By noon, all commanders had to report to the staff, and we believed that we would get orders for the operation. After an hour and a half, we were told that Paulus had returned from OKW with the order to hold the cauldron at all costs, as the Caucasus army would be cut off otherwise. We all made long faces because now all we had were our hopes for Manstein to keep us going.

Everybody on the road on the Don heights now scattered, and we also were pulled off for new fire service operations. For this purpose, the next morning we were ordered to get briefed at the staff. With our tank, the only runner, we drove to the general. His bunker (there were several) also was located in the steppe. A double sentry asked for our assignment. The company commander identified himself and went into the command post. We also climbed out of our tank and had a look at the area. In the rising sun between two bunkers, we noticed a giant pile of complete winter suits. Unnoticed by the sentries who were making their rounds, we carried out a brief fitting. Apart from the boots, everything went quickly. When we tried to return to the tank with our valuable booty, the sentries noticed us. But we did not follow the order to bring everything back, and when an officer arrived and repeated this order, we did not obey it right away. The guard was immediately alerted and threatened with a loaded and locked machine pistol. A short discussion with the officer did not bring any success, so we all were very bitter about it. Later, we learned that two days later a Russian tank force found this area, and the Germans burned these precious goods before fleeing. Since even our company commander could do nothing about it, we returned to our unit with our operations order.

In the meantime, we had only six operational tanks left. Units of the Romanian Army, which were operating in the southern part of the Kalmuck steppe, had been overrun and beaten back by the Red Army. This entire army was reeling back in blind panic. The German Army command tried to plug this gap by shoving in German troops. This included our unit with six tanks, which was to be ready to march in ninety minutes. We don't know what awaits us there. The distance we had to travel would be about forty kilometers. The weather was cold, 22 degrees below zero, with icy winds and snowdrifts from time to time. For the first twenty-five kilometers, everything went well, but then the snowdrifts increased, and the road markers could barely be made out. Now and then, there was a tactical sign that indicated which units were in this area.

Suddenly, horse-powered Romanian units showed up in front of us. Here one truly could say, "Man and horse and wagon—the Russian has beaten them." The first ones still tried to clear the road for us, but as we advanced, nobody did that anymore. Judging by their equipment, this unit was incapable of stopping the heavily armored units of the Red Army. The time passed, and it became progressively darker; our company commander ordered a halt. There were two reasons for this: first, we could not wage a battle by night, and second, there was the danger in the chaos of the cauldron of suddenly finding ourselves in a Russian sector of the front. Over the radio, we formed a hedgehog position, and guards were posted for the night. Our "911" took the first watch from 8:00 to 10:00. The night was relatively quiet, apart from the flares, which generally marked the course of the front line. There was no contact with the enemy. We found out that we still were several kilometers from the main line of resistance. There was nothing to eat anymore, as we had already consumed our daily ration of one slice of bread and sixty grams of conserved meat in the afternoon. But we made do with one bottle of diluted rum that we still had. This was not very much for five men. We quickly rolled ourselves in our blankets and slept until dawn.

By morning, there was mighty artillery and machine-gun fire, and everyone was ready for battle immediately. By radio, we were all ordered to load our special shells in case we bumped into T-34s. There was no food or drink, and we moved out straightaway. After a short drive, we found out that the T-34s had made a mess of it all. We not only ran into Romanians but also scattered groups of German infantry who were exhorted to turn around by our company commander. Seeing our six tanks, they followed us; some rode on top of the tanks. We still had half an hour's drive before we made contact with the enemy. The Russians here didn't have T-34s, but they had antitank guns. The infantry had to dismount, and it started. We fired some rounds from our guns and our machine guns. As we fired, we discovered that the gun of our Panzer III ejected the shell only halfway. Therefore, we had to pull out the rest by hand; it was very hot. This was a powerful obstacle to our fighting power.

By midday, we reached the actual main line of resistance without major contacts with the enemy. About 500 meters in front of us was a thick hedgerow in which the Russian infantry had dug in. We were in a small ravine so that our tank had cover but a bad field of fire. Our company commander contacted the staff of our resident infantry in order to prepare a common attack. Suddenly, there was a mighty roar of engines, and out of the hedgerow, a T-34 burst forth. Now we were shocked and expected more. But nothing happened. With his barrel threateningly pointed in our direction, the T-34 drove down his sector of the front line. After about a kilometer, it turned around and drove back provocatively, without firing a round. After an hour, it showed up to do the same maneuver again. It certainly was his objective to lure our firepower, but we did not do him the favor. In the meantime, it had become 3:00 P.M., and this provocative ride had been repeated several times without any success.

Then it was decided that this position had to fall before the onset of darkness. Two men of each tank crew had to disembark with a machine gun to reinforce the infantry in their positions. Three men remained in each tank with the guns, and I was ordered by our company commander to drive back to the repair shop with our driver to have the gun fixed. My boss, Wilhelm Hermes, and Herbert Schwertner remained with the infantry. I was really pleased with this decision, since it meant I would have a roof over my head.

AN OBSTACLE RIDE

The drive was far from simple. According to the advice of our boss, we only needed to concentrate on the tactical sign of our unit to arrive. (These signs showed a fence with a horse jumping over it.) So we moved off. I stood in the turret, and we communicated over the internal radio. But already the first decision was difficult, as our tactical sign pointed away from the main road, but we followed the direction. After a drive of several kilometers, we saw a small village in front of us in a valley. It was about 4:00 P.M., and it already was getting dark. In front of the village and to the right, a single house stood, and as we approached, we saw flames rising up from the rear of the house. Two "chained dogs" (military police) were standing guard there. Our first thought was that we can get something here. So we made for the house and dismounted.

The chained dogs told us to move on, but we had become curious as we could see cases and boxes in the burning part of the house. We tried to enter the house, but the chained dogs did not allow it. But should we leave all to the flames? So we mounted our tanks, went into reverse, and collapsed the old block house. The flames got air, and we got the schnapps, cigarettes, chocolate, and English biscuits—a rich booty. The chained dogs meanwhile had concluded that we were not to be trifled with since our driver, Alfons, had threatened to use his weapon. Now we loaded up whatever our tank could carry—four boxes with twenty-five bottles of schnapps each, five boxes of 500 tablets of chocolate each, several thousand cigarettes, and three boxes of biscuits. We had become fully unfit for battle, and we were conscious of having done a punishable deed. But we had taken the booty not only for ourselves, but also for the entire unit, as far as it still existed.

We now turned toward the village that was on our line of march, which was located on the western bank of a totally dehydrated stream. Here our pioneers had laid a bridge that could carry only eight tons; with our eighteen tons, we could not cross. Next to it to the right, there was a second ford, but the steep embankments of the stream—which would pose no obstacle in dry and non-frosty weather—nearly became a death trap for us. But we had to go forward if we were to reach our unit. On the valley floor stood a twelve-ton Panzer II, which had tried to take the slope umpteen times but had slipped back again and again. Now we stood behind it. The mutual shoving did not help. In the meantime, it seemed like the Russians had noticed the position and were firing artillery and mortars in our direction. I tried to convince some truck drivers who were high on the bridge to pull us out, but most were not up to the challenge; others made themselves scarce when shells burst. Would this be our end? Suddenly, a three-axle Krupp with a tow rope showed up. It hooked up in front of us. First, the Panzer II in front of us went up, and then it was our turn. Gratefully, we donated ten bottles of schnapps, fifty chocolate tablets, and a carton of cigarettes to the three-man crew. They were very pleased with this, and we were happy to be out of this sticky situation.

Meanwhile, it had become dark, and as we were forbidden to use our lights, we drove on using our night-lights. It was very difficult for me to watch out for tactical signs, as none could be overlooked. We communicated over our internal radio. At places we could not oversee or junctions in the road, we dismounted and decided together what to do. Apart from flares in the distance, there was no sign of life. We were alone in the icy cold steppe, with the main line of resistance then near, then far away. By midnight, the area became more animated; now and then, we passed a few parked vehicles with guards. But they were not Russians. As we saw our tactical sign again, we stopped and noticed some trucks. We dismounted and asked a guard about our whereabouts. The information was positive since there were units of the 24th Panzer Division here. The repair company was farther back, and we decided to spend the night here. Quickly, one more bottle was opened, and everyone took a hefty draught, and then we rolled into our blankets and slept.

At the crack of dawn, we got exact directions, and after driving for an hour, we arrived at the repair shop. There the first breakfast was going on, and we received a hot cup of coffee. In addition, we got our daily ration of one slice of bread and sixty grams of tinned meat. When duty began, we reported to the repair shop commander and told him our problem. He generously put a one-ton prime mover at our disposal for our great baggage; we gave some to the repair crews and made our way to the trains. Here we were greeted as if we were Santa, but it was not divided up until the combat units returned. By afternoon, we got our Panzer III back from the repair shop in a well-repaired state, and our five tanks eventually returned. There were no losses in men, but two of our tanks had suffered mightily. Our joy was great; everyone was still alive, and there was a great deal to tell about the last twenty-four hours.

The combat group had not had an easy time of it. The T-34 had continued to provoke and ventured out more and more. This was too much for the three Panzer IIIs, and the first shells left the barrels. The T-34 was hit but not wounded. As the Russian subsequently fired, it was in the right position for the Panzer IV with the long barrel. The first shell was a direct hit, and before the T-34 could turn around and make himself scarce, the second hit him and put an end to him. This colossus now stood burning and didn't move anymore. From the terrain in front of us came a mighty fire of infantry weapons with mortars and *ratschbumms* (small artillery pieces with short range but high penetration). For our task group, this was the beginning of the counterattack in conjunction with the infantry.

Four Panzer IIIs launched the counterattack, with the big Panzer IV remaining in reserve. With powerful bursts of fire and tank support, the whole matter was cleared up in one hour. The enemy had not counted on our strength and left his positions head over heels. These were expanded upon overnight by our people and handed over to the infantry the next day. We withdrew. On the other hand, two of the Panzer IIIs had suffered serious damage that could be fixed only by the repair shop. Now we had a look at our booty and divided it. Everyone in the fighting unit—thirty men in all—received a bottle of schnapps, five packets of cigarettes, and five bars of chocolate. Subsequently, a tin of biscuits was divided. The rest was handed over to the kitchen for storage.

In the evening, we got our daily rations, which were swallowed down with a swig from the bottle, and then we slept. Our tank was our place of rest; sometimes, it was somewhat uncomfortable, but at least we had a roof overhead. The morning was spent rather quietly; everyone tried to wash, brush his teeth, and shave since this was not possible everyday. Then we were ordered to do technical work on all our weapons and instruments. On that day, the sun was shining for several hours, which was a relief for us. For the first time in a long time, we had a hot midday meal. We got dried vegetables with plenty of horse meat—a special treat for our hungry stomachs. When we asked where the meat came from, the answer was that we took a half-starved horse from the passing Romanian units. The day was spent in quiet, and even mail was distributed. I got two letters from home. In the icy cold tank, the mail was read and answered straightaway. I had only two field post stamps left to send my dear ones at home a message and let them know I was alive. I could not tell them that we were in the Stalingrad cauldron, but I drew a circle, and my family understood.

By this time, we were in the vicinity of the village of Karpowka, a small town in the Don steppe. On the second day of our stay, our commander was called to the commanding general's command post, and we already suspected new orders. After his arrival at 3:00 P.M., we were given our new orders: "The new task! Comrades, tomorrow we have the task to reconnoiter the sector of terrain on Hill 218, the so-called White House, where we have had contact with the enemy before, but where everything is still unclear. This will be done by the '911,' the '912,' and the long-barreled Panzer IV. The rest will remain here. There will be no infantry support; we are left to our own devices."

This was another suicide mission. That's what I thought. Everyone could now adjust physically and morally. After an unquiet night, the engines warmed up in the morning. A quick swig from the bottle and the daily rations as breakfast, and then we were handed four daily rations which I got at the administration. At exactly eight o'clock, we said good-bye and drove off into the unknown. We depended on our company commander to find the place of our operations since he had a good general staff map. After about two hours, we reached Hill 218, and shortly afterward, we found the White House. It was no more than a steel-like building with a locked door. Apart from some tufts of steppe grass and some wood, there was nothing to be found. So we mounted up and continued.

In front of us, there was nothing but steppe with some snow and foggy weather. Visibility was about 500 meters. On our radio, I picked up incomprehensible conversations, which disappeared once again. We eventually reached the peak of the hill. Suddenly, to our left and right, large terrain covered with small bushes appeared, which grew into groups of trees fifteen meters high. Those to our right were lower than those to our left. In single file, we drove through the middle of the forest. The wall of fog in front of us broke up a little, and at about two kilometers distance, we could make out the silhouettes of three T-34s, which were standing at right angles to our course to our left. Over the radio, I informed everyone, but they had seen them already. So we had to be careful here. We drove forward a few hundred meters, until we were fifty meters from the edge of the wooded area. Here my commander posted the "912" to the left in the woodland, with the direction of fire to the left. He positioned the Panzer IV to the right in the terrain, with the direction of fire to the right. We remained standing in the middle of the road with our aim at six o'clock (toward the rear).

To conserve fuel, we all had to switch off the engines. Now we had to wait. All tank commanders had opened the upper turret hatch and were observing the area with their binoculars. All of a sudden, there is a rifle shot; our commander half-falls into the turret and shouts, "These swine!" What had happened? Close to our tank, a Russian sniper must have lain in wait, and he had given our Cuno (that was the Christian name of our commander) a grazing shot to the head. The field cap and the skullcap had been penetrated and the hair had been singed a little. This was the first shock. The aimer and loader then got out to the left of the turret; Cuno also joined them. They searched the entire area but found nothing—no sniper, no rifle; it was as if the earth had swallowed him up. All three boarded again in order to regain some composure.

After about thirty minutes, we heard an increase in engine noises. So we increased our vigilance. Then the noise got stronger and stronger, and to our left came a T-34 at full speed. In all the tension, we had forgotten that we could not drive at all since our electrical starter was broken, and we could get our Panzer III moving by cranking the handle. But in order to achieve that, two of our men had to get out. At the time, this was impossible because the second T-34 had arrived and nearly rammed us as it curved away between us and our Panzer IV into the woodland. Fortunately, the T-34 had turned its gun toward the rear and was not immediately ready to open fire. On the other hand, our Panzer IV had switched quickly and put an end to it with a direct hit. The first T-34 had suffered the same fate as the second one, but we had not seen that. Over the radio, we communicated that we had seen three T-34s, so one more was in the offing. In the meantime, we had turned our gun in the direction of twelve o'clock in order to be able to help firing in case of a trap. But our engine still was not turning. So Schwertner and I went out to crank the engine. We succeeded, and our Panzer III could move again. Now we stood and waited.

Over the radio, we discussed the situation and praised the Panzer IV crew. We decided to wait thirty more minutes and then leave the theater of fighting. The fog had closed in again, and the view had gotten worse. The black smoke of the two burning T-34s could hardly be seen. When after thirty minutes we wanted to begin moving and checked out the situation, we heard engine noise in the distance. So we got into the vehicles and paid attention. We had heard well; up came our number three—slower and more wary, though. He turned his gun to the right, then to the left, feeling out the vicinity; all was not well here. Our Panzer IV had moved his position to the front a little, and our Panzer III moved a little to the rear in order to increase the field of fire for the Panzer IV. Suddenly, the T-34 fired into the wood blindly. That was the moment that our Panzer IV made its deadly hit. Three T-34s were knocked out quickly behind one another; that was unique for our unit since we would have fared badly without the Panzer IV. All three left this scene of battle and discussed the remainder of our mission outside the small woodland. We concluded that apart from these events, there had been no contact with the enemy. So we decided to return to our base, which we reached by evening. Another day had passed without any losses, even though it had plenty of excitement. Our boss said good-bye and drove to the staff to make his report.

OUR LAST ACTION AS "FIRE DEPARTMENT"
Our operation as "fire department" led us from Kalach on the Don via Marinowka, Karpowka toward Pitomnik, Gumrak, across the railway line toward Gorodiche, the northernmost salient in the cauldron. For several weeks, fierce battles had been raging here. The positions changed hands daily. By day, our troops sat in the prepared positions there. At night, in a snow storm, which was blowing impenetrably from the east most of the time, all of a sudden the Russians were standing in front of the trench. There was little resistance from our side. Whoever managed to save himself had to make his way out in a flight to the rally positions, which were better garrisoned and armed. It simply was a tactical innovation of our infantry units to garrison the first line of defense weakly in order to keep the losses to a minimum.

It was, however, of vital importance for us to hold the area in order to prevent the Russians from entering Stalingrad. And the Russians attached great value to seizing this sector of the front line since it was the shortest way into Stalingrad. In this area of the northern blocking position, we now were mixing it up for days. At dawn, with the infantry, we had to retake the positions that had been lost overnight. We succeeded in doing that by day, though two of our tanks were left on the battlefield and both had suffered direct hits from a *ratschbumm*. Only a few crewmembers got out in one piece. The worst in these actions was the miserable weather and not being able to make out the enemy, who was hiding well-camouflaged behind snow walls. The white snowsuits of the Red Army men completed the camouflage.

One morning we were almost caught. We drove up to the invisible position when all of a sudden three Russians and a *ratschbumm* appeared in front of us. With great presence of mind, our driver pulled our Panzer III in a sharp turn to the left and was able to catch the small gun and the three Russians with the right track. For us, it was a great shock—and for the Russians, too, because they stood in front of our tank as if turned to stone. They were moved off as prisoners by the infantry that accompanied us. The shock was all the greater for me, and I was still busy with warming up the machine-gun mounting with our heating lamp inside the tank. And it was even worse because I had taken off my shoes and was sitting in the tank in socks. For me, it was a warning for later actions.

DECEMBER 14, 1942

Exactly a year ago today, I had arrived home for a three-week leave; my parents and sisters were very excited. This December 14 was to be the last operation for me and the entire crew. By afternoon, our company commander came back from the O group. In a briefing with the tank commanders, he announced the following: in the northern blocking position, the Russians have penetrated our main line of resistance over a depth of 600 meters and a width of 400 meters. Reconnaissance has shown that the Russians have some infantry, some antitank rifles, some heavy machine guns, and some mortars there. Our mission was to use our Panzer III and short-barreled Panzer IV there. The remaining long-barreled Panzer IV cannot be used because it has no shells.

We were to be accompanied by three SPWs (*Schützenpanzerwagen*, or armored personnel carriers) with full crews (about thirty men) and equipment. The commander was of the opinion that this would not last long, and we were clear about everything. We'll move out for the attack at 3:30 P.M. Everyone now was thoughtful; war was not a game. An hour later, we drew cold rations for five days once more. I was charged with the administration and the distribution. By afternoon, we had some warm food, and everyone got half a liter of horse meat soup with dried vegetables. It was better than nothing, and overall, it was warm. By 3:00, the three SPWs rolled up for the attack. At exactly 2:30, our two crews were ordered to mount up and move out. The road to the scene of the action was not long, about four kilometers.

It was already getting a little dark; the weather was clear with a temperature of 25 degrees below zero. About half way there, we were contacted over radio by the staff with the order to delay the attack by thirty minutes. We stopped and checked everything again. Then we noticed a Russian reconnaissance aircraft at low height. It was circling around for a while and then disappeared. It was obvious to us that it was reporting our movements. The thirty minutes did not last long for us, and we got the idea of eating our daily rations. We all were hungry, but the boss ordered that everyone was to consume only half a slice of buttered bread, which I was to prepare. Hermes, the gun aimer, still had three bottles of diluted rum and took out a bottle. Before we had drunk the first round, I buttered the slices and handed them out. We would have liked to eat more, but no longer could stomach it.

There still were six more minutes to go. The commander ordered, "Panse, give us a few musical notes." With my mouth organ over the microphone, it sounded as if it came over the radio. What does one play in such a situation? At exactly 4:15 P.M., the call came over the radio: "Men, here we go!" In the meantime, it had gotten dark, and the moon arose over the heavens; it grew cold. Along the way, we passed a knocked-out T-34, with burned-out containers lying all around. We continued up a hill, at whose summit we could make out a trench system. On the other hand, there were many dead soldiers lying around there. The snow lightly covered most of them, and we could not be sure which nationality they were. The three APCs drove about fifty meters to our right.

When we crossed the summit, all of a sudden antitank fire opened up from our left flank. Now we knew we had reached the Russian main line of resistance. Halfway to our right and in front of us, the Panzer IV took position. Still we did not return fire. We kept going forward and looked out to make out the exact positions. Suddenly, there were the first hits on our gun mounting. We noticed at impact that these were not ordinary shells; each impact rained sparks. The fire increased constantly, and we also returned fire several times as well. Again and again, there was this serial red glow in front of us. Now we were certain that these were not the simple antitank rifles, but that some antitank guns were firing at us as well. The skies were continuously brightened by star shells fired by the Russians. We could clearly make out what was going on. By driving to and fro, we changed positions in order to force the Russians to change their aim at us again and again. While doing this, we had to take care not to present our flanks to the enemy because we had weak armor there. About thirty meters in front of us, the Panzer IV was doing the same maneuvers. Via the radio, we inquired about the situation with the Panzer IV, which already had reported some hits.

This tank was of a new type, which we had gotten in Krepp. At some locations on its outer hull, it had three-centimeter-thick reinforcing plates; behind it, there was a hollow space of five centimeters. This had the advantage that a shell would mostly penetrate the outermost layer but would have its angle changed and therefore could not easily penetrate the main armor. The entire exchange of fire already had lasted ten minutes, and the hits on our frontal armor became more virulent—a sign that we were closing in on the enemy guns. All of a sudden, there was a new hit, and only the right track was still turning—according to our driver, Alfons Bartsch, who reported this over the intercom. There were some attempts to continue, but we did not advance anymore; neither did we retreat. We found out that we had been hit in the left-side transmission and were not capable of maneuvering anymore. All that was left to us was to bail out. The boss gave the order for it in succession: aimer, loader, and then it was to be my turn, but the boss had orders to inform the Panzer IV about our situation and counsel them to fight their way back to the T-34, which we had passed in our advance toward the main line of resistance. There we were to report our situation in the infantry command post. In bailing out, we used the turret hatch away from the enemy, since we did not want to run the risk of being shot by Russian infantry. In order to do this, everyone had to pull himself up in the turret and drop himself backwards into the snow. It all went well; our driver was the last to bail out.

What could we do now, without a roof over our head? No one could take anything with him. In our black tankers' uniforms, we clearly stood out against the snow. There was no time for debate because some shells had again burst on our badly hit Panzer III, and the splinters flew all around us. Everyone wanted to save himself. Our orders were clear: just avoid falling into Russian hands. In between volleys of fire, we again and again heard the Russian battle cry—"Urraah!"—that went through marrow and bone. The Panzer IV maneuvered away from us. The boss and I both looked for tank tracks in the snow and tried to get to the road by crawling and sliding. The other three had disappeared. Now and then, we tried to get forward with bigger leaps. At each leap, we had to rise up in our black uniforms, providing a good target for the enemy. They were firing at individual men with antitank guns, and we felt each shell hiss overhead. Our repeated attempts were without success.

We crawled about 400 meters on our bellies to our own main line of resistance. For us, it was a battle for survival; no one wanted to die or fall into Russian hands. While we were having a short breather, we saw three pillars of smoke. When we looked closer, it became clear that these were our three armored personnel carriers burning there. They had not managed to penetrate the enemy's main line of resistance very deeply, and all three probably had been knocked out by a direct hit. We were down another thirty men. We had covered only 400 meters, and the Russians were still behind us. We had to keep moving. Where could the other three be? It was bitterly cold; my hands were stiff, and I hardly felt my feet as snow had come into my shoes while I was crawling. I had left my gloves in my tank. But in exchange for that, I had my plate with radio documents (secret material) hanging from my arms, and I pulled them through the snow. In the meantime, we managed to reach our MLR through diligent crawling. But nothing moved; there was no trace of German soldiers, just dead soldiers everywhere. Here we tried to make a second pause; our strengths were at an end. Only fear drove us forward.

All of a sudden, we heard the howling of the Stalin organs. I thought that this would mean our end. We both quickly pulled in some corpses in order to take cover behind them. The first salvoes passed overhead; the second ones came a lot closer. Suddenly, there was a muffled impact and a detonation in our direct proximity. We both lay on our backs, and I felt a sharp burning sensation at my lower belly. When I groped there, I noted a hole in my trousers. The pain wasn't that bad, but my neighbor Meyer had taken some shrapnel in the left lower arm. Now we waited for the next salvoes, and we quickly pulled in some more corpses for cover. But nothing came, and instead, we heard the terrifying cries of the Russian infantry. So we had to get to our feet quickly and move off again. After the Russians had had fired some flares, we saw the knocked-out T-34 about 150 meters in front of us. Now we tried to get closer to our objective in some leaps. The Russians still were firing with their antitank guns. But these rounds probably were not aimed at us. They tore up the containers and barrels near the T-34. But we had to go there. Ten minutes later, we made it. Right under the T-34 was the entrance to the infantry command post. When we got there, Lt. Herbert Schwertner of the infantry and Alfons Bartsch welcomed us. Now only Wilhelm Hermes, our aimer, was missing.

In the bunker, it was cozily warm, and we remembered that we had gotten something from a shell. My fingers had swollen up in the meantime, making it difficult for me to open my trousers. The medic in the command post concluded that a piece of shrapnel as big as the nail of my little finger had gotten lodged in the skin of my belly. It did not sit deeply and could easily be removed by the medic. Afterward, I got a tetanus injection against gangrene. On inspection, the chief's wounds looked more serious. He had deep holes at two places in his lower arm. The medic was able to remove one splinter, but the second was lodged more deeply and was so big that only a doctor could help. The first aid here consisted of only a bandage and an injection. Now he had to await transport to the rear. A sudden noise at the entrance to the bunker made us sit up, and in the entrance stood Wilhelm Hermes. Now the joy was great; all five of us were alive and together again. A vivid discussion ensued, and everyone described his dramatic escape. At the same time, we also started making plans. Wilhelm had seen that our tank was still standing where we abandoned it. In it were our very private possessions and our five-day rations. We decided that we had to go there as long as it wasn't burning. The chief, however, warned not to begin such an undertaking; he would take care of replacement rations himself.

Alfons Bartsch, our driver, could not sit still, and he, Hermes, and Schwertner had already slipped out of the hole. The chief and I were incapacitated, he with his wounds and I with my frozen parts. The infantry lieutenant contacted the staff via the field telephone and told them that five men awaited transport here. A few minutes later, our regiment called us, and we quickly reported the situation. They promised to come and pick us up. According to their report, our three adventurers had closed with the tank up to 300 meters. The constant firing of star shells from the Russian side lit up the battlefield as if it were day, and Red Army men were seen moving toward our tank. At the same moment, there was a mighty detonation with a burst of flame, and our Panzer III was on fire. Now everything was over; our home was aflame; our possessions were lost. We were homeless under the icy cold steppe skies.

The three returned disappointed and downcast. Then a small one-ton tractor rolled up in front. The five of us bade farewell to the platoon commander of the infantry unit and his comrades, and we rolled back in our vehicle. After about fifteen minutes, we were directed to a bunker near the regimental staff, in which four men already were living. But it was so spacious that eight men could fit in there without difficulty. The chief was driven to the field hospital for treatment there. After a successful operation, which mainly consisted of dressing flesh wounds, he was brought to the regimental staff in order to report on our failed attack there.

In the bunker it was warm—which wasn't exactly the best thing for my frozen hands and feet. At about 9:00 P.M., the bunker door opened, and we found four men whose tank had been knocked out. At the orders of the regimental commander, a big plate of still-warm pancakes and a big can of real coffee were placed on a table for us, and we were wished a hearty appetite. We were blown away that something like that still was available in the cauldron. Without hesitation, we piled in and wolfed down the food. Our hosts in the bunker also got something. Fortune and misfortune are that close together.

We nattered on throughout the night, and everyone related his escape. On leaving the tank, Herbert Schwertner had noticed a rail embankment about 200 meters to our left and managed to reach it and cross it under the fire of the anti-tank gun. So he got out of the field of fire. Alfons Bartsch, who had been with us at the start, had walked toward the Panzer IV, which had still been maneuvering and firing, and wanted to take cover there. He had stumbled and fallen and had been overrun by the tank—luckily not by the tracks—and the hull had pushed him deeply into the soft snow. When the tank had gone, he took a look around; all his limbs were still safe and sound. Then he made off toward the railway embankment. (This is the railroad that runs via Alexandrowka, Stalingradski, and Orlowka back toward Stalingrad. Our actions in the northern blocking position took place within this curve.) Under cover of the embankment, Alfons made his way to the infantry positions, where Herbert Schwertner already was waiting for him.

Wilhelm Hermes, our aimer, had struck out to our right. In the many ups and downs that the Russian fire forced on him, he reached a shell scrape and jumped in. He hardly gave any thought to a short break when a shell burst in the immediate vicinity and covered his hole with big frozen clumps of earth. In the first moments, he thought, "It's over." But his limbs still were in one piece, and with his penknife, he began to hack away bit by bit. As he saw some light again, he heard again the cries of the Russians outside and dared not get out of his hole. Only after it had gotten quieter did he continue his tiring work and try to lift the hard clump of earth with his last strength. "First of all, I took stock of the situation," he reported. "When I noticed nothing, I crept out, oriented myself quickly, and saw our former main line of resistance 100 meters behind me. I gingerly made for it and suddenly was challenged: 'Password!' which I did not know. Now I found out that I was right in front of the very weakly held MLR. I had a short conversation with the infantryman, and when he recognized my black tankers' uniform, he said, 'So you were those which were running around out in front?' When he inquired about our tank, I confirmed that it was standing there knocked out in front. The infantryman showed me the way to the main command post, and that was the bunker under the T-34."

I already had described our suffering. So ended our last action with the Panzer III. We sat with our heads down. We had no more than our lives, which are valuable enough, but for a soldier, that's only half of it. Totally exhausted, we lay down on the cots with two blankets and slept until the morning.

During the night, we were tortured by hunger, even though we had been fed well. My frozen hands and feet had swollen mightily and hurt a great deal. The night was quiet, and once more, we could undress down to our underclothes and stretch out on a hard but comfortable cot. What would happen to us tomorrow?

The next day, our quartermasters brought us a pot of hot coffee—though we had no mugs, which had been burned in the tank, along with my eight boxes of Attika cigarettes and four big packs of Krim tobacco, which I had been saving for my next home leave to please my father. All had become prey to flames. So that morning we drank the coffee from the mugs of our comrades in the bunker. There was nothing to eat since we could not demand anything from the little that was left to our comrades. Overnight, blisters had formed on my hands and feet, and I had to find my way to the first-aid post. Once I arrived in this bunker, the doctor diagnosed me with second-degree frostbite. He put an ointment on my hands and feet, renewed the bandages, and told me to come back tomorrow. Once we got to the bunker, my comrades were sitting down and dividing things. What had happened? The boss had thought of us and had sent a cooking kit, a drinking mug, fork and knife, a greatcoat, a blanket, and one complete set of underclothes and socks, a bread bag, and a bag. He had thought of our necessities. We still had nothing to eat. I lay down on my cot and resigned myself to my fate.

Alfons Bartsch had always taken care of our extra rations ever since he had opened the backpacks of some dead Russians and took their iron rations. Mostly they consisted of three loaves of bread and two blocks of compressed oats, which yielded a tasty soup when immersed in hot water. By the afternoon, Alfons had returned with 850-gram tins of veal and pork, in addition to a complete loaf of bread. So we had something to eat once more. And where had he found all this? He found our own field kitchen, and after a march of eight kilometers, he explained our situation, and he was pitied. He also brought a towel, a bit of soap, and a razor for everyone.

In the afternoon, our boss returned. He had his left arm in a sling. He inquired after our well being; apart from me, everyone was well. His driver handed out cold rations for five days. These were 500 grams of bread per man, a box of pork of 850 grams for two men, and three bottles of diluted rum. Now we had reason to have a party. We didn't tell him about what Alfons had "found." One bottle of rum was opened straightaway and made the rounds. Then we came to discuss the future. We no longer had a tank, and of the seventeen tanks in Krepp with which we had started, only four still existed. Two of those could no longer be repaired. On the other hand, the crews were still complete.

The long-barreled Panzer IV was out of ammunition, but the short-barreled Panzer IV, which had carried out the attack with us, was still operational. We still had twenty men—one of which was wounded, one half frozen, and eighteen fit. What will now become of us? The chief said, "Tomorrow, I'll have you all transported to the rear. In the rear with the trains, there are plenty of empty bunkers that you can live in. What will happen after that is still unclear." He then turned to me and said, "I very much regret that you caught the worst of it, but we have a good doctor in the rear, and he'll quickly have you fit again. You'll live in bunkers in the closest vicinity. Do you have any other worries?" I told him we had only one razor, one toothbrush, and no toothpaste for the four of us. "I'll make a note of that," he said. He made his good-byes and disappeared.

Day and night were really quiet. We had food and drink but had to divide it. In the morning, we got ourselves two mess tins of hot coffee and had breakfast. Subsequently, I was brought to the first-aid post by Hermes and Schwertner. My wounds were brushed up again, and I was given new bandages and had to return the next day. My comrades brought me home again; walking was very difficult for me, especially on the left foot. Once we arrived there, Alfons gave me a pair of cutdown Russian felt boots. He had found them when he learned that I had problems getting into my shoes. I thanked him; they were truly valuable for me. The five of us were good comrades.

We took care of each other, including our boss, who, before I started serving in his tank, I had thought of only as a very punctual and strict person. I later learned that he could be a good comrade as well.

Shortly before lunch, our vehicle, an armored half-track, appeared to pick us up. Hermes and Schwertner quickly ran off one last time in order to fetch us a hot lunch. They were lucky and brought us each half a liter of warm ogre soup with meat—something we had not eaten for a long time. After lunch, we grabbed our belongings, bade farewell to our hosts, and disappeared with the half-track. The drive across the steppe to our trains lasted less than half an hour, and we arrived in the Pitomnik area. There we looked around for a suitable bunker near the first-aid post. We arranged everything quickly. Our division had established itself well in order to spend the winter here. At the time, no one knew that the cauldron was coming and the front was approaching us. In our bunker, eight men could make themselves at home comfortably. We had six two-tiered bunks, as well as a proper gun oven, a table, a home-built field stool, and cases with shelves made out of planks. The bunker was located about 1.5 meters below the earth. The roof consisted of railroad crossties, a layer of iron plates on it, on top of that yet another layer of crossties, and on top of that another fifty centimeters of earth. We concluded that only a direct hit by a bomb could have any effect on us. We quickly gathered wood since there was plenty lying around from the bunker building, and we got the stove going.

It was a bright, lovely winter's day, about 20 degrees below zero. We did not need too much time to furnish our new home. It was more important to inspect the vicinity. Bartsch and Hermes went out to make a detailed report on everything. Schwertner stayed with me, and we made ourselves comfortable in the bunks and soon fell asleep. When both comrades returned, it had already gotten dark outside. Alfons, like always, was a great success in "organizing" things, and he brought an entire loaf of bread, a box of veal, and a bottle of diluted rum. They also had located the field kitchen and reported our presence for the days ahead. Furthermore, there were five wax candles as booty. The box of veal was warmed up on the stove, and we each had two slices of bread. The bottle of schnapps made the rounds, and for us, it was a robber's banquet. Both our scouts had reported that the kitchen was about 300 meters away and the bunker of our battalion doctor was located about 50 meters away. Our boss had his quarters with the staff, and our arrival also had been reported there. The office of our former company was in our direct vicinity. So far everything was clear. Soon everyone was asleep in the warm bunker. The night was spent in relative quiet; only faint engine noises could be heard.

The next morning, we learned that the field aerodrome of Pitomnik was nearby. From there, Ju52s and He111s resupplied the encircled 6th Army by night. After breakfast, Schwertner accompanied me to the doctor. A medic unwound the bandages, and Dr. Rocholl had a look at the wounds. He said, "That looks bitter, but we'll try our best." The wounds were cleaned, the remaining blisters were cut open, and the scraps of skin removed. Everything was cleaned once more, an ointment was rubbed into it, and I was bandaged up once again. This time, I only needed to return in four days. For me, these frozen parts were a horrible sight: everything looked like raw meat.

I spent four days in the bunker, and my comrades took good care of me. They obviously meant the best, but I felt ill. Not only did the wounds hurt, but I was also incapable of helping myself. I could not even go to the toilet without help. On the fourth day, I was brought up to see the doctor once again, and after the opening up of the bandages, he was of the opinion that my wounds were improving. Again, everything was washed off with a yellow medication, rubbed with ointment, and bandaged. I returned to the bunker until the next time.

The days grew increasingly boring for me. My comrades went out to reconnoiter everyday, but one of them always stayed with me. One evening, they returned and said they had run into Waldemar Fockin. Waldemar was a *hiwi*, a Russian in German uniform who served as translator for our company. From a Russian POW camp in Germany, he had been assigned to us, and he spoke German well. He was from Moscow and was a radio mechanic—an engineer by profession. Waldemar was in great demand in our company, especially when we were still moving forward. He was the sixth man in the tank of our company commander, and as soon as prisoners were taken, Waldemar had to translate the interrogations. At this time, he now accompanied a German truck driver to Pitomnik every other day in order to fetch supplies. Even before the cauldron, we had become close friends since I had to replace our killed master radioman, and Waldemar, being a tradesman, helped me out really well. And so it happened that one evening, Waldemar came to our bunker and paid me a visit. Joyously, he embraced me and said, "My best friend, so sick. What can I do for him?" I made it clear to him that this would take time. I proposed to him that he move into our bunker. He agreed, and two days later, Waldemar moved in with us. He retained his job with the truck to Pitomnik.

On the second day, he told me that a quarter loaf of bread was hidden away under my blanket. I was to tell no one about it, however, share it with nobody, and eat it only furtively. If he had been caught taking the loaf, it would have meant death for him. As long as Waldemar was with us—until January 15, 1943—he gave me this ration of bread. He also told us that on the airfield, there were giant tents stacked with supplies, all good stuff. But we still got only 100 grams of bread and 60 grams of meat or lard per day.

On Christmas Eve, our field kitchen handed out tea with rum, a slice of bread for each, a block of horse meat, a bar of chocolate, and a pack of cigarettes. Alfons, like always, had scrounged a bottle of diluted rum, and we spent the evening in our warm bunker, lit by candles. Shortly after Christmas, the Russians stormed the airfield and took or burned the army's total fourteen-day supply. About this time, we had to move, withdrawing to the field aerodrome at Gumrak.

OPERATIONS WITH COMBAT GROUP EICHHORN

One morning, a dispatch rider arrived, and our boss told us that we were to see him. With the support of my comrades, I also humped along. We reported according to regulations and had to take our places. He gave a short speech, honored us collectively, and regretted the sad end of our common operations. He had a short story to tell about everyone. He then turned to me and said, "You, my dear Panse, have suffered most of it, and instead of the frequency tables, you should've gotten yourself a pair of gloves. But you always were a conscientious radioman. That's why I got you into my vehicle and kicked out the 'loose contact' [the former radioman]. By the way, are you still mad at me that I made you train so well in crawling across the ground? With you in the right and me in the left track, we got forward real well. That was a ticklish situation for us. But we were lucky, and all five of us are still alive. What now is to become of us, I do not know. To judge from the current situation, the rest of our unit will be formed into a combat group without tanks under the orders of Captain Eichhorn. Neither Panse nor I will be able to take part in this operation."

He ordered the batman to bring five glasses and a bottle of cognac. We toasted, and he wished us all the best in the battle of encirclement. Subsequently, an entire loaf was cut into five parts, and each man was given his part with a block of horse meat. The boss said, "So my friends, what I am dividing with you is my Christmas gift from the staff. I did not want to eat it alone but instead share it with you since we went through thick and thin together." Finally, we drained the bottle of schnapps. With a thank-you, we bade good-bye to our company commander, Cuno von Meyer. "Boys, keep your ears to the ground and best of luck!" Those were his last words. We had never seen our "old man" in such a fatherly mood.

Thanks to the special care of the battalion doctor, Dr. Horst Rocholl, my frozen parts had improved markedly. A thin skin covered the afflicted parts on my hands. According to the doctor, the healing process was progressing well. I wasn't surprised, since I had been eating a double ration of bread everyday.

Between Christmas and the New Year, we had to evacuate our bunker and move to the vicinity of the small field aerodrome at Gumrak. Here there were hundreds of completed personnel bunkers. We found one, and together with Waldemar, we made ourselves comfortable.

Hunger, cold, and lice were our continuous companions. How long would this last? Was there any hope of salvation anyway? We all were of the opinion that Russians would kill us all. Silently, I had reconciled myself to my fate. I could not flee, I could not fight, and all I had left was my pistol. Could I do this to my parents and my sisters? No one would learn how my life had ended. These thoughts kept me busy when my comrades were out with the aforementioned combat groups and shock groups. I decided that it was not yet time. The leaflets that were dropped by the Russians over the cauldron exhorted the encircled troops to surrender. Everyone was guaranteed food, drink, and life. What was one to believe? Our propaganda or their leaflets? Then there was the exhortation by German officers and soldiers who were already in captivity to lay down our weapons and switch sides. We were guaranteed a healthy return after the war. Again, who to believe?

When the bunker door opened in the evening, I counted my comrades; all were present. Of course, I had taken care to heat the bunker properly. Most of the time, there was nothing to eat because they ate before they went off to the battle. I could offer them only a small slug of tea, and if they were willing to talk, I could learn whether the mission had been easy or difficult. Only now and then did our field kitchen have warm soup for our fighters. At the beginning, the battle groups had thirty men, but no action passed without loss.

By New Year's Eve, I was very content with how my wounds were healing, which my doctor confirmed. I could move around a little. The right foot was almost completely healed, but I still could not wear a shoe on my left. In the afternoon, rations for five days were to be drawn. Bartsch and Hermes collected them. Once again, we got dried vegetables and horse meat. For now, there were no operations. So we spent the day in the bunker. The mail also had to be collected. I had three letters—from mother, Hilde, and Erika. The joy was great, and I was content. Lying on the bunk, I read each letter three times. In my thoughts, I was home with my loved ones.

On the same day, there was no contact with the enemy, but we were well aware that hardly two kilometers away, the Russians were lying on the other slope. Apart from some reconnaissance parties, the Russians kept quiet throughout the day. It became dark; the night was cold and frosty. We sat down to the communal evening bread at out table with 100 grams of bread and 60 grams of tinned meat, as well as a mug of tea. After dinner, everybody went to his bunk.

Every bunker had to furnish a guard for a certain period of time; guards had to walk around a certain section of the bunkers for a certain amount of time. Schwertner of our bunker had guard duty from 10:00 P.M. to midnight. Most of us had fallen asleep by the time Schwertner was summoned to his post. He clothed himself warmly and disappeared into the cold starry night. He was on his post for only about fifteen minutes when mighty infantry fire was heard. They were rifle shots, mainly with tracers and many colorful rockets. The fire increased, and the shells rained down on our height in great number. We all jumped down from the bunks and got dressed. Then Herbert entered the doorway and shouted, "The Russians are coming!" Now we waited for orders, but none came. Everyone quickly looked outside to see the fireworks. Infantry fire without artillery support really wasn't a sign of a serious attack. Even so, the situation was not good.

The most valuable thing to us was supplies, and we still had enough for four days. In short order, we decided that we should eat everything quickly so that the Russians could not get their hands on it. Besides, what are 400 grams of bread and 240 grams of tinned meat for a starved soldier anyway? Less than half an hour later, the supply box was empty, and our stomachs were full. But still no Russians were coming. Alfons Bartsch had a look to see what was going on. He got dressed, got his machine pistol, and went out. After about twenty minutes, he returned and explained the situation. There had been no thought of an attack; the Russians simply had been celebrating the new year—according to his time, two hours earlier than us. We had full stomachs now but would have to go hungry for four days. How were we to survive that?

At midnight, there were fireworks from our side as the year 1943 began. There was no cause for celebration in the cauldron. We were starved, frozen, and burned out according to Arno von Lenski, our divisional commander. Here there was nothing to save anymore. But the OKW (Wehrmacht supreme command) demanded that we fight on and hold on until the end. The next day came, and there was nothing to eat. To tell the truth, we didn't even feel the hunger anymore. Alfons got two mess tins of hot coffee, which even had some sugar in it, and much to our surprise, he also found a bottle of diluted rum.

January 1 was a lovely, though frosty, day, which passed without any trouble. We had thick ogre soup with tinned meat in the afternoon. The bunkers wre warm, and the candles heightened the cozy feeling. By evening, Alfons put two tins of vegetables on the oven. Everyone stared at the green beans: where had they come from? Alfons told us not to ask, and we handed him our mess tins. Waldemar got his share, too.

The next day, there was no operational order for our combat group, which had started off with thirty men but now had only seventeen men left. The dying did not stop. In the evening, when Waldemar returned from his supply run, he silently placed half a loaf of bread on the table and then said, "Friends, eat. What I've done for you is punishable by death, but hunger hurts. The cauldron will not last long anymore, and so I don't care whether the Germans shoot me if I'm caught or the Russians shoot me later as a *hiwi*. As German soldiers, you've always been good to me." Silently, we collected the bread, and Alfons thanked him and told him to be careful. We knew that he ran a great risk.

Now I just had to report to the doctor every four days. A very thin skin began to grow over most of the open bits. Only three toes were open on my left foot, but I could shave and wash again. It was progress.

The first weeks of January went by, and it became clearer day by day that the Russians were compressing the cauldron. We could look out to the front, and everyday, we had to reckon that the enemy would show up on our doorstep one night. With regard to weapons, we had nothing with which to oppose the Russians anymore. The few heavy guns or mortars had little ammunition left. Most vehicles were standing around and had no petrol. The few vehicles that were absolutely vital to sustaining life were given fuel from aircraft, which was tanked out

Gumrak airfield had to be evacuated on January 16 because the Russians were close to capturing it. We grabbed our meager belongings and disappeared in an Opel Blitz in the direction of Stalingradski. Again on a slope, we moved into badly constructed bunkers. Stalingradski no longer was a field aerodrome; only the occasional Ju52 touched down here. The entire slope was filled with bomb and shell craters so that landing here was very risky. Resupply of the troops now took place only by airdrops by parachute at marked drop zones. The end of the cauldron was closer.

Before we had moved toward Stalingradski, our unit was told to give up Waldemar to a collection point. We did not know the reason. Often, *hiwis*—there were several hundred of them in the cauldron—were left in a camp and abandoned to the Russians. It was a sad day for us, not only because he had brought us extra rations right up to the last day but also because he had become a true comrade. Alfons gave him a padded Russian uniform and a pair of felt boots (Valenki) so that he would not fall into Russian hands in German uniform. He bid us farewell with embraces. Turning to me, he said, "You were my brother. We got along so well." With tears in his eyes and a short wave, we left, never to see Waldemar again.

We knew our days were up. What would happen? Would we ever seen our homes and loved ones again? The shock-troop operations of Combat Group Eichhorn (which was the name of our new company commander) were carried out daily, but without any result. The Russians were in front of us, about 600 meters from our bunker. This position could be maintained for only a couple more days, and then all that was left to do was to flee into the city of Stalingrad.

Thanks to the intensive treatment of Dr. Horst Rocholl, my frozen parts had improved very well. Apart from a few small bits, all had healed. I tried to move outside a little, and in the end, I had to look around for a pair of boots that fit. Close to our bunker, there were six loaded trucks of our company, which were always dragged along from one move to another. When I had the time, I looked through every individual vehicle. The first vehicle had spare parts for tanks, track links, etc. The second had a reserve field kitchen, and a stiffly frozen horse lay in its cauldron. No wonder, then, that from time to time we had horse meat, while no horse had been seen for weeks; that was because our cook had unhitched several horses from the Romanians at a suitable opportunity. The third vehicle was a French Renault. Here I found what I had been looking for—our former storeroom. I got whatever I needed: two undershirts, one overshirt, gloves, a motorcycle overcoat, two blankets, a pair of motorcycle boots, a motorcycle pullover, two pairs of underpants, and even a pair of leather boots, size 44. I also found a box with lighters and a glass container with ten fuses, which were always good to have at this time of year. I organized a backpack for myself, and my kit was complete.

Once I returned to the bunker, I unpacked everything. When my comrades returned from operations that evening, I told them about my scavenging and gave away all that I had, except for two lighters and 200 flints, which I kept for myself. Why all this? I morally and psychologically had prepared myself for captivity.

On January 17, our combat group had to undertake a heavy attack to clear a hill in front of us to prevent the Russians from observing our positions. But Dr. Rocholl freed me from it by telling the company commander I still was not fit for combat because of my frostbite. Our combat group suffered great losses; only ten men of seventeen returned. That was a heavy blow. All three of my former crew returned. In the bunker, they told that their orders were to attack the enemy in a wide open snow field in their black tankers uniforms. This was madness, but orders were orders. We knew every soldier who had been killed and were deeply shocked.

On January 18, Meyer, our old company commander, visited the bunker. He had heard about this attack and was deeply shaken. After all, all these men were comrades with whom he had started his offensive from Kursk to Stalingrad in June 1942. It is the soldier's fate to risk his life daily and hourly. This last attack was badly prepared and was carried out without artillery or mortar support. But what role could humans play anyway? The cauldron would be finished soon, and all would be lost. I don't know whether everyone thought this way, but I did. My life was to end at twenty-two years, and I didn't want that.

Cuno had come to explain to us that on orders from above, he would be flown out with sixteen other high-ranking officers in order to take command of heavy tank units outside the cauldron. He wanted all of us living members of the former 9th Company to make a list with our home addresses so that he could give messages to our families. When he turned to me, he said, "I'd love to take you with me, as you cannot fight anymore with your frostbite. I'll see what can be done. The list was made and handed over to Meyer. There was no flight ticket for me, as I had not been wounded seriously. Despite all of Meyer's exertions, I stayed behind on January 20 with tears in my eyes.

The emergency airfield at Stalingradski, which could only be used by aircraft at their own risk, was nearing the end of its use. The last Ju52 landed on January 22, 1943, and the three-man crew slept one night in our bunker with us. We agreed that the next day they would take our mail with them. As a gift for letting them spend the night, they gave us a so-called Führer package with all sorts of sweet things. After we all had eaten our fill, we sat down to write. I sent last greetings to my parents; my sister, Anneliese; Hilde; and my girlfriend, Erika. No aircraft landed after this.

The next morning, we drank coffee with the crew and said our good-byes. With great sorrow, we looked at the three courageous pilots who started their machine and disappeared in the clouds. Apart from our radio—which reported that everything was fine in the heroic battles in Stalingrad—we no longer had any link with the outside world. We still had our big UKW receiver, which once belonged to the company; it was transported on a truck and powered by a twenty-four-volt battery. Stalingradski did not remain in our possession for long. Starting on January 23, mighty artillery and rocket (Stalin organ) fire indicated that we had to disappear from here quickly.

So we packed our stuff into four trucks and disappeared in the direction of the city of Stalingrad, which was one big pile of rubble. It looked ghostly. On this day, we had to cover about forty kilometers, and in the night, we arrived at the tractor works in North Stalingrad. There was not much time to find quarters, and we moved into a U-shaped complex of ruined buildings. The vehicles were parked in the courtyard, and we looked for an appropriate shelter, which we found in a staircase. The first floor still had a blanket, and there was a cellar window to the southern side. The shelter was just big enough for four men. The next morning, we expanded our shelter and found a stove. Though it consisted only of an iron can, it heated very well. While scavenging in the individual ruins, we even found a pair of mattresses. The radio was brought in and started up.

During the first two days, we looked at our surroundings, which were in ruins. Our little mob, as we called it, consisted of only ten men of the combat group, two cooks, and two men of the office, which still existed but was out of work. Of course, we looked out for the field kitchen and the first-aid post, which I had to visit from time to time for my treatment. You could see how tense and skinny all these people had become. Without the will to live, everyone faced the question of when and how his end would come. Over the radio, we learned about the situation at the front. Basically, the entire cauldron had been compressed onto the city.

The Russians were trying to split up the city that stretched for seventy kilometers along the Volga. Within the city, they encircled Stalingrad north, middle, and south. In the north, we, the remains of the 24th Panzer Division, were stuck, as well as the remains of the 16th Panzer Division, the 14th Panzer Division, and other units. Masterfully, the Red Army had managed to first liquidate Stalingrad South and then Stalingrad Middle. Tens of thousands of soldiers fell here—"killed for Führer and Fatherland," "fallen on the field of honor"—these were slogans that no longer could influence the morale of the troops. Half starved, frozen, burned in their tanks, and eaten by lice—this was the end of the German Army.

The actions of Combat Group Eichhorn in the next days of street fighting brought more and more losses. Both Wilhelm Hermes and Herbert Schwertner became victims of this crazy war, Hermes with a round through his lungs and Schwertner with one through his belly. But it went on, even if only for a few days more. I was not exactly fit for the front, which was attested to by a doctor's report. Along with a comrade who had been wounded in the lower left arm by an explosive bullet, I spent every evening at the crossroads of the Tractor Works to keep a fire going to show the supply planes where to drop their supply bombs. Everyone had to lend a hand in order to lengthen the resistance; that was our task during the final days in the cauldron.

In the meantime, wood had gotten scarce in the ruins, so that we kept ourselves busy with collecting some during the daytime. The fires were placed in a twenty-by-twenty-by-twenty-meter triangle. The aircraft that were flying in knew this marking. The supply bombs they dropped often drifted far away from the center because of the weather. It was the job of search troops to recover these bombs and their contents and bring them to collection points for distribution. To the last day, each man got 100 grams of bread and 60 grams of meat or fat. Military law still ruled in Stalingrad, and anyone who stole supplies was court-martialed and shot.

On January 30, Hermann Göring held a great speech in the German Reichstag, which we heard as well. Amongst his boastful praises, he listed the heroic battle of the 6th Army in Stalingrad, namely its destruction, in which the last commanders blew themselves up with their units. That was a big lie, since it was certain that we still were living and that what moved to our left and right had not blown itself up either. We did not know that the cauldron at this time still contained about 90,000 men. But we now knew one thing: that we did not exist anymore, that all of us were counted as killed. Did the battle here still serve a purpose? There was a murderous bombardment for twenty-two hours per day. Only during the afternoon from 4:00 to 6:00 did the bombardment taper off. I do not know why the Russians chose this timeframe.

Russia was in the grip of a deep winter, but a mess tin of clean snow could not be found anywhere—the earth had been churned up that much by bombs and shells. So we were ground down pitilessly, and we had nothing with which to oppose it.

On January 31, a rumor ran that our divisional commander, Maj. Gen. Arno von Lenski, had been negotiating surrender with the Russians. By the evening, the conversation was confirmed officially, and all weapons were silent. We were not aware of any conditions. The next day, these were made known to us. On February 2, the rest of the 6th Army capitulated at eight o'clock in the morning. All combat was to cease; all weapons were to be handed in at collection points. The guns were to remain in their positions. Every officer and private had to surrender to the Red Army, either individually or in units. Everyone was allowed to take personal objects with him in his baggage. The wounded were to be cared for. All who did not put up any resistance were guaranteed their life as well as a return home after the war.

On the morning of February 1, I visited Dr. Rocholl for the last time. He had a look at my hands and feet and said, "We just managed that. The left foot still has some open spots, but I'll bind it up freshly once more and will give you ointment and some bandages so you can treat yourself. Look out for a second case of frostbite on the same spot, as this will have consequences. I wish you all the best; perhaps we'll one day meet again." I thanked him for his troubles and wished him all the best. Soon I was out of the cellar and returned to my comrades.

Officially, we still had three man of our crew left. Alfons Bartsch was the best off as far as health went, as he had suffered nothing. Wilhelm Hermes had been shot through his lungs; apart from some complaints with breathing, he felt well and did not want to go to the hospital. My frostbite had healed a little. The three of us wanted to remain together at all costs. Then there was Spalenke, a former radioman of the 3rd Platoon, an Austrian, and two office Wallas from our company—I can't remember their names. No one knew what had become of Eichhorn, our last company commander.

Six soldiers and three NCOs were the remnants of the 9th Company. In late April 1942, it had proudly marched off into the field with 145 men and survived the cauldron with six men. Were we the lucky ones to survive this hell? We did not know what awaited us in captivity. We looked toward it with mixed emotions. We sat in our staircase and discussed whether we could trust the Russians. Our opinions varied, but no one thought the Russians would kill all of us. We abandoned any thought of killing ourselves and thought we might be able to break out.

In the early hours of February 2, Alfons and Wilhelm would try to break out and reach German lines, even though none of us knew where that was. All six of us assembled their march packs. First, I tried my size forty-four boots. I had no problems with the right one, but the left one didn't fit. I forced it on. I packed my backpack with overcoat and tins. There were still all sorts of stuff to put on: underclothes, two pairs of socks, my black tank uniform, and a blue work overall, a normal gray greatcoat, an overcoat, and two pairs of gloves. I did not want to freeze again.

With the capitulation, the courts-martial were abolished, and everyone could do as he pleased. So we could get something to eat for ourselves. My comrades left me in the cellar to guard the house, and the others moved off. After an hour, everyone had returned and unpacked all kinds of good stuff—conserved sausages, tinned ham, tinned butter, fresh bread, tinned fish, powdered pudding, tinned vegetables, all sorts of things that we had not seen for months. There was also diluted rum and blocks of ground coffee. Everything was divided properly, and a big orgy of consumption was begun. In sewers under the city, my comrades had discovered a supply depot and had gotten plenty of supplies in short order. Three men returned for a second time and returned with schnapps, chocolate, and a sack of tinned vegetables. Spalenka and I prepared one more bag with five tins of vegetables for us, all for the march into captivity. We ate for the entire afternoon and into the evening. Our jaws were aching from all the chewing.

At 5:00 P.M., we lighted our marker fires as before, and once again, the aircraft showed up. Did they not know that we had capitulated? We were well cared for and did not need anything anymore. The water bottles were filled with schnapps in order to keep warm. Now all we had to do was step out in front of the Russians with hands held high—a horrible thought for a once-elite army. But we were vanquished; we had no choice. By midnight, our little oven was heated up thoroughly one last time, and then everyone crawled into his corner and was alone with his thoughts. I thought of home, of all my loved ones, and wondered whether I would see them again. The future was uncertain. We feel asleep until we were awakened by the cold. That was at four in the morning. After the stove had been heated up once again, everyone boiled a block of coffee for himself.

No one was hungry since we had eaten well in the previous hours. Bartsch and Hermes indicated that they would begin their attempt to break through to the German lines now. Each took his pistol, some hand grenades, a bread sack, and some supplies. Then they made their good-byes and disappeared.

We wished them luck. Now we sat down thoughtfully and waited for the hour of eight o'clock. In a heating shaft, we hid our pistols and thirty tins of conserved vegetables, which we no longer could take with us. In the meantime, our friends had been gone for an hour. Perhaps they were lucky; perhaps they already had been shot. Shortly before six o'clock the tent flap in front of our door opened, and our two comrades entered. They had tried to break through at several locations, but the main front line had been manned so strongly that they could not find a hole. So they resigned themselves to the same fate as us. With apprehension, we waited for eight o'clock. Outside it was quiet; not a shot rang out. There was an eerie silence. We had chosen the exit to the inner courtyard, and at 7:45, we prepared to march.

THE MARCH INTO CAPTIVITY

At exactly eight o'clock, the Red Army men came for our ruins. They filed along the houses to our left and right—one each with three men in the inner courtyard. They announced their arrival with a salvo from their machine pistols. Now there was no way back for the six of us. I was the first man to come out of the ruins with my hands raised; the others followed. When the young Red Army man indicated to me that I could lower my arms, I was pleasantly surprised. His next question was for a watch. Although it was broken, I had to hand mine over to him. He put it away, and in return, he gave me half a loaf of bread from his backpack. Each one of my comrades now had to hand over his watch although the Russian no longer had any bread to give them. Then he waved to us to show that we should proceed. That was a positive first impression.

Our route led to the next collection point. German soldiers streamed out of all the ruins. I was amazed at the mass since we rarely had seen anyone else during combat operations. Once we arrived at the collection point, we looked for acquaintances, but we could not find any. Several hundred had already been assembled here—not everyone had blown himself up like Göring had suggested. Then came a second positive surprise. I already have indicated that we carried some baggage with us. We struck up a conversation with an older Russian major and his female translator, who accused me of being an SS man. When I reacted in amazement, she said, "You are wearing the black SS uniform, and in order to hide it you have put on an overall over it." I explained that I was a tanker and not an SS man. She was not satisfied with this, and I took off my overall to show her that as a member of the army, I wore an eagle on my chest, whereas the SS men wore it on the arm. My explanation satisfied her.

Spalenka and I had put down our boxes with tins but had not kept sight of them in our dispute with the translator, and a Red Army man took them. Spalenka reported that to the major, and before the man was out of sight, he had to return and return everything to us. As punishment, the soldier got a few blows on the head and a kick up the backside from the major—another gesture that gave us food for thought: the Russians aren't all that bad. Until the afternoon, we moved from one collection point to another, and the number of German prisoners grew and grew. The last great collection point was in a wide valley outside the city.

THE BEGINNING OF THE DEATH MARCH

The first baggage checks were carried out in this valley, but only a few pieces of luggage were taken away. I gave my raincoat to an NCO from the office who did not have anything other than his thin army overcoat. Now the big march began; infinitely long streams of men passed by along the horizon. Later, it was established that there were 90,000 men, "men who had blown themselves up"—what a bald-faced lie by a German statesman. The march went east and went on forever into the darkness.

The roads grew worse, and the snow looser and deeper. It was sheer torture to advance with this baggage. So we agreed that each one of us was to ditch one bag. It was still a tiring march. After a while, we also ditched the second bag. This was a difficult decision to make since it contained our food. We had been starved for long enough. But what mattered here was to keep going in the great mass—or else lie down and freeze to death. Then the six of us decided to try to stay at the head of the big column. When we reached the head, five of us would sit down and rest while the sixth would keep standing and watch out for the tail of the column. Then everyone was awakened, and we marched back to the head of the column, where we repeated the process. We kept this going the entire night. We had learned that small groups of Russian rear-area men would lie by the road to rob German prisoners and kill them if they resisted. Frontline troops, on the other hand, were usually generous and humane.

The death march, as we called it, seemed to last forever. We asked Russian horsemen who passed us by how long the road would be. They answered, "Skora budit domeu" (Soon you'll be home). So it continued for the entire night. Everyone's strength fell, and so did the marching tempo. The cold was bitter, and we feared that if we took a swig of schnapps from our water bottles, our lips would stick to the bottle. For me, the situation got worse as my groin began to swell, but I did not want to throw away anything else, so I had to bite my teeth and hang on. After a while, we noticed in the skies that day was coming. Again, we asked a Russian horseman how far we were from our objective. He answered us, "I scho pertvazit" (Another fifteen kilometers). That was a ray of light, but we did not know whether we could believe him. Then we saw something that looked like houses in the distance. Was that to be our objective? My swollen groin became worse and worse, and I could only take short steps; my marching tempo slowed down remarkably. Luckily, there were no Russian rear-area units around anymore. The village, our objective, became clearer and clearer. Alfons Bartsch took my backpack from me to carry it. In hope that the village, which was about three kilometers away, would offer quarters, we agreed that four men would go ahead quickly. Hermes and I would follow slowly. The four went off, and the two of us tried to get ahead as fast as we could make it. We had to rest in the snow several times since I could barely put one leg in front of the other.

One hour later, we reached the village with the name of Dubowka. It was a large village, maybe even a small town. The prisoners were lying down completely exhausted in the road. Suddenly, Bartsch showed up, and we were all delighted to be reunited. All six of us had survived the fifty-three-kilometer death march. For me, it was the biggest physical exertion that I had ever endured in my young life; there were only three toes of raw meat on my left foot. With all my strength, I tortured myself forward to this objective, but I wanted to live and not croak like a dog. I had the help of my comrades. During these hours of struggling for survival, real comradeship showed itself; we were there for each other.

As the day went on, 45,000 men were sheltered here provisionally. The other 48,000 prisoners, who had been diverted along the way, were marched off in the direction of Beketovka and had been sheltered there. We were placed in five empty grain storage silos with two floors, with 10,000 men to each silo, 5,000 on each floor. The place was crowded, and everyone sat down on his pack. We slept sitting up. The many people in the room radiated warmth so it was warm in there. The shelters became less crowded as hundreds died everyday. This wasn't surprising. It had been a difficult winter, with daily temperatures well below zero and with only 100 grams of bread and 60 grams of meat or fat per day for two months. We were starved and without strength. Many had frostbite on their hands or feet. A large number had been bitten by lice. And now these run-down and weakened men had faced a fifty-three-kilometer march. It took a superhuman effort to survive these exertions and the illnesses to which we were vulnerable, like thyroid fever and dysentery.

This was the end of the once-proud 6th Army. Only several thousand men survived this misery. I was one of these few. Despite everything I experienced and witnessed, I had the good fortune to see my home and loved ones again.

A tank amid the ruins of Stalingrad.

Soldiers gather in a plaza surrounded by rubble.

Saving a comrade from the ruins.

CHAPTER 2

The Road to Stalingrad: Nemesis on the Volga

Joachim Stempel

"**B**ehave yourself to the last moment as is fitting for a proper soldier!" my father, Lt. Gen. Richard Stempel, told me before the end came at Stalingrad on January 25, 1943.

Stalingrad—the triumph and loss of a German army—continues to provide fodder for research as well as for explanations and arguments. In the military historical literature on the battle of Stalingrad, there is an insurmountable mountain of books, professional articles, and other works that deal with the operational thought, strategic actions, situation reports, and command decisions regarding the progress of the battles between the Don and Volga Rivers in 1942–43. Historians research the causes of the catastrophe. I'm not a historian—I was simply "there," committed, highly motivated, and convinced of the correctness of my actions.

The following record should be seen in that light. It is based mostly on my personal experiences as a foot soldier, not on the exemplary situation map of the commander—and certainly not the commander in chief. From a young age, I had to shoulder military tasks and responsibilities under extreme conditions unknown to the modern generation, which has experienced nothing comparable.

My story is, of course, subjective. It takes the form of a "diary" in which daily entries are made about each day of fighting. This is supplemented by reports, letters home, and other documents. I present my story in chronological order—without

Joachim Stempel.

any explanations, without any retrospective analysis, without any sarcastic looks forward, and without any modern knowledge. It was important to show what really took place behind the official reports, announcements, news, and other publications, behind the naked numbers, the boastful reports, and strange place names. I've tried to convey the efforts and suffering, the courage and bravery, the sacrifice and misery, the poverty and continuous deprivation, the bitter abandonment and hopelessness, of the soldier in battle, as well as his loyal comradeship and fulfillment of duty.

To make this especially clear, every personal story is preceded by the limited and precise expressions of the Wehrmacht communiqué for that date, as far as it makes any mention of the situation and the fighting in my own sector and shows the development of the general situation. I've also included corresponding reports from the War Diary of the Armed Forces High Command (OKW). The stories of the last weeks in Stalingrad—during which there was no possibility of writing letters, much less of transporting them home by mail and during which the keeping of a diary also stopped—were written from memory. They still remain so clear and vivid as they tower over everything I experienced before and after.

In the inferno after the battle, the Red Army captured 93,000 prisoners, of which only 6,000 ever saw home again. I was allowed to be one.

"NOW MARCH TO STALINGRAD AND REACH THE VOLGA!"

August 14, 1942: Departure from Stalino with the 14th Panzer Division to the East

On July 19, 1942, the 6th Army received the order to attack Stalingrad. It read:

> The 6th Army is to take possession of the landbridge between the Don and Volga north of the railway Kalach-Stalingrad and secure it in an easterly and northerly direction. The army will cross the Don and

then advance with its heavy units to the area directly
north of Stalingrad up to the Volga, all the while securing the northern flank, while at the same time,
detached forces penetrate into Stalingrad from the
north and take it.

Accordingly, on August 14, I was ordered to command an
advance detachment of the regimental staff and received the
following orders:

- to reconnoiter the ordered route of advance on accessi-
  bility, obstacles, etc.
- to mark the route
- to scout out and note down billets for the battalions
- to scout out and note down a billet for the regimental
  headquarters
- the possibilities of securing and guarding the sites
- to make sketches
- to designate a starting point for the subsequent march

And so we set out at dawn this morning in order to build
up a great lead on the column of Panzergrenadier Regiment
108. First, everything goes smoothly, and we reach Shakhty by
way of Novotscherkask. Then it's onward to the Don. Here the
landscape changes greatly. We move east of the Donets where
the wide agricultural grounds have already given way to the
Don and Kalmuck steppes. East of the Don, only more steppe
awaits us. The ground is flat and devoid of trees; it possesses a
depressing boredom—heat, dust, and wide spaces without
shadow. Nothing notable is visible on the horizon. Despite the
heat of more than 50 degrees Celsius, which calls to our minds
the desert, we are nevertheless thinking how all this will look in
winter: snow, winter storms, icy frost. Don't think about it! Not
now, while we're sitting on our motorcycles, sweating. Driving
does not offer any relief either. Heat and dust—nothing else.

Late in the afternoon, we reach the first billet area and
prepare the billets, locate a site for the regimental headquar-

ters, and put traffic directors on the road to guide the battalions to their designated areas. Then the columns arrive. Everything takes place in quiet and complete discipline. The men quickly get established and set up guard posts. The regimental commander is not satisfied with his billet, which is too primitive, and the staff is looking for an alternative. But in this village, none is to be found. No one else has proper billets, not like we had at Stalino. The night passes quietly, and I busy myself again with the operations we are currently carrying out.

In oppressive heat and pressured by sand storms, Panzergrenadier Regiment 108 rolls farther east, raising a great cloud of dust and sand. We have to maintain contact with other troops of the 14th Panzer Division. A motorcycle platoon is always out in front to mark and indicate landmarks, reconnoiter designated areas, and build up the guard posts. Then we wait for the other units to arrive and billet, and we start talking about the advance route and billet areas for the next day. Finally, we tend to personal care and make all preparations for the following morning's march.

The war diary of the OKW mentions our operations more than once. On August 16, 1942, it says: "Attacks on the northeastern flank of the 14th Panzer Division were beaten off." And on August 20, it says: "Enemy attacks on the right flank of the 14th Panzer Division were beaten off. The enemy forces encircled at the railroad station of Abganerowo were eliminated and attacks with tanks north of the railway station were beaten off as well. The bridgehead north of Stalingrad was expanded, the emergency bridge over the Don was completed."

Panzergrenadier Regiment 108 now marches over that bridge in the deep south. The Don is behind us. This is a giant river, more than 1,870 kilometers long, and comes from a source in the central Russia. Below Rostov, it flows into the Sea of Asov, in the Gulf of Taganrog. Especially important is the fact that west of Stalingrad, the Don approaches the Volga to a distance of 55 kilometers in a large bend and then curves away again. In front of us is only steppe now, in which everything expands in bright sunshine and glittering endlessness. We leave the giant dust clouds that tower over the entire wide open land and darken the skies behind us. Now we are coming; now it is our turn.

August 21, 1942: Across the Don to Aksai, Abganerowo, and Tinguta Railroad Station

On August 21, 1942, it is noted in the OKW war diary: "24th Panzer Division, in its advance east, has reached the southern edge of Lake Zaza and advances north toward Zaza. There the enemy is stronger. The 14th Panzer Division fights in the heights northwest of Zaza and near Tinguta railroad station, on the left flank our own troops and Romanian troops have advanced further north and have thrown back attacks of the enemy."

The Bolsheviks defend themselves desperately and bitterly contest every foot of soil. They want to make a stand at the Don; they want to stop our attack cold. As we know from prisoners, Stalin himself has worked on this army and sworn them to fight this battle between Don and Volga. We feel this increased resistance, and every fight causes mounting losses. In an abandoned red command post, we find written sources, orders, sketches, and even handbooks. In one of these, a Russian infantry handbook for combat from 1941, I find the following directive:

> The infantry is to have no fear of encirclement and should know how to take up a defensive ring and break out of it in complete order. When the infantry is encircled, the commanders have to maintain command strictly in their hands. A strong defense in all directions has to be organized, and all measures are to be taken to prevent the enemy splitting up the one encirclement into many smaller encirclements. The break out from an encirclement can only take place on orders of the highest command authority. It should be carried out in good order and in no case in small groups.

It is not to be wondered, therefore, that the enemy tries to force a decision here and now. We will learn how this will look when we are not capable of subjecting the Russian to our will, as we have grown used to. But our attack draws us closer and closer to the city. Especially in the north, our troops boldly advance toward the Volga and Stalingrad, while we're battling the Russians southwest of the city on the railroad at Tinguta station. We find more heat and dust, wide open steppe, and enemy field positions that are perfectly camouflaged and putting up bitter resistance. We are learning what kind of city this is, the objective of such fighting, which the Russians do not want to give up at any price.

Stalingrad lies on the western bank of the Volga and has a north-south expansion of 40 kilometers. Geographically, it is parted by the valley of the Zariza Stream, which flows into the Volga. The most remarkable and important features are, from north to south, the Rynok suburb, then Spartakowa, the tractor works, the gun foundry "Red Barricade," the bread factory, the iron works "Red October," the Lazur chemical works, the expansive business area with the "Red Square" north of the Zariza down to the south toward Kuporosnoje and Jelschanka. Inland, the city extends from the Volga to five kilometers over rising heights on a ridge. Behind this, the land sinks again slightly toward the west. We are now thrusting here in this forward area after conquering the Soviets' outer defensive positions. There are individual villages located there, which increase and grow more dense as one moves toward the town—workers' settlements, city buildings, silos, oil tanks, and water towers. In between all that, railroads split off in all directions with high railroad beds and deep railroad cuts.

This makes for a confusing chaos with all sorts of obstacles that can turn into hell for an attacker. And today, August 24, German soldiers stand close to the suburb of Rynok on the high rising western bank of the Volga. It is located nearly 100 meters above the stream, which here has a width of about 2,000 meters. Here is the watershed between Europe and Asia, which our tanks, now standing on the high bank at Rynok, are trying to cut with their fire. A proud feeling comes over all of

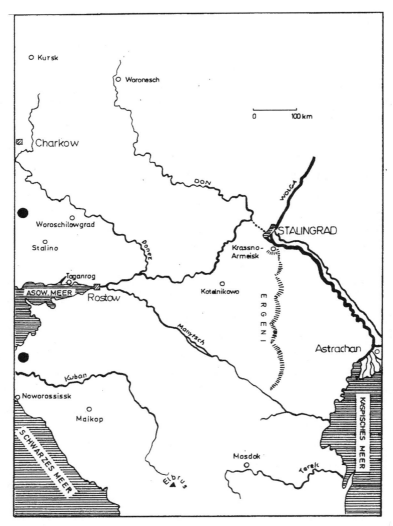

Stalingrad and environs.

us. Now it's our turn. We'll take the town from the south, and when we stand at the Volga, we'll be standing before the very gates of Asia.

August 25, 1942. Breaking into the Defense System in Front of Stalingrad and the Attack on the South of the City

On August 25, 1942, the Wehrmacht communiqué made known: "Northwest and south of Stalingrad the attack gained more ground despite desperate Bolshevik resistance. Fifty-two Soviet tanks were destroyed. Fierce day and night attacks of the Luftwaffe against the enemy rear area, especially against Stalingrad, caused major fires and great destruction in arms factories and military installations." In the OKW war diary, it was noted: "The attacks on the Panzer divisions on the right flank of the 4th Panzer Army have grown more feeble. A stronger enemy is south of the Volga-Don canal. All attacks on the railroad at Tinguta were thrown back. Those enemy elements encircled here were destroyed."

On August 26, the Wehrmacht communiqué reported: "In the area west of Stalingrad, the enemy was thrown back eastwards in bitter fighting. Stalingrad, which is the scene of major fires, was attacked day and night by the Luftwaffe with high explosive bombs." The OKW war diary also describe it: "Repeated enemy attacks on the positions south of Stalingrad were beaten off. Strong pressure on the advancing parts on the right flank of the 4th Panzer Army."

Dust and the great heat take their toll on us as well as the continuous nervous tension and the high degree of necessary attention. The fine sand of the steppe manages to penetrate all parts of the uniform, and the uninterrupted wind blows away everything and covers it in a ghostly white-grey. No, Stalino is weeks and weeks past. It is stunning to see how quickly people are capable of adapting. But it won't last long here—our advance and attacks are unstoppable.

On August 29, the Wehrmacht communiqué reports about these battles around Stalingrad: "In the Stalingrad area, the German troops continue their attack against partially extensive enemy fortifications. Multiple counterattacks were beaten off."

On August 31, the Wehrmacht communiqué reports: "South of Stalingrad, German troops penetrated the enemy positions, annihilated strong Soviet forces and are standing 25 kilometers south of the city. Night attacks of the Luftwaffe caused expansive fires in Stalingrad. Railroad targets and aerodromes east of the Volga were attacked with good results."

Now we have arrived in the suburbs of the city and in the deep system of enemy positions. And there are more deeply echeloned and well-crafted field fortifications in front of us. Here it becomes clear to all of us why the Russian resistance is so successful. Dug-in tanks are scarcely visible, with their guns aimed just over the cover. Flamethrowers turn the entire killing ground that we have to cross into a sheet of flame. Closing with the enemy causes losses. And yet we have pierced deeply into the Russian defenses and hope that their resistance will diminish in short order. Behind the long rolling heights lies Stalingrad. Gigantic plumes of black smoke are rising to the skies there, and at night, a bright gleam of fires covers the entire city.

On September 1, the Wehrmacht communiqué reports: "South of Stalingrad, infantry divisions and fast troops expanded their penetrations into enemy positions and in a rapid advance took possession of an important ridge in the direction of the city. An enemy armored train was destroyed. Intense operations by the Luftwaffe contributed to shattering the enemy resistance. In the past night strong bombing attacks were carried out against Stalingrad and several airfields east of the Volga."

On September 3, the war diary of the OKW reads: "Southwest of Stalingrad, German and Romanian divisions have advanced beyond the railroad of Stalingrad-Kalach and now are fighting northwest of Woroponowo station, ten kilometers west of Stalingrad. The units advancing from the northwest are close to linking up with the forces coming up from the south. In between them the enemy tries to stop the forces trying to link up."

Today, like past days, again saw bitter fighting with the retreating enemy. The Bolsheviks fortify any high ground and obstacle and, as before, defend themselves with determination and bitterness. They hang on to their excellently fashioned dugouts and make use of every useful section of ground to weaken our still present impetus and stop us cold. Again and again, there are these damned dug-in T-34 tanks, which are difficult to spot. Most of the time, they are spotted too late. They completely hose us, and the fields in this wide-open steppe offer no cover from their tank shells. In a concentrated hail of fire, our grenadiers are pinned down, and onto them, the Russian flamethrowers hiss and spit their load and cause horrible and hideous casualties.

Overhead are our dive-bombers and close-support aircraft, our Ju88 bombers, which drop their bombs on the Russian positions and bunker systems. Added to that are the rocket launchers located close behind us. They fire their screaming and howling projectiles over our heads into the enemy—a hellish inferno in which no one knows whether fire is enemy or friendly. The attack makes progress only slowly in the scorching heat and raised dust clouds.

September 3, 1942. Panzergrenadier Regiment 108 Suffers Severe Losses

The losses in men and materiel are high, way too high. In these days, about three quarters of regimental officers have become casualties—three quarters! My nineteen-year-old "orderly" has fallen. My driver has been severely wounded; one of his arms has been ripped off. I myself suffered minor cuts from splinters. This is how the losses of Panzergrenadier Regiment 108 look during the operations against the fortifications west of Stalingrad:

1st Company
2nd Lieutenant Harter killed (during a penetration into enemy positions with a "Hurra" and entrenching tool in hand)

2nd Lieutenant Menges wounded

2nd Company
2nd Lieutenant Möbius severely wounded
2nd Lieutenant Wittiber wounded

3rd Company
1st Lieutenant Haensel severely wounded
2nd Lieutenant Häring wounded

6th Company
1st Lieutenant Schade killed
1st Lieutenant Gräfe killed

7th Company
1st Lieutenant Richter severely wounded
1st Lieutenant Seidel severely wounded
2nd Lieutenant Plasil wounded

8th Company
1st Lieutenant Hollenweger wounded
2nd Lieutenant Wurst wounded
2nd Lieutenant Rüger wounded

10th Company
1st Lieutenant Schöne severely wounded
2nd Lieutenant Kaufmann killed

12th Company
2nd Lieutenant Göbel killed

These losses leave behind huge gaps. Who would have believed at Stalino that after so short a time of renewed operations and after such a complete bringing up to strength, the battalion would have been decimated so much? And all before the fight for the city of Stalingrad itself!

The attack is to be driven forward without a break to deny the Russians time to entrench themselves and expand the trench systems and defensive positions even further. Today I have been given the task of providing security for the regimental command post. We have to expect enemy bombardments of artillery and rocket launchers, the so-called "Stalin's organs." Suddenly, a large armored personnel carrier bears down on our position. In a thick cloud of dust, our divisional commander, Lt. Gen. Ferdinand Heim, dismounts. On his neck is the Knight's Cross of the Iron Cross, which he was awarded this very day.

"Where's the regimental commander?" he asks.

"Down there, general," I answer, pointing toward the steps that lead to the underground cellars.

The general descends, and after quite a while, he comes to the surface again, mounts his personnel carrier, and goes to visit the battalions.

On September 5, the Wehrmacht communiqué has this to say about our front sector: "In the theater of operations of Stalingrad, the German assault troops took multiple fiercely defended and recently expanded field positions. Enemy counterattacks were thrown back." On the same day, the OKW war diary noted: "Strong enemy in well dug-in positions west of the Don 'knee' south of Stalingrad. Panzer and infantry divisions are attacking, coming from the west, on the Stalingrad town center, about four kilometers from the Volga, in severe fighting."

At this time, we are closing in on this city, which is defended so toughly by the Russians, only arduously, meter by meter. It is unbelievable to see the bitterness and desperate courage with which the Soviet soldiers defend this point that is so important to them. But we do not let up, and despite high losses, the attack is carried forward without pause. We're not to give the Bolsheviks a break in the fighting; we're to keep the pressure mounted on them. Even so, more and more clearly, the question is asked: "How are we to carry on like this in the days and weeks to come?" The muster rolls of the companies have been decimated, and there is no mention of replacements. Where would these come from, anyway?

On September 7, the Wehrmacht communiqué reported:

In the battle for Stalingrad, German and Romanian troops again gained ground in heavy fighting. The enemy renewed its heavy relieving attacks from the north against the German blocking positions using strong infantry and armored Units. All attacks were thrown back bloodily, and 108 enemy tanks were destroyed. Panzer and motorized infantry divisions, supported by air force and antiaircraft units, played a decisive part in this. Day and night attacks by the Luftwaffe are aimed at the town area. Furthermore during the night airfields east of the Volga were bombed.

The OKW war diary provides this additional information: "The XIV Panzer Corps continuously attacked the enemy since the early hours of the morning with tanks. The attacks on the whole were stopped. At some locations the enemy succeeded in breaking into our own positions using fresh troops. Only the use of all available reserves enabled us to throw the enemy out of our positions and reestablish the main line of resistance."

September 8, 1942. New Job: Aide-de-camp with the 14th Panzergrenadier Brigade

Today, when I got back to the regimental command post from operations with my motorcycle platoon, I was immediately ordered to see the regimental commander, Colonel Schmidt. I brush off my dirty and dusty clothes, order the night-watch roster for the command post, and make my way to the staff bunker. In an earth bunker, dug deeply and covered with earthen works, I find the officers, noncommissioned officers, and men of the staff. I report to the commander. He does not even allow me to sit down but tells me in a service-like fashion: "Stempel, effective immediately, you are transferred to brigade staff. Report there today. New job: aide-de-camp with the brigade commander, Colonel Freiherr von Falkenstein. Understood?"

I am dismissed and climb up to the light and fresh air. What's the meaning of this? Now out of the deepest mud, I hand over my platoon. What am I supposed to do at brigade, anyway? Orders are orders, and who can tell what they're good for? Who knows what happens tomorrow or the day after that? Everything here can change in such a short time. What will this battle yet demand from us?

I go to see my men and say my good-byes. A sergeant major takes over command of my motorcycle infantry platoon in my absence. We know each other well; all will continue as before. Then I report my departure to the commander of Panzergrenadier Regiment 108 and drive to the command post of the 14th Panzergrenadier Brigade with a lot of mixed feelings. It's not far, and therefore, I arrive quickly. Here I am ordered to report to the commander early the next day to carry out my duties.

On September 8, the Wehrmacht communiqué reports: "In the fortress area of Stalingrad, German troops in the face of tough resistance took further positions on the heights. Strong bomber and close-support squadrons supported the fighting of the army. The Volga bridges south of the city were bombed day and night."

On September 9, it reports: "In the fortress area of Stalingrad, armored troops pierced strongly defended enemy positions and in bitter fighting took the domineering high grounds west of Stalingrad. Overnight the city and Soviet airfields east of the Volga were bombed." On the same date, the OKW war diary notes:

> The panzer and motorized infantry units repositioning themselves around Stalingrad once again launched an attack against this overall strongly fortified city. The southern part of the city and the Volga are under fire from artillery with forward observers. The enemy tries to hamper the advance of our troops by massive sorties. In order to provide relief the enemy once again attacked the northern front of the XIV Panzer Corps on three locations with massive forces.

My new job gives me an overview of the job of a staff. Here things look different; here the operations of the lower units are guided; here we are informed constantly about the situation of the enemy. My situation has changed completely. I escort the brigade commander to the regiments of the brigade, to the superior staffs and neighboring units. I plan these drives for the commander and drive myself to situation conferences and order groups. And then I have to present the decisions and anything remarkable to the staff. I'm there when the daily reports from units come in and hear how the report for the division is prepared. It is an interesting job, and the nights are comfortable: I lie in a hole in the ground covered with a groundsheet.

On September 13, we are to have a "big day." The Wehrmacht communiqué for the day reports: "In front of Stalingrad, the assault troops fought themselves forward towards the edge of the city despite the severe enemy resistance after storming multiple enemy fieldworks and penetrated the southern part of the city. Enemy relief attacks from the north were thrown back." The OKW war diary elaborates on this:

> The attack against Stalingrad progresses slowly against the toughly defended fortifications on the edge of the southern suburbs. Parts of the panzer and motorized divisions that attacked south of the Kalach-Stalingrad railroad managed to reach the industrial area of a southern suburb. Here there is severe fighting. Likewise the infantry and panzer units that are advancing on the middle and northern part of the city continue to advance south and east. From the north the enemy repeated its vain attacks on the positions between the Volga and the railroad.

Throughout the night, there was a massive operation by Soviet bombers. The attack of the Soviet Air Force lasted from 7:30 yesterday evening to 4:00 this morning. Apart from that, there is constant artillery fire of all different calibers coming down on our positions and deep into the rear area as well. Likewise, from time to time, we are subjected to fire from the

Stalin organs. Although the results cannot be compared to the massive noise and the great number of simultaneous impacts, there are many killed and wounded every time. Two hours ago, our command post was hit by such a "layer." When the smoke had gone and the dust had settled, we saw the losses and the damage that had been caused by this. I also have gotten some scratches. But who here is without bandages and plaster?

It is clear that the Russians will not give up the city at any price. They're trying everything to keep us from penetrating this traffic center that is so important to them. It is almost two months now that we've sunk our teeth into this fortified front, and the impetus of our attack died down a long time ago. The superiority we had until now cannot help us move forward anymore. But we must gain the western bank of the Volga on the entire length of the city. And how do things look on the Soviet side? We do not get much information from captured Red Army men. And the deserters? They tell us wild stories.

Soviet Account of Their Defense of the City

How the Soviets viewed this phase of the battle is made clear by the following extract from *The Soviet Army: A New Type of Army* by Schatagan and Prussanow:

> During one month, the Soviet troops managed to stand up to the high pressure of the enemy. The exemplary steadfastness and the tough resistance of Soviet soldiers foiled the enemy attempt to overrun the defenders, move across the Don and break into Stalingrad. This gained the Soviet leadership the time to reinforce the defenses of Stalingrad and to take the necessary measures. The Communist Party organization of Stalingrad organized 15,000 workers and Kolchoz farmers to build fieldworks. The Soviet troops fought with a determination not seen before. But they were forced to withdraw under the pressure of a numerically superior enemy. By the 13th of September,

the fascists had managed to reach the town edge of Stalingrad. The heroic defense of the city began. 75,000 inhabitants of Stalingrad fought in the ranks of the Soviet forces. The workers of Stalingrad labored day and night despite the murderous bombing attacks and the incessant artillery bombardment of the city. Even when the enemy was less than a kilometer from the "tractor factory" and the enemy's guns were firing at it over open sights, the work in the factory halls was not stopped. In these horrible days the factory reached the highest productivity of labor and daily built dozens of tanks, which rolled straight to the forward positions from the factory gates. Their crews were the workers that had built the tanks.

It was like that day by day. The resistance grows stronger, and the fight is carried out without mercy.

The Battle for the Railroad Area and the Grain Elevator
A few days ago, four lieutenants arrived from home from our replacement depot in Dresden. Early in the morning, they shook me awake in my hole in the ground and tore of the tent square covering me. What a joyous reunion! My comrades von Erdmannsdorff, Versock, and Laube. We shook hands, and there was a short report about the current situation. Laube was already killed yesterday. I was shocked, even considering the general coarseness and callousness.

Today witnessed another massive operation by our aviators, who are coming and going all the time. Again and again, the close-support pilots and our comrades in the Stukas dive down upon the enemy positions and the factory works of this big city. All of a sudden, there are Russian fighters in the air. Where are our Me 109s? They've already gone to take on the next wave. Two of our close-support aircraft have been hit. They come down in flames over there. And the Russian anti-aircraft artillery is firing from all barrels. Now they've gotten a Stuka that was coming in to attack. He comes down vertically, and a big pillar of smoke, black and dark, rises to the heavens. My God! Three hits by the Russians in only a few moments! That is something we have not seen before.

Yet the next squadrons are already approaching high in the skies. Some are diving in front of us on nearby targets; others at great altitude continue to fly east. In flights without break, this takes place in front of us. They dive down on the Russian positions with the noise of their howling of sirens and pull up sharply after dropping their bomb, and off they go. And the other bombers fly across the Volga and drop their destructive loads in the wide and endless woods. Who of us can guess at what has been amassed there in preparation for a renewed counterattack? From our brigade command post, we can look across to the land, which spreads away on the eastern bank of the great river. It is an imposing view.

On September 14, the Wehrmacht communiqué reports:

> In the fortress battlefield of Stalingrad the assault troops of the Army pierced the fortifications on the edge of the city in the face of particularly tough resistance, strongly supported by our artillery, and stormed the commanding heights northwest of the middle area of the city. In futile counterattacks the enemy lost twenty-nine tanks. Strong Luftwaffe forces intervened in the battles and attacked recently brought up Soviet forces east of the Volga with good results. During the night airfields north and east of the city were bombed.

I live through all of this from the armored personnel carrier of the brigade commander. First, we drive down to an advanced observation post and remain there in a covered position. We listen in on the radio traffic of our units, and it quickly becomes clear what an important day this is going to be. Today the 6th Army will take the key area of the actual city, the famous Mamai-Kurgan. This hill, which has been noted as Hill 102 on German and Soviet general staff maps, controls the entire city center. That is why both sides want to gain and keep possession of it at any price. Today it is in German hands, the prerequisite for a continuation of attacks into the city itself, down to the Volga. Colonel Freiherr von Falkenstein also drives down to the command posts of the panzer-grenadier regiments, and only late in the evening do we return to brigade command post.

On September 15, the Wehrmacht communiqué includes the following report: "The victorious storm of German troops on Stalingrad, excellently supported by units of the Luftwaffe, is gaining more ground."

September 22, 1942. Stalingrad South Has Been Taken
The Wehrmacht communiqué elaborates on the action:

> The battle for Stalingrad is characterised by the remarkable toughness and determination of the enemy. The 94th Infantry Division, which was attacking south of the railroad, penetrated the southern suburb and beat off enemy counterattacks from the direction of the Volga. North of the railroad a division managed to penetrate through the city and take the water plant on the west bank of the Volga. North of this, parts of another division managed to penetrate into the city in the face of tough resistance.

At our brigade command post it is broadcast in the evening briefing that the Stalingrad railroad station has just been captured—this time once and for all. In five days, it was evacuated and retaken fifteen times by the Russians. But now it is securely in German hands. And with this, the majority of the southern city has been taken—all except for one building, which rises from the southern edge of the city and towers over everything. It is a giant grain elevator, where bitter fighting still rages.

On September 18, 1942, the OKW war diary reports about this operation:

In the Beketowka area, there was lively river traffic in both directions on the Volga. The 94th Infantry Division took the road bridge over the Zariza and the area east of the rail bridge. West of the rail bridge, the 24th Panzer Division cleared the quarter and the gully south of the Zariza. The division stands on the southern bank of the river and has made contact with the 71st Infantry Division, coming down from the north, which is mopping up the district south of the barracks area and around the central railroad station.

In the Wehrmacht communiqué of September 19, it is indicated that on the previous day, 120 tanks and 77 enemy aircraft were destroyed. And the war diary records the critical situation in which we often find ourselves. But it is always unified. And so today we can read:

In the city area of Stalingrad, the 29th Motorized Infantry Division took over the southern sector of the 94th Infantry Division and in doing so freed more parts of the division for the assault. By the afternoon, the 94th Infantry Division gained a small strip of the west bank of the Volga south of the Zariza in hard house-to-house fighting. North of the Zariza, the 71st Infantry Division cleared the western part of the city to the railroad.

Strong enemy forces (up to three regiments) broke through the landbridge on the railroad south of Kotluban and penetrated to Borodkin. Further enemy forces are approaching from the northwest. Thanks to the brave behavior of the outer flanks of both divisions that were flanked by the enemy tanks and after a concentric counterattack with tanks, assault guns and anti-aircraft guns on the encircled units, these were destroyed and the old main line of resistance was secure in our hands again. Attacks south of Kotluban failed. All in all, until now, 106 enemy tanks have been destroyed and numerous prisoners rounded up. Individual fights behind the front are still in progress.

September 21, for the first time, brings a remark that is of particular importance to me. In the OKW war diary, it is written: "On the left flank of the 371st Infantry Division, multiple enemy advances were beaten off. On the southern front of Stalingrad, the 14th Panzer Division broke up attempts by the enemy to close in on their positions. In Stalingrad, on both sides of the Zariza, some housing blocks were taken in heavy fighting. The battle continues."

Today, as on the previous days, I am constantly in advanced observation posts and among the regiments and battalions with the regimental commander. Strong Russian counterattacks are expected everywhere. The movements and preparations of the enemy allow no other conclusion. The Russian attacks against the 371st Infantry Division indicate that the Soviets are trying to split up the cohesion of our concentrically attacking troops. I would not have believed that I would be on the same battlefield as my father after so short a time. On the situation map, I see the positions and the course of the main line of resistance of all divisions, including our regiments and battalions. What will the coming weeks and days bring us?

On September 22, the OKW war diary reports: "In the area around Stalingrad the 14th Panzer Division beat off an enemy attack against the right wing. The district southeast of the Southern Railway Station has been cleared down to the Volga. In the grain elevator the enemy still holds determinedly. North of the Zariza the 71st Infantry Division took building blocks east of the party building down to the Volga."

Now we've finally attained the southern edge of the city. The fighting is meter by meter. It really is a bestial battle for every bit of ground, for each undulation in the ground, each gully. The losses it brings are unimaginable on both sides. Directly in front of us are the big, wide, and confusing factories and workshops in which work is still going on. With binoculars, one can clearly see how tracked vehicles roll out of the halls and then disappear into the maze of ruins and the remains of other installations—that is, when they're not hit by our antiaircraft guns. Everything here is unbelievable, surpassing everything seen before. And our artillery fire of all calibers and our bombing attacks tear into this without pause. Smoke and dust rise against the skies and darken the piercing sun. And yet we see again and again that newly completed T-34 tanks leave the factories. As prisoners reveal, they are either driven to the front and handed over to the troops there or they roll straight into battle.

What is happening here in these days cannot be described. Our heavy artillery fires over our heads from its firing positions far behind us. Directly behind us, the division artillery is firing overhead, and so are the rocket launchers, which, with their "screaming and moaning," make even us "old fighters" jump in the nearest hole for cover. The roaring, gurgling, and hissing is horrible—straight over our heads! Next to and in front of us, 88mm antiaircraft guns are firing over open sights at targets that suddenly are spotted in the factory and work areas. It is a hellish noise. And then, out of the blue sky and without any prior warning, Soviet artillery and Stalin organs impact among us.

Then the brigade commander gets the report: "The grain elevator has been taken!" First, a battalion had attacked there, and after five days, parts of three German divisions finally took this important point. With this, the southern part of Stalingrad has been taken, the traffic vein of the Volga has been cut, and the industrial center that existed until now has been destroyed.

September 23, 1942. With the Brigade Commander among the Battalions and to the Soviet Fighting Positions

Today, September 23, the brigade commander again wants to drive to the regiments and battalions in order to receive reports and get a picture of the current situation. For this reason, I prepare the maps and check the fighting positions and the roads leading to them. Then the brigade commander,

against the current trend, wants to go all the way to the front
to the command post of the 2nd Battalion of Panzergrenadier
Regiment 103, which is operating in the positions on the
heights northwest of Beketowka. They've just taken this important bit of ground, and that's where the brigade commander
wants to go next.

We mount the armored personnel carriers, and the radio
links are up, ready for "attention!" We're rolling at high
speed in a southeastern direction to the panzergrenadiers.
Now and then, Russian artillery fire hits the area, which is
abandoned and looks like no-man's-land as we drive into it.
No command post is visible here. But left and right of us are
dug-in grenadiers, who look up from under their steel helmets in amazement, as if they want to ask what this armored
personnel carrier is doing out here on the front. The fast
ride goes on. No one stops us—the commander of the 14th
Panzergrenadier Brigade wants to go to 2nd Battalion of the
103rd! The road then descends into a valley, and there in
front of us, at three o'clock, stands a small hut. As we're driving down to it, all of a sudden earth-brown shapes jump up
from behind the house. They're standing as though they're
rooted to the ground.

A hail of bullets is coming in our direction. Russians!
"Stop! Reverse!" The driver tears the armored personnel carrier around. "Tempo!" Rifle, machine-gun, and antitank fire!
A veritable hail of projectiles ricochets, and we are hanging
bent over and stooped in the armored half-track. The excellent driver zig-zags up the long hill again. The rounds hiss,
explode, and whistle around us, hitting the antennas and
bouncing off the sides. As we are driving up hill, the sides
offer only makeshift protection, and in our open-topped vehicle, we offer a good target for the Bolsheviks. In a stormy ride,
and turning again and again from one side to the other, this
zealous noncommissioned officer behind the wheel drags us
up the hill until we're out of the range of the astounded Russians, straight through our own advanced positions to the
brigade headquarters.

They're already waiting for us here, since people know about our "expedition." When we dismount from the armored personnel carrier, we are showered with congratulations for our "second birthday." The commander immediately orders a round of champagne in order to celebrate the avoided imprisonment and the undamaged return.

In the days ahead, the Wehrmacht communiqués bring only brief descriptions of the battle in the built-up area of Stalingrad. We're able to advance only extremely slowly and have to deal with Russian counterattacks constantly. On September 27, the Wehrmacht communiqué reports: "In the city center of Stalingrad, the infantry stormed several bunker complexes and housing blocks and, supported by dive bombers, advanced on several positions down to the Volga." And in the OKW war diary is recorded: "On both sides of the mouth of the Zariza the 94th and 71st Infantry Division began an attack early in the morning against tough enemy resistance and by midday had reached the banks of the Volga. The Russians still hold out in nests of resistance on the quays. North of this on the railroad loops of the factory area enemy attacks were beaten off."

The operations on September 29 were described as follows in the OKW war diary: "In the Stalingrad area, the 100th Jäger [Rifle] Division regrouped and attacked in a northeasterly direction. The division took two-thirds of the meat 'combinate' [factory]. The 24th Panzer Division cleared the western part of the metallurgical works of "Krasn. Oktjabr" [Red October] and took the district southwest and west of the 'Red Barricade.' The northwestern elements penetrated into the Barrikady district."

On September 30, it further reports: "In Stalingrad, the 100th Jäger Division held off several enemy counterattacks, but had to give up a group of houses north of the meat 'combinate' to a numerically superior enemy. The 24th Panzer Division west of the Bread Factory advanced two kilometers to the railroad and in the morning hours again took hold of the temporarily lost Barrikady district in severe house-to-house combat."

It is unbelievable how the course of events here is developing into a war of positions. The fight rages for each house, each factory hall, for railroad cuts and walls, for each cellar. What we all fear seems likely to come true—that we'll be fighting here in winter.

October 1, 1942. Penetration with the Romanians in the "Lake Sector" South of Stalingrad. The 14th Panzer Division Cleans Up the Situation.

While on October 1 the Wehrmacht communiqué emphasizes the uncommonly brave behavior of a German panzer corps that holds the northern blocking position against all enemy attacks and now is penetrating into the northern part of the city, the OKW war diary tells of the fighting in the southern part of the city:

> South of the penetration location at the VI Romanian Corps the detached southern group managed to hold on the line Scharnud-Sadowoje against enemy attacks of unknown strength. At the penetration south of Zaza the enemy managed to break through the front of the 1st Romanian Infantry Division, which fell back to the southwest and northwest. The 14th Panzer Division, which was brought up as reinforcements, was able to stop the enemy with the tanks and motorcycle riflemen that had arrived first, retook the heights and pulled the parts of the Romanian units that yielded back into the attack. This contained the penetration. On the northern flank of the division, the enemy took Dubowi Owrag. The enemy could be stopped by a counterattack. South of Stalingrad, an enemy attack was thrown back. The 100th Jäger Division and parts of the 24th Panzer Division penetrated into the Krasnij Oktjabr district and the "Red Barricade." Several attack columns were driven forward to the railroad. Northeast of Barrikady an attack of battalion strength was beaten off.

So there it is. Together with other units of the 14th Panzer Division, we are suddenly pulled out of the front at Stalingrad. Who'll close the holes we leave behind? Who'll continue the attack in our sector? Are "new" units brought up? We don't know. We have a new task that has to be carried out at once and with the greatest possible dispatch: "New operation in the Lake Sector!" That is south of Stalingrad, where the Russians managed to break up the front of our allies, the Romanians, with a large-scale attack, in order to attack the German divisions that are fighting in the flank in Stalingrad and cut off their communications and lines of supply. It is to be dealt with quickly so that we can return to the Stalingrad sector.

On October 2, the OKW war diary explains in great detail:

At the breakthrough positions south of Stalingrad Sadowoje seems to have been retaken. Confirmation is still lacking. The 14th Panzer Division, with only weak forces, managed to reestablish the situation east of Plodowitoje in the shortest time possible. In an exemplary attack the enemy was thrown back, and by leading the Romanians forward, the old positions were retaken again. Dubowi Owrag is partially in our hands but is still the scene of mop-up operations. A reconnaissance in force by the enemy in front of the 297th Infantry Division was repulsed bloodily. In Stalingrad, after fluctuating fighting, the attacks aimed at the northern flank of the 100th Jäger Division were beaten off.

Our attacks here are carried forward in an exemplary fashion as if on maneuvers and immediately have the expected success. The Russians bug out and retreat. In a very short time, the "mess" here can be cleaned up. The Romanians also are to be seen again and can come forward again and occupy anew the positions retaken by our units, which had been theirs in the first place in the Kalmuck Steppe and on Lake Zaza. For one night more, we will hold these positions together with the

Romanian infantrymen, and after that, new assignments await us. In front of us is a wide, open, slightly undulating country. Here no approach can go unnoticed. But will the Romanians hold this line, without us to back them up? Hopefully. The weather is bright, sunny, and rather warm, even at night. So there is no reason to leave the positions here and go searching for houses.

On October 3, the Wehrmacht communiqué reports: "South and north of the city, strong relieving attacks failed after severe fighting. Forty-one Soviet tanks were destroyed in this. German and Romanian air forces attacked the enemy supply traffic on the railroads of the Caspian Sea and in the area of the Lower Volga." The OKW war diary contains the following about this day: "The attack of the 4th Romanian Infantry Division in a southeastern direction from Sadowoje was stopped. At the lake front south of Zaza, enemy attacks were repulsed. The enemy managed to retake Dubowi Owrag. Strong enemy attacks against the southern front near Stalingrad were repulsed. One penetration could be contained."

And on October 4, the OKW war diary explains further: "At Sadowoje, the 14th Panzer Division moved into the assembly area. At Stalingrad, several enemy attacks south-east and east of the Barrikady were beaten back."

Today we are pulled out of this sector, to be kept in readiness as a "fire brigade" in the rear of the Romanians. That is quite good on one hand, but on the other, we can be sent into the "really deep shit" at a moment's notice. From today, Colonel Freiherr von Falkenstein leads the 14th Panzer Division, as Lieutenant General Heim has taken over command of the XIV Panzer Corps. So now I've "landed" at the divisional command post in order to be at my commander's disposal at all times. It seems like I am in "another world." Here people are under almost peacetime conditions—situation conferences, the coming and going of staff officers, signals officers, dispatch riders. Here everything comes together; here is the heart of the command of the 14th Panzer Division.

On October 5, the Wehrmacht communiqué once more carries a detailed depiction of the events in our sector of the front:

> In the battle for Stalingrad, infantry and panzer units in close cooperation with close-support aircraft took further parts of the northern city area in dogged house-to-house fighting. The Soviets suffered severe bloody losses; nine tanks were destroyed. Night bombing attacks were aimed at Soviet airfields, artillery positions, and railroads east of the Volga. In the battles on the Don Front, the commanding general of a panzer corps, General of Panzer Troops Freiherr von Langermann und Erlenkamp, wearer of the Knight's Cross to the Iron Cross with Oak Leaves, died a hero's death in the front line. On his side, the commander of a Hungarian division, Colonel Nagy, died in the fight for the freedom of Europe.

The OKW war diary in addition reports: "The 14th Panzer Division, together with the 4th Romanian Infantry Division, attacked from Sadowoje. In the first assault the old Romanian positions could be retaken."

Today I witness this "clean-up" on the map at the divisional command post about 60 kilometers south of Stalingrad. A Russian penetration of the Romanians must be cleaned up by an attack of German tanks and panzergrenadiers. The situation is corrected very quickly—and without any severe losses. That all sounds so simple, so sober, so routine. And yet I know exactly how it looks "down there" with the squads, platoons, and companies. When the names of places, units, times, and losses get here in reports, it is clear to all at the divisional command post that the Romanians have far too little heavy weapons, far to few armor-piercing weapons, to be able to face these Soviet attacks with any success. And so German units, which of course are missing elsewhere, must be kept in readiness everywhere as fire brigades. Only these can carry out the counterattacks needed to reestablish the old situation for the time being.

On October 6, replacements arrive—young, freshly trained soldiers from Infantry Training Battalion 108 in Dresden. There are recruits among them that I trained in March and April. Now they're coming to the field army and then even to this front, Stalingrad. These boys won't have an easy time of it in this hell.

October 7, 1942. German Prisoners of War Are Bound Up by British Troops during Their Attempted Landing at Dieppe.
On October 7, the majority of the Wehrmacht communiqué consists of a publication of the Armed Forces Supreme Command about the tying up of German prisoners by the British during their attempted landing at Dieppe. The statements made about this subject by the British War Ministry are confounded by eyewitness accounts. The Armed Forces Supreme Command feels itself to be forced to order the following:

1. From October 8th at 12 o'clock in the afternoon, all British officers and men captured at Dieppe will be bound up. This measure will last until the British War Ministry states that in the future it will give truthful accounts of the shackling of German prisoner, or it has gotten the authority to enforce its orders with the troops.

2. In the future, all terror and sabotage troops of the British and their auxiliary troops who do not behave themselves as soldiers, but as bandits, wherever they operate, are to be killed mercilessly in combat by German troops.

We do not have problems like that here. We know exactly what the Bolsheviks do with our comrades who have fallen into their hands. We have lived through it when we've found them:

slaughtered, treated bestially, and tortured. Reprisals would not have any effect here. There are no "laws" here.

On October 9, the Wehrmacht communiqué once again is silent on operations on the Stalingrad front. On the other hand, the further developments regarding the treatment of prisoners of war is covered.

> The British government has not addressed the fact that despite the earlier and current hypocritical statements of the British War Ministry, German prisoners were tied up in a rough manner. Therefore, on October 8th, at 1200 hours, 107 British officers and 1,269 noncommissioned officers and men were put in chains after having been informed about the reason for this. Military chaplains, medical personnel, and wounded and sick personnel were not chained up. On October 8th, in the evening, the British War Ministry made public that from October 10th at noon, a similar number of German prisoners will be chained up. If that happens, the Wehrmacht Supreme Command will order the chaining up of triple the number of British prisoners.

In the OKW war diary for today, it can be read: "South of Stalingrad strong enemy movements east of Sadowoje. A very lively activity by aviators in the vicinity of Plotowitoje. In the Stalingrad area, the Russians for the first time fired the heaviest artillery. Our own artillery is active against enemy resistance nests and fortified house-blocks with effect."

Now it is finally our turn. We move off toward our new operational area. We quit the steppe here, south of Tundotowo, and are transported to the northern part of Stalingrad. With everything packed, loaded, and ready to march, we are waiting only for our marching orders. Earlier, I once more—and for the last time—had the opportunity to exchange a few words with my father over a field telephone across a distance of 120 kilometers.

While we are waiting, I dash off another letter for the people at home. Who knows what is coming for us and when we will have the next opportunity?

Today, shortly before our advance "up again" toward Stalingrad, I would like to write a long letter. We're supposed to enter into house-to-house fighting in northern Stalingrad. As we have received some replacements, we will certainly, and as quickly as possible, throw the Russians out of town completely! By the way, among the replacements are recruits that I trained in Dresden in March–April. I have already met up with some of them. From a neighboring house, where a signals platoon of the division staff has a radio, I've laid a line toward my digs. We have a few headphones, and so we hear the music for the weekend from back home! Well, you can imagine how emotional that makes one. The room has very small windows. My greatcoat and blanket have been spread as a bed on the ground, and one lies on them and look at the skies above.

October 11, 1942. The Battle for the "Dshershinskij" Tractor Works.

On October 11, the Wehrmacht communiqué reports:

In continuous battle at Stalingrad, enemy formation areas were destroyed by effective artillery fire. Relieving attacks of the Soviets north of the city failed. In local operations on the Don Front, several enemy fighting positions were destroyed and prisoners and captured weapons were brought back. In the time from September 29 to October 9, 356 Soviet airplanes were destroyed in aerial combats, 66 were shot down by antiaircraft artillery, and another 18 were destroyed on the ground, so that the complete losses were 459 aircraft. In the same period, 36 aircraft were lost on the Eastern Front.

On October 14, the OKW war diary describes a situation report at the Führer's Headquarters: "Marshal Antonescu has asked that the 5th and 8th Romanian Cavalry Divisions not be transferred to the 4th Panzer Army, as winter quarters for both divisions cannot be prepared. The Führer decides that both divisions are to join the 4th Panzer Army anyway. The Romanian 3rd Army on October 10th took over its sector on the Don before Kletskaja. The 6th Army yesterday launched another attack on Stalingrad."

On October 15, the Wehrmacht communiqué reported: "At Stalingrad, infantry and panzer units broke the grim resistance of the Soviets in housing blocks and barricade positions and advanced deep into the northern part of town. Bomber and Stuka squadrons in continuous operations destroyed enemy bunker and artillery positions. Enemy relieving attacks were repelled with high and bloody losses." The OKW war diary for the same day reads:

> LI Army Corps [Stalingrad], at 0730 hours on the 14th of October 1942, launched an attack, and in an advance with the 14th Panzer Division, it managed to reach the housing group in the southwestern part of the tractor works, while with an advance by the 305th Infantry Division north of it, she also managed to penetrate and storm the housing group northeast of the Tractor Works. On the northern edge of town, the 389th Infantry Division also managed to gain ground in its attacks eastward.

Now our division has again been in action with the city as the focus of our attacks. The fight for this industrial center and the surrounding housing blocks is difficult and exhausting. We have to contend with unbelievable losses here. The days on Lake Zaza with the Romanians are well behind us now. Now the great struggle for the city center has begun. The resistance here is determined and fanatical. With all means and newly brought up forces, the Bolsheviks are trying to retain hold of

the western bank of the Volga in this sector. Here in the northern part of Stalingrad, the toughest and deadliest battles take
place. Something like this has not yet been seen in this war—a
concentration of fire in the smallest space possible, operations
by people under the most brutal conditions, man against man.
It is not wrong to compare this event with the attritional battle
of Verdun in World War I. There in six months, more than half
a million German and French soldiers were killed.

"Each soldier a fortress. Behind the Volga, there is no land
anymore for us. Either fight or die!" With these slogans, the
commander of the Soviet 62nd Army, Gen. Vasily Chuikov,
whips up a fanatical fighting mood. The Russian resistance
grows more and more bitter; our losses grow higher and
higher, the units weaker and weaker in personnel strength and
fighting power. Reinforcements are needed. They are brought
up, some even by air. But the battle for the tractor works here
in the north of the city is a unique horror. The battle in the
factory halls is horrific. Red Army prisoners and deserters are
rare these days, and those that are collected at the brigade
command post are reclusive and somewhat rebellious. Above
us, even over the biting, black clouds of smoke from the burning oil tanks that pass overhead, the squadrons of our Luftwaffe fly their operations without pause.

October 15, 1942. The War Diary of General Chuikov, CO of the Soviet 62nd Army.

On October 15, the war diary of the Russian commander of
the 62nd Army, General Chuikov, reads:

> 0530 hours: Like yesterday, the enemy has started today
> with a reinforced artillery reparatory barrage on the
> front of Mokraja Metschetka–"Krasnij Oktjabr" district.

> 0800 hours: The enemy is attacking with tanks and
> infantry. The battle is raging on the entire front.

0930 hours: The attack of the enemy on the Stalingrad Tractor Works has been beaten off. At the courtyard of the works, ten fascist tanks are burning.

1000 hours: Tanks and infantry have overrun the 109th Guards Rifle Regiment of the 37th Division.

1130 hours: The left wing of the 524th Rifle Regiment of the 95th Rifle Division is overrun. About fifty tanks are rolling over the regiment.

1150 hours: The enemy has taken the sport grounds of the Stalingrad Tractor Works. Our units which have been cut off fight on in the encirclement.

1200 hours: The commander of the 117th Rifle Regiment, Guards Major Andrejew, has been killed.

1220 hours: A radio message from a unit of the 416th Regiment from the hexagonal housing block: "Have been encircled, ammunition and water available, death before surrender!"

1230 hours: Dive-bombers attack the command post of General Scholudov. General Scholudov is without radio communications in a neighboring bunker that has collapsed. Take over the communications to the units of this division.

1310 hours: Two bunkers in the army command post have collapsed. One officer is sticking in the mass of earth with his legs, but we can dig him out".

1320 hours: Through a pipe we have pumped air into the bunker of general Scholudov.

1440 hours: The telephone link with the units has gone down; we have switched to radio and mutual confirmation by signals officers.

1525 hours: The headquarters guard has entered combat.

1600 hours: The connection to the 114th Guards Regiment has been severed, its situation is unknown.

1620 hours: About a 100 tanks have penetrated the grounds of the Tractor factory. The enemy's air force is overhead as before and is attacking us with bombs in low level flights.

1635 hours: Regimental commander Lieutenant Colonel Ustinow requests that his command is post to be bombarded, as he is encircled by sub-machine gunners.

1700 hours: The signallers can only write down with difficulty the radio messages of the units, that continue to fight on even though encircled.

2100 hours: Another radio message of the 37th Guards Division: "They're still fighting."

On October 16, the Wehrmacht communiqué reports: "At Stalingrad, a panzer division in a bold nightly attack managed to penetrate down to the Volga, and then in cooperation with infantry units took the northern part of the factory suburb of the big 'Dhershinskij' tractor works in intense house-to-house and street fighting. Strong aerial forces flew strikes to soften up the enemy, while fighter units stopped any counter moves from the enemy air force." And the OKW war diary adds: "The attack by the 6th Army on October 15 led to the complete taking of the northern part of Stalingrad, including the tractor works and the brick works. Parts of the 14th Panzer Division broke through to the edge of Rynok."

October 17, 1942. The Battle for the "Red Barricade" Gun Foundry.

On October 17, the Wehrmacht communiqué tells about the progress of the battle: "At Stalingrad, infantry and armored units in close cooperation with incessant aerial forces and Luftwaffe antiaircraft artillery continued their enthusiastic attack despite bitter resistance, overran several strongpoints and dug-in tanks and penetrated into the 'Red Barricade' gun foundry." And the OKW war diary continues: "Parts of the 14th Panzer Division and the 305th Infantry Division advanced in a southwesterly direction into the grounds of the foundry; simultaneously an attack of own forces was launched from the brickworks on the river bank. The fighting here continues."

In these days, the brigade commander only rarely leaves the command post. He is in the situation room constantly and follows the incoming messages and the way the situation is developing. And yet at the end are the successes of the 103rd and 108th Regiments, as well as that of the 64th Motorcycle Rifle Battalion. Joy and satisfaction rise over all negative impressions. The objectives of the attack have been taken; the Russians have been thrown back everywhere. Our tanks give us space in which we have the possibilities to act and have an effect in this labyrinth of houses and factory halls.

On October 18, the Wehrmacht communiqué brings the following report: "At Stalingrad, the attacking forces broke tough enemy resistance, stormed all works of the 'Red Barricade' gun foundry, and after the bloody repulsion of determined counterattacks, we threw the enemy out of the adjoining district. Heavy attacks by strong Luftwaffe units supported this battle and destroyed many guns on the eastern bank of the Volga."

The next day, October 10, the Wehrmacht communiqué reports: "In the northern suburb of Stalingrad, German troops took another group of houses from the Soviets. The fights to clear the factory area of the 'Red Barricade' gun foundry still continue. Close-support pilots mainly bombed the strongly fortified strong points of the 'Red October' factory." And the OKW war diary adds: "In the northern part of the town behind the front, Russian resistance flared up again in individual nests of resistance."

It slowly is getting colder here, with long rains; snow showers announce the coming of the Russian winter. Will we experience it here? All this now adds to the difficulties of the battle. The losses in men and materiel have risen so high that it simply cannot be imagined that the units that led the attack from the beginning are to remain in operations.

On October 21, the OKW war diary notes: "In the battle for Stalingrad parts of the 305th Infantry Division after regrouping attacked the housing block north of the gun foundry. Further data about the progress of the attack are still lacking."

On October 22, the Wehrmacht communiqué reports: "In the battle for Stalingrad, in determined man-to-man fighting, bitterly defended earth bunkers and barricade positions were taken. The focus of the German air attacks was on the enemy strong points in the northern part of the city. Continued relieving attacks against the front north of the city were completely annihilated with the support of the German and Romanian air forces."

On October 23, the OKW war diary notes: "The preparations for the attack of October 23, 1942, in Stalingrad were completed. On the northern front between the Volga and Don, the enemy repeated its attacks with support by individual tanks. All attacks were repulsed."

In cold but sunny weather, the attack is renewed. The Bolsheviks finally are to be thrown down the western bank of the Volga and destroyed. But the Russians defend themselves with unbelievable bitterness and toughly hang on to their positions—with their backs to the Volga. Again hundreds of dive-bombers fly at the enemy and drop hundreds of bombs on the small strip of the western bank of the Volga—there where the

Russians have dug themselves in "to their necks," there where they're still holding out in the ruins.

Today I learn that Lieutenants Ullrich and Winkler have been killed. I talked to both only a few days ago—Lieutenant Ullrich at the division staff, Lieutenant Winkler at the 108th. The divisional cemeteries keep on expanding. It is depressing and difficult when one learns of the number of losses and the names of one's own comrades. I experience this not only in my direct vicinity. When the brigade commander is briefed on the situation at the regiments and battalions, I always hear the discussion of our own losses and the losses of command personnel. In particular, this day of attack has demanded horrible sacrifices. How are these gaps to by filled anyway? They have to be filled since the city has to be taken in its entirety. The entire western bank of the Volga must be in our grasp in order to attain a continuous main line of resistance, save forces, and form the necessary reserves.

STALINGRAD. THE LAST FEW METERS TO THE VOLGA

October 24, 1942. Taking Command of a Company in the 2nd Battalion of Panzergrenadier Regiment 103 in Stalingrad.
On October 24, the Wehrmacht communiqué reports:

> At Stalingrad, infantry and armored units renewed their attack, threw the enemy back out of several streets in hard house-to-house fighting, took the majority of the "Red October" factory, and advanced down to the Volga. The enemy positions were under the hail of bombs of the continuously operating bomber and dive-bomber aircraft, who furthermore attacked enemy artillery positions on the islands in the Volga and east of the river in day and night attacks. In the north of the city weak enemy relieving attacks failed.

The OKW war diary notes:

South of Stalingrad, the artillery of both sides fired harassing fire. The 79th Infantry Division gained the railroad on the western edge of the metallurgical works (first objective of attack) and with assault troops advanced to the middle of the works. The big work halls were taken. The fighting still continues. The 14th Panzer Division cleared out resistance nests in the bread factory. According to unconfirmed reports a detachment of assault troops of the 79th Infantry Division has penetrated down to the Volga. On the landbridge north of Stalingrad multiple attacks with individual tanks were beaten off by the 60th Infantry Division.

Early in the morning, I am ordered to the brigade commander, Colonel Freiherr von Falkenstein. Here I get a new task: "Report to Panzergrenadier Regiment 103. There you are to take over the remains of the Panzergrenadiers as company commander. The commander of the 2nd Battalion is Capt. Erich Domaschk. This is a detachment. Afterwards, you are to return to brigade. Best of luck!"

I report my departure. At the brigade command post, my things are quickly packed. After that, I am taken in a jeep to the command post of Panzergrenadier Regiment 103. It is very difficult to get there with the impacts of artillery shells and the labyrinth of obstacles. And yet we arrive there after only a short time. In the ruins of buildings, I descend into a cellar where the regimental staff has nestled itself. Then I am standing in front of the commander of Panzergrenadier Regiment 103, Lieutenant Colonel Seydel. I report to him and am greeted with joy, as out in front there is no officer anymore that can lead the forces of the regiment that have shrunk to a company. I get a short briefing; everything else will be told to me by the battalion commander. The last hundred meters down to the Volga are at stake. They have to be taken.

Here comes a corporal who is to lead me to the main line of resistance, to the battalion. Immediately, we report our departure and work ourselves forward. The corporal, in fully torn-up and muddied uniform, takes me in the direction of the front to the battalion command post—over mountains of rubble, through collapsed buildings, and through the remains of halls and factories. Everywhere projectiles strike the walls that still stand. Onward, onward! Over shattered rails, through hollows with loose stones and iron beams that have come down, then again through factory halls, in which parts of machines, work benches, and material of all sorts lie around, toppled, destroyed. From the iron girders that are still standing hang wavy metal plates and wiring. Chaos! Here and there, explosions from infantry guns impact, low-trajectory shells whirring around. Cover! Down! The surprising artillery bombardments give us an indescribable feeling of revulsion.

Finally, we arrive. The battalion command post is in a cellar. Here the staff members work; here the runners sit down on the ground; here the radios stand in a corner; over there the signallers sit at their equipment. An eerie scene! It grows even more eerie when I enter an adjoining cellar and recognize the battalion commander. After my report, he stands up and looks at me. We don't know each other, as I belong to Panzergrenadier Regiment 108. He's a tall figure. He extends his hand to me, tightly controlled but in a relaxed way. He exudes an incredible calm. The adjutant, First Lieutenant Meisel, also comes up to brief me on the situation and give me my orders. There are about forty men in this company, the remains of the battalion, the last panzergrenadiers in the regiment. Here I finally learn everything that I have to know.

Another NCO is to take me to the company, which is led by a senior sergeant. I report my departure and climb up the staircase toward daylight, out of the rubble of the gun factory and toward the Volga. We jump from cover to cover, crawling behind the remains of walls and hearths that still stand and indicate where once houses stood. Just a few more mounds of rubble and refuse and then we're there. We climb into a potato cellar, down a rickety ladder. Here is the company command post from which the remains of Panzergrenadier Regiment 103 are led. The senior sergeant tersely briefs me and concludes with the words, "In ten minutes we'll attack!"

I take one more look round. To continue the attack, we position ourselves up the ladder among the broken walls and the iron rubble. This must once have been a factory hall. The senior sergeant, an experienced and battle-tested NCO, has a good knowledge of the ground, which looks like an abandoned landscape of craters. Behind every piece of cover, behind every wall, and behind every mound sits the enemy.

October 24, 1942. Attacks to Take Possession of the Administration Building of the "Bread Factory."

Then it is time. In front of us is the administration building of the bread factory. Here come our Stukas. We're attacking! Meter by meter, we crawl forward, following the bombs that the Stukas are dropping in front of us. The howling of sirens, explosions, breaking, splitting, fountains of mud by the exploding bombs. Salvos from the Soviet guns crash around us; the nauseating explosions force us to take cover. Then shells from our own artillery howl overhead. The Soviet artillery continues to shake the earth and hit the factory walls with a noise like that of an underground train entering a station. It's unbelievable; one can understand nothing anymore.

We continue to jump from crater to crater, from earth pile to the remains of a wall, and now quickly to the block of a house, then to cover. Once again, the fire of the Soviet guns comes down on us. Onward! We have to seize the last hundred meters to the Volga. But the Russians are hanging tough, and they bitterly contest every hole in the earth, every pile of rubble. Snipers lurk everywhere, hitting us in the flank and inflicting bloody losses; they are hiding all around but cannot be spotted at all.

As it slowly gets dark and the view becomes too unclear to see much, we stop the attack and take up positions to be safe from nightly surprises and be able to spot every enemy approach. There's much activity: runners to the platoons, platoon commanders to the infantry. The killed are recovered and the wounded prepared for transport. Evening reports are made and sent off to battalion. None has any rest—everybody is wide awake, ready for anything. A questions hangs over everything: what will tomorrow bring? Just now, our food carriers have been taken out by the Russians behind us. They rise up out of tunnels that lead behind our front line and wait in the dark for runners, ammunition, and food carriers, ready to overwhelm and kill them.

As the Soviets are still lurking in some buildings of the bread factory in front of us and to our right, we attack again today. We prepare ourselves, look at each other once more, and check the watches—now! We advance slowly, meter by meter. It takes hours to reach the next objective. We set up covering fire, working our way forward, pressed close to the earth, and looking for even the smallest possibility of cover. We continuously look around us—where are the Russians lurking? And then we see them again, directly in front of us—the heads of the Red Army men, only fifty meters from us.

Explosions blast brightly, and debris flies around our ears. We take on more losses, dead and wounded. My God, how many will we have to recover and drag back tonight in the darkness? To our right, motorcycle riflemen attack again. We can hear their cries and their firing. Smoke from burning buildings is everywhere, from the oil tanks to our left and the glowing remains of the factory halls. Then all of a sudden, our Stukas come up again. We fire white flares so that they can immediately recognize our forward lines and drop their bombs on the enemy as close to us as possible. White and yellow-white flares rise up everywhere. "Here we are!" How can the planes possibly see where the German outposts are? They curve and circle—then suddenly dive. With a deafening howl of sirens, they come diving down—far in front of us, directly in front of us, and—my God!—also behind us. More giant craters are made; smoke and dust clouds and fountains of earth darken everything. We can see nothing.

Now machine-gun fire erupts independently from the various groups, accompanied by cries, shouts, and engine noises.

The Soviets are counterattacking! I can make them out, thirty or forty meters in front of us. They are bent over and not wearing steel helmets, just caps. Now we're covering them with fire from all weapons. We need an artillery barrage! Red flares! Quickly! Our artillery comes in howling. Mortar projectiles whir and whistle. The Soviets are still there. Taking cover now has no use.

Hour flows into hour, day into day, of bitter fighting. On October 27, we assemble again. Though tired and exhausted, we still have the will to force a decision. Immediately after breaking cover, our men fall dead and wounded in the first few meters. Get down! Take cover! Who's firing on us? Where is the damn fire coming from? There—in front of us! The Soviets have taken up positions in front of us behind walls and dark piles of earth. I order: "Go! Flank them on the right and left flank. We'll fire on them from the front." And it's working; we're taking them out; they're surrendering. We wave at them to come closer, and under fire, some Soviets manage to reach our positions.

By evening, we finally have taken possession of the administration building of the bread factory. We count on a Russian counterattack, which will undoubtedly come soon. But for the moment, all is quiet. Therefore, the platoons and groups are organized differently for the night. We set up positions in favorable terrain from which we can flank the Russians when they get close. When they come up, we'll shower them with concentrated fire. I establish the company command post out here directly behind the groups, again in a potato cellar but centrally located with useable communication connections to the platoons and the groups. We dig in, even deeper into the earth.

Then I am ordered to battalion command post. I make my way there, moving through a lunar landscape, back to the battalion command post, which can be found in the cellars of the gun foundry. That is not simple in this darkness and in the terrain that has been ploughed over and under. After I finally get there, I first report the situation of the company to the battalion commander and explain the events of the day's fighting.

Subsequently, I am briefed for tomorrow's attack. The battalion commander, Captain Domaschk, will be with the company in person, with all men of the battalion staff. We shake hands and off I go.

How long can this man-to-man fight, this fire at the closest of distances, be kept up? I do not know. But it surely cannot last very long anymore, not with these casualties and losses. But perhaps we'll manage the remaining few hundred meters tomorrow. The Soviets are holding out in the steeply falling slopes to the Volga, where no fire can reach them. The prisoners have indicated that high Russian staffs have their bunkers there. They are sitting in their rocky slopes, and each evening, they send new men into battle. We have no more and are living in shell craters and holes in the earth, and we still have to take them in front of us. Stalingrad is almost completely in our hands. Only the bit in front of us remains—a small Soviet bridgehead that is of paramount importance to the Bolsheviks for the continuation of the defense of this horrid city.

October 28, 1942. Attack between the "Red Barricades" and "Red October" Factories to the Western Bank of the Volga

On October 28, the Wehrmacht communiqué reports: "At Stalingrad, the German attack east of the bread factory penetrated to the Volga and thereby brought about the fall of a larger housing area occupied by the enemy. Units of the Luftwaffe intervened in these battles with good results. South of the city Soviet relieving attacks were repeatedly repulsed in heavy combat." The OKW war diary further elaborates:

> During yesterday afternoon, the enemy once again west of the Volga attacked the positions of the 371st Infantry Division south of Stalingrad. Using tanks and strong artillery he succeeded in expanding the penetration of the previous day and penetrating into the southern part of Kaporoschje. The breakthrough was blocked off, countermeasures have been put in

motion. The 79th Infantry Division, in an attack, took
the remaining parts of the "Red October" metallurgical work. North of it elements of the 14th Panzer Division and the 305th Infantry Division attacked towards
the Volga from the Bread Factory and the "Red October" works and made it to the river bank, including the
tank farm. North of it elements of the 305th Infantry
Division are engaged in hard battles between the gun
foundry and the Volga.

During the entire night, I get not a single moment of rest.
Machine-gun and rifle fire is heard continually; flares light up
land and sky without pause. Meanwhile, the planned operations for the morning run through my head constantly. And
then it finally is time!

The morning comes, the sun rises, and it will again be a
warm day for the season. Today we are to take the banks of the
Volga River. Even the battalion commander has a steel helmet
and machine pistol, with several staff soldiers following him.
Once more, we discuss the way the attack is to unfold, then we
assemble, supported by our artillery and all heavy weapons. We
leave our positions and work our way forward meter by meter.
But only a little later, our attack has been spotted. Enemy rifle
and machine-gun fire slams into us and forces us into cover.
Then the "big lumps" arrive—Soviet artillery and heavy mortars. It is exploding and howling in from all sides. I'm hit in
the left hand. But we have to go on; I can spare no time to
check out what happened to me. Onward, onward, in any way
possible! Just don't stop! The men give it everything, all they
have in their power, all that is possible.

In the last building of the housing complex that still
belongs to the bread factory, there is no more resistance, so as
ordered, we make a left turn onto the collapsed houses in
front of us. From there, we should be able to see the Volga. But
we see nothing; we hear only Russian shouts and commands.
They're only thirty meters in front of us, well camouflaged and
difficult to spot. Their roaring fire meets us and forces us to go

down really low. We crawl into the earth, using any sinking ground, every pile of rubble. In a bomb crater behind us, we collect our wounded and pull the dead out of the hail of Russian bullets. We're lying here in front of our objective, so close to the Volga; at most, it's fifty meters away. But we cannot advance any farther. It is simply impossible.

The battalion commander goes back to the rear and promises me that we are to get replacements during the night. But we'll have to hold this position here. Perhaps we'll get a real "draught from the pint" of replacements and not just a few drops, as we have until now. Then we should be able to take this last bit.

As determined and bitter as the Russians defend here and try to hold the riverbank, they are also attacking my father's infantry division wildly and determinedly, again and again. How would things look over there today in this awkward situation?

October 29, 1942. Repelling Counterattacks in the "Front Outpost" Close to the Western Bank of the Volga.

On October 29, the Wehrmacht communiqué had this to say about our sector of the front:

> At Stalingrad our troops, after repelling several counterattacks stormed other parts of the industrial area and the housing block. Relieving attacks by strong enemy forces, supported by tanks, against the German positions south of the city, as always until now, collapsed with heavy losses to the enemy. Apart from carrying out strong operations over the city the Luftwaffe during night and day bombed enemy airfields, artillery positions, and troop movements.

Meanwhile, the OKW war diary recorded:

> During the morning the enemy attacked the 371st Infantry Division several times and was repulsed. By

afternoon a massive attack before the entire front was stopped and collapsed. The break-through at the Volga was sealed off. The housing blocks taken yesterday in Stalingrad were cleared of the enemy and other sections of the street between the "Red Barricades" and the Volga were stormed. A relieving attack on the 60th Division between Volga and Don collapsed in our own fire.

Early in the morning, after a surprise barrage by our artillery, we go in again. Immediately, we are forced to take cover in a raging torrent of all sorts of infantry weapons. We cannot advance this way, and we won't succeed in closing with the steeply descending banks of the Volga or in throwing the Bolsheviks back over the Volga. They offer bitter resistance and do not retreat a meter. From our present positions, we can see the bank of the Volga—the ridge before the steeply descending slope—and cover it with our fire. But it's unreachable for us. That's where the Soviet staffs must be located, leading and organizing the resistance.

We are now receiving fire from three sides and are pinned down by the Russians in our shell holes, and since we're so far out in front, we once again have terrible losses. We can't even lift our head out of cover anymore to have a look around. The Russians are lying thirty meters opposite us, no more than that. Behind them are their commanders and commisars, and behind them is that wide stream, the Volga.

In the warming afternoon sun, we are stuck in our holes, waiting for renewed support from the heavy artillery. Finally, it breaks loose. With a cry of "Hurrah," the Russian infantrymen storm from their positions and try to overrun us. Quickly, we leave cover, and everybody opens fire. We can hold them, and once again, we repel the attack. The Soviets can't force us down on our knees, but our losses are great. How shall we deal with the next attack?

Now we are lying opposite one another, and we wait for the rapidly falling dusk. Only then we can move freely again and

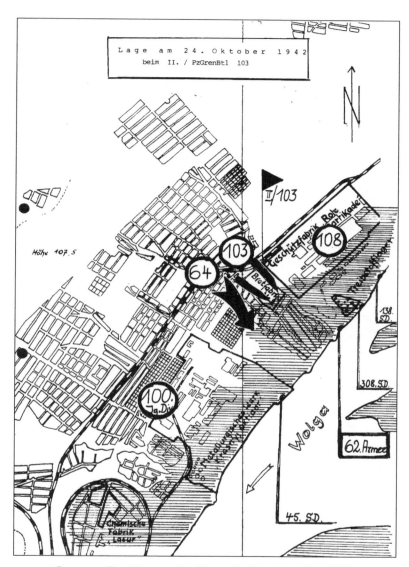

German Positions at Stalingrad, October 24, 1942.

control the open field. As all field telephone lines are jammed and broken down, it is only by radio that contact with battalion can be maintained. I end my situation report with a strong demand: "We can only hold here, when we get reinforcements!" Immediately, battalion replies: "Hold at all costs! Replacements will be led forward during the early hours of the night!"

As we jot down this radio message, our machine guns rattle again, followed by cries and shouts. It is time again: the Russians are attacking. It is not completely dark yet, and I can make out the Russians that are storming our position. Machine pistols are set on full automatic. Quick-firing rifles crack. Bright tracer rounds are flashing and shaking around us as if drawn by electric wiring. We have to hold! Hand grenades, machine guns, continuous fire, hand grenades! But what's going on out there? On the right flank, our own people are walking? Get back! A group wants to evade on its own! I shout at them: "Remain in positions! Hold them! Hold them!" And the Russians are behind them. Our orders are to hold! So we must climb out of our holes. We jump over our own men and attack into the flank of the advancing Russian infantrymen, with constant fire from all weapons. We throw them from their trenches and shell holes, which had been in our possession just now. The Russians flee, or they keep lying down dead. A group from my company that had fallen back and broken its protective cover is now lying dead or wounded.

"Positional Warfare" in the Main Line of Resistance between "Red Barricade" and "Red October."

Once again, the enemy assault has been repelled. The main line of resistance is in our hands as it was before. How often can we do this? It is enough to make one cry. Who is killed today, lying wounded and unattended in holes in the earth, waiting for the protective cover of the night when they can be transported away? At 2300 hours, there are noises behind us again—rattling and whispering. Are those the food carriers already? No. Here they come: "replacements"! There are eighty young soldiers from the Field Replacement Battalion. At their head is a young officer, First Lieutenant Ferch. All are eighteen or nineteen years old, and they haven't fired a round in anger yet. Added to that, more men from the rear area are joining us—convalescents and soldiers returning from leave. Group leaders also are present. My God, how strong we are all of a sudden!

The subordination has been prepared by battalion; we just have to divide them among the platoons and groups. That is done quickly. The first lieutenant is dependent on cooperation with me. He is older than I am and has come from home to this hell with a clean jacket, clearly visible badges of rank, bright uniform collar, and officer's cap. The entire night we're squatting on a few covered stacks of coals and potatoes. In the fading light of a few candles, I brief the lieutenant on the situation and orders for the morning, describing the area in front of us and the events of the past few days. Apart from that, we constantly hear the monotonous flood of words from the observer, who is standing on the stairs of this cellar and reporting what can be seen and observed outside: "White flare . . . 200 to our right . . . muzzle blasts on east bank of Volga . . . rifle fire at the second group." And so the reports and observations continue throughout the night, as always.

On October 30, the Wehrmacht communiqué reports: "At Stalingrad, the attack was continued with support from dive bombers and the ground gained in the last battles was cleared. Ferries and boats on the Volga laid under effective fire of our artillery. South of the city yesterday, relieving attacks supported by tanks collapsed before our own positions in the defensive fire of all weapons and the bombing attacks of all weapons." Recorded in the OKW war diary: "South of Stalingrad, the enemy, supported by artillery, attacked at the old penetration location, on the western bank of the Volga. He was thrown back in hard fighting. The newly gained positions in the metallurgical works and the 'Red Barricades' factory were cleaned of the enemy even further. Counterattacks north of the tank farm were repulsed."

By morning, a Russian artillery bombardment begins—drumfire, forty minutes long. Then all of a sudden, the shells land far behind us—the Russians have shifted their fire to the rear. Now they're coming at us, jumping from cover to cover. One moment, they disappear in order to resume their fire from another position. Our position is now subjected to the fire of heavy 120mm mortars. We return the fire with our machine guns and hand grenades. We have frightful losses, especially with the new ones, since we cannot remain in cover while holding off the enemy. Men cry out: "They're coming!" Then there are shouts in Russian—medics are needed. The Russians have broken through on the right. The platoon there counterattacks immediately and ejects the Bolsheviks. First Lieutenant Ferch carries it out with two groups. Next to me, he jumps out of the trench and quickly falls back into it. A 2cm shell has shattered his head. The good, brave first sergeant leads the few men in a counterattack into our positions, cuts off the Russians that have penetrated, and destroys them. An enemy attack has again been repulsed.

Many of the lads who arrived overnight have been killed in their first firefight. They were killed as soon as the first bullets flew. Now we have to recover the dead and wounded. We pull them back into areas that are outside the effect of enemy fire. But we have to fight on amidst the many groaning and complaining wounded. There's no movement yet in no-man's-land that would indicate that the Russians are readying for a renewed attack. I offer a few comforting words to the moaning wounded: "Wait until dark. Then you'll be fetched; then you'll be cared for; then you'll get out of this hell!"

These words are hardly uttered when Russian artillery opens up again. The earth is quaking with the impacts; fountains of sand and mud pour down on us again and again, taking away our view. The Russians are coming again. Request artillery fire! Immediately, red flares go up: "Enemy attacking!" Finally—it seems like an eternity—the shells of our artillery scream overhead into the enemy's rear areas. With this, the enthusiasm of their attack dies down, and the Bolsheviks remain lying down in front of our positions. Slowly, the firing dies down. We have control of no-man's-land. It is getting dark, and the time has come to prepare measures for later. We remain highly alert, though, because at long intervals, the enemy launches surprise bombardments on us. We now recover our wounded and dead and take them to the rear, bringing ammunition and supplies back to the front. The evening report must be compiled, and so runners are sent to the battalion command post.

On October 31, the Wehrmacht communiqué has only few remarks to make about our sector of the front: "At Stalingrad, storm troop operations gained further ground. As a result of his high losses, the enemy has stopped his attacks south of Stalingrad." The OKW war diary likewise was terse: "South of Stalingrad, an enemy attack was beaten off by the 371st Infantry Division; likewise, an attack south of 'Red October.' Preparations for the conquest of the remaining halls of 'Red October' have been completed."

October 31 began without any special events. We were to hold but launch no new attacks; orders for the continuation with support would follow. The Russians also are behaving quietly at the moment, suspiciously quiet. In no-man's-land, nothing can be seen, which leads to the conclusion that a new attack is imminent. So we can busy ourselves in our holes in the earth improving our positions; we are finally able to clean our weapons and order our tools. All day it remains quiet. Tense, we await the coming night . . .

On November 1, the Wehrmacht communiqué reports: "South of Stalingrad, the enemy resumed his attacks without any success. An attempt to ferry several Soviet battalions across the Volga north of the city failed completely. A number of large boats were sunk, the mass of the enemy force was destroyed or taken prisoner." The entries in the OKW war diary for today offer little extra information:

South of Stalingrad, the enemy continued his attacks against the 371st Infantry Division with air force support. In Stalingrad the attack, gained further ground

despite bitter resistance and multiple enemy counterattacks in the north-eastern part of the metallurgical
works gained further ground. North of Stalingrad
(south of Winnowka) the enemy tried to land on the
western bank of the Volga with two or three battalions.
The majority of the attacking battalions were
destroyed, the rest were compressed into a tiny area.
Four large boats were sunk.

We are lying here as if we had been nailed to the ground.
At the moment, we cannot lift our head above the ground.
Instead, we lift up a steel helmet over the edge of the trench
with a plank. Every time we do that, fireworks erupt. After only
a short while, the damaged helmet is no longer useable even
for this purpose. But there are many steel helmets lying damaged, bent and torn by shell splinters. Our losses are frightening. From October 28 to November 1, we lost seventeen killed
and thirty-three wounded in the company. All in only a few
days! Anyone can calculate when his turn will come.

A young lieutenant comes into my hole in the ground in
the company command post and reports to me. He's straight
out of weapons school and came here to the 103rd via the
replacement unit. For the briefing, I order the platoon commanders to come see me so that the "new guy" gets to know
them straight away. Now we again have a second officer. This
gives me the ability to make my way to the battalion command
post. Once there, I report to the battalion commander, Captain Domaschk. I brief him on the situation and report to him
in detail how things are looking with the company. After that, I
learn something about the "big picture." At my father's division, like before, "all hell broke loose." The Soviets are attacking there night and day, including with their air force—when
our fighters are not in the skies. It was supposed to have been
very, very critical! The Russians over there are trying with all
their strength and energy to penetrate into the southern part
of Stalingrad. But the 371st Infantry Division has repulsed all
these attacks. If only I could talk to father once more about his

situation and the situation here with us. He won't know that I am fighting as a company commander in Panzergrenadier Regiment 103 for the last few meters for the Volga.

On November 2, the Wehrmacht communiqué brought only a brief report about the situation in our sector: "South of Stalingrad, new tank-supported attacks of the enemy failed. North of the city the Soviets once again tried to land without any success. Two gunboats and several landing craft were sunk, a gunboat was damaged and several hundred prisoners were taken." The OKW war diary additionally reports:

> An enemy attack on the boundaries of the sectors of the 297th and 371st Infantry Division was repelled. Likewise a west-bound Russian attack at the city power plant failed. Elsewhere front corrections were carried out, and smaller counterattacks were halted. No new ground was gained for us. In renewed attempted landings of the enemy south of Winnowka another 250 prisoners were taken and several boats were sunk.

Today was full of excitement and tests for the nerves. From over there in the woods on the eastern bank of the Volga, Soviet batteries of all calibers fire their "packages" into our sector. It simply does not stop. But our artillery also is constantly covering the edge of the bank, a few meters in front of us, with surprise bombardments. We also rain machine-gun fire and bursts of fire from machine pistols on attacking or reconnoitering Russians. They are very close. The firing comes from all directions. Then the ricochets whir and whistle down on us from the rear. Only when our Stukas appear—when they're circling over all of us in order to pounce down on the enemy suddenly—do we have a short break. But the planes' rear gunners have barely fired their last rounds when they pull away and the 'fireworks" down here open up again. So it is necessary for us to be prepared for battle at any moment.

Tonight I want to send a message home. But first I eat and compile the evening report. Then I write:

Yes, you surely cannot imagine the last phase of this wrestling! No! No one can! The many, many losses! Every evening under cover of darkness we get about ten men replacements, from the hospitals, from staffs, from the rear areas! A small gang, this Panzer-grenadier Regiment 103! With this company I have taken parts of the famous bread factory, and after the cleaning of an enemy-occupied housing block, I have penetrated to the Volga. With the company, I control the bank of the Volga from here. You can imagine what we're going through here! Boy oh boy! It is unimaginable! From three sides we receive continuous fire by snipers. That's why we continuously have these high casualties! And we have to hold, hold under all circumstances! Three weeks of man-to-man fighting without a break, house-to-house fighting, man-man fighting! There's no way one can sleep!

The Russians are about thirty meters away! Washing, shaving, all of this is done away with! I already have a respectable beard. Only the food is fabulous! Always special rations, butter, sausages, white bread, chocolate, schnapps, cigarettes, and so forth. But all that can only be "wolfed down" in the mud and misery over here! We have lice and are in tatters! Today the Bolsheviks again laid a drumfire barrage for forty minutes, and we could only fold our hands and say, "Amen!" It cannot be described how it howled, hissed, shrieked, and exploded. What will happen next? The gods or the devil only know! If I will ever get back to brigade, I do not know.

So now I close for today. I am not capable of reporting more. All the best and Sieg Heil!

On November 3, the Wehrmacht communiqué reports:

At Stalingrad, the heavy offensive fighting for housing blocks and streets was continuous. Dive-bombers continued their attacks against the bitterly contested resistance nests in the northern part of the city. Despite determined resistance, the enemy lost further ground. His continuously repeated counterattacks failed. Bomber units disrupted the rail links east of the Volga and the ferry activities across the stream for a long time.

The OKW war diary adds: "Continuation of the battle for the industrial area of Stalingrad. South of the brick works, our own troops took hold of the banks of the Volga. In the northern part of the city as well, battles for the individual housing blocks are still continuing."

Until now, it has been a bit "quieter" today. But what does that mean? Like before, we cannot lift our heads out of cover. Russian snipers zero in on us straightaway. Constantly, we stand ready to break up a Russian attack with all weapons. But nothing is moving; only bombardments by the Soviet artillery and heavy mortars keep us down in our dugouts. In our positions, it is warm—a summery warmth—as the sun is still shining brightly in the cloudless sky.

On November 4, the OKW war diary has recorded for the current day: "371st Infantry Division beat off enemy attacks in company and battalion strength. In the southern part of Stalingrad several enemy reconnaissances in force from the direction of the city power plant and in the metallurgical works were beaten off. Likewise, the remaining nests of the enemy in the southern corner of the brickworks were broken up."

Events at the company were the same as in the days before. We still cannot lift ourselves out of our holes. Immediately, we receive aimed fire—two killed and five wounded, who were hit as a result of carelessness. In no case can we remain in this position. We must attack or "correct" the front. There are no other options.

On November 5, the Wehrmacht communiqué said: "At Stalingrad, storm troop operations were carried out. An enemy strong point was knocked out, enemy assaults thrown back. Army covering detachments on the Volga sank a large river steamer. Heavy air attacks were aimed at enemy strong points west of the Volga 'knee' and battery positions east of the stream." And the OKW war diary records: "In the battle for Stalingrad, a strongpoint in the northern part of the water works was taken. Furthermore, the rear areas were cleared up. Also in Spartakowa, some housing blocks, which put up a tough resistance, could be taken into our hands."

Shortly after midnight, First Lieutenant Meisel arrives at the company command post. I get orders to withdraw to the old positions on the eastern edge of the gun foundry at 0230 hours. The reason for this measure is that our daily losses are so high that being overrun is now becoming a real possibility. I immediately adapt the order and organize the change of position with regard to the order of withdrawal, covering fire, and passing through our lines. And on the dot at 0230, we assemble noiselessly and with large intervals. The Russians seem not to notice. Without losses, we get back into the positions we know. Now a correction has been completed, and we are out of the bulge that has cost us so many losses. Now the Bolsheviks cannot flank us anymore. Although we have not given up any sector of ground that is decisive, the very thought of the large sacrifices that the attack cost us here is enough to make one despair. Such great casualties in the advance in these labyrinthine, difficult-to-control workers' settlements on our front—and now all that was in vain? No, one simply cannot think of that now. One has to see the total task, nothing else. Something must happen if we are to conclude the battle for this town successfully.

On November 6, the Wehrmacht communiqué has little to say about our sector of the front: "The combat activities at Stalingrad were limited on November 5 to lively storm troop actions from both sides and the repelling of individual advances by the enemy. The railroads east of the Volga were attacked by bombers all day."

It is unfathomable. We hardly have nestled ourselves in our positions, and here the Russians again are in front of us, at most fifty meters away. So they did notice it when we withdrew.

And now we are again in range of their infantry weapons. The sniper fire starts again; only this time it is not flanking fire. And yet we cannot get out of our cover. Immediately, the Russian marksmen fire wildly at everything that becomes visible on our side. The lieutenant that was posted to us several days ago wants to leave the company command post in order to check the communications trenches, with which he is not familiar. I do know them and explain to him that this intention is out of the question during daylight. I order him several times to stay in cover until everything is dark. But he cannot be dissuaded from his plan. In his conspicuous uniform, he climbs out of the trench, walks a few meters, and collapses after being hit by a sniper.

Struck in the lower abdomen, seriously wounded, he's lying in front of us. How are we to help him? How are we to get him? It takes a long time before we are successful. He's crying with pain—the bullet has hit his testicles. In daylight, we cannot recover him. He can't lie down, sit, or stand up—it is horrid. The battalion doctor comes forward to sedate him here. While we continue to endure firefights with the Russians and try to protect ourselves from surprise bombardments, an armored personnel carrier is driven up to the closest cover. The lieutenant is carried there meter by meter in tiresome recovery work. Stooped really low, every movement draws fire. Then they're finally there, and the severely wounded man, with folded upper arms, is hoisted into the rear of the carrier. Here the doctors have to await the fall of night. The lieutenant can be heard constantly—his complaining, his moaning, his whimpering. Sometimes it is quiet, and then it comes again, horribly strengthened.

Soviet salvos are coming down on our positions again. Behind us, the "big packages" of the Soviet heavy artillery strike. By dusk, this fire lessens and becomes an irregular harassing fire. Now the time has come to transport the seriously wounded back to the aid post. For me, the time has come to prepare my evening report. The platoon commanders give their situation reports and hand over their opera-

tions sketches, which have to be assembled into a single com-
pany-operations sketch. After the men who have brought us
food and ammunition have finished over here, they take the
report to battalion with them. It always is a difficult road
through the labyrinthine settlement in the darkness, which
makes it easy for Russian parties to surprise and overwhelm
our men.

On November 7, there are only two lines in the Wehrmacht communiqué: "In the Stalingrad area, only local battles
took place. Bombers and dive bombers attacked battery positions and villages east of the Volga."

The entire day we have "contact with the enemy." The Bolsheviks are lying fifty meters opposite us. They do not mount
attacks. The artillery fire—from time to time supported by
120mm mortar fire—continues throughout the day. But our
artillery also is pounding the ridge of the riverbank that lies in
front of us. We cannot see anything but are in constant tension
because something has to happen.

On November 8, neither the Wehrmacht communiqué
nor the OKW war diary has anything to say about the situation
at Stalingrad. Over the past few hours, nothing has changed
here. Yet we have the feeling that something decisive is developing. We cannot remain lying here. Nothing is gained by
doing that. So we must attack in order to throw all Russians
down the bank of the Volga before winter sets in. Therefore,
engineer battalions are to be drawn up, which are to finish
"the remains" in cooperation with us. As I have learned from
battalion, the engineers are already behind us in the rear area
and are practicing the taking of enemy bunkers and fortified
field positions with storm troop operations. In fact, we have
enough fresh units to gain victory with one last strong effort.
We are in an optimistic mood.

On November 9, the Wehrmacht communiqué is once
again silent about our situation. The landing of the Americans
in North Africa towers over our actions here, and more is
reported about this. The OKW war diary also is silent about
our stagnating operations.

On November 10, the Wehrmacht communiqué gives only one sentence about our situation: "At Stalingrad, storm troop activity." And the OKW war diary for today concludes: "South of Stalingrad, assembled enemies were destroyed by Romanian artillery. Our own artillery fired on enemy battery positions on the eastern bank of the Volga. An enemy attack on the metallurgical works was beaten off with bloody losses to the enemy."

We are fighting positional warfare. World War I must have looked like this. We lie fifty meters apart and are tensely waiting to see who'll attack first. I believe it will be us. When the engineers are ready for the attack and have come forward to us, that will be the moment for the attack. We learn nothing about the situation in Africa. The Führer is supposed to have spoken about the situation in Stalingrad. It will be taken with assault troops. Well, we are not capable of mounting anything bigger anymore. If only the engineers would come!

On November 11, there's only one line in the Wehrmacht communiqué: "At Stalingrad, lively assault troop activities." That is all that is said about the situation at Stalingrad. Today, other events occupy all attention. It is the situation in southern France, where German troops have occupied the hitherto unoccupied part of France to prevent an imminent British-American landing. In the OKW war diary, it is reported about us here: "South of Stalingrad, an enemy advance was stopped by Romanian artillery shortly before our own lines. Attacks from the east and the south on the metallurgical works were thrown back with high enemy losses. Our own artillery shelled at and put on fire an enemy motor boat north of Stalingrad."

Once again, we had a big day in the skies. Without a break, our bombers pass overhead and drop their loads in the Russian-occupied part of Stalingrad—especially to the right of us on the metallurgical works, in the flats that are still standing. For us, that means that we have less danger of snipers operating there for the time being. So the focus of the fighting has moved away from us here. Hopefully, our comrades over there succeed in driving the Bolsheviks out of the remaining parts of the industrial area and into the Volga.

The Enemy Armies East Bureau of the Army General Staff provided the following "Short Estimation of the Enemy Situation on November 12, 1942":

In front of the army group, the outlines of the planned attack, suspected by the allied armies, are becoming more and more clear. Apart from the spotted formation of two masses of troops in front of the flanks of the Romanian 3rd Army, the indications of a massing of forces farther to the west also increase; especially in the Kalach area (radio traffic of the 63rd army with six or seven unknown units, suspected slotting in of the 1st Guard Army, railroad traffic towards Kalach, bringing up of elements of the 5th Tank Army [?], counterintelligence reports about troop movements in the Kalach area), possibly also in front of the Hungarians.

The total picture of the build up of forces is still unclear with regard to location, site and scale, possibilities for an attack soon are not visible yet. An estimation of the total enemy plan is not yet possible with the unclarity of the picture, however, an imminent attack against the 3rd Romanian Army with the objective to cut off the railroad to Stalingrad has to be taken into account; with it the German forces standing further eastwards can be threatened and a withdrawal of the German troops standing at Stalingrad can be compelled, which would free the waterway over the Volga. The forces available probably are too weak for further reaching operations (at this time in front of the right wing of the 3rd Romanian Army are available sixteen rifle divisions and one to four tank brigades, in front of the left wing seven rifle divisions and three cavalry divisions). Whether a large offensive across the Don against the 8th Italian and 2nd Hungarian Army—objective Rostow?—after the operation against the Romanian 3rd Army is to be expected or whether the enemy apart from the offensive operations against the Romanian 3rd Army will launch limited offensive operations against the Italian 8th and Hungarian 2nd Armies, is something which cannot be determined yet. The report of an officer taken prisoner, who names the objective for the attack as the railroad Orozowski Stalingrad, seems to confirm this line of thought.

In planning signed: Gehlen
F.d.R.
signed: Wessel
Captain of the General Staff

On November 12, the Wehrmacht communiqué reports: "At Stalingrad, shock troops threw the enemy out of further housing blocks and strong points in bitter assaults. Army artillery and antiaircraft artillery of the air force sank five large ferries and cargo cranes on the Volga. Artillery positions and supply communications east of the river were hit heavily by aerial attacks." In the OKW war diary is remarked: "At Stalingrad, further bunkers of the enemy in the area of the water works and the chemical factory could be taken. Enemy attacks from the south on the 'Red October' works could be repulsed. East and northeast of 'Red Barricade,' storm troop operations were successful. Several housing blocks were taken. At the juncture between the 6th and Romanian 3rd Army, the enemy repeatedly attacked without success."

Today the Russians try their luck with us. Again and again, they launch attacks during the entire day. They no longer come at us frontally but from the labyrinthine terrain of the metallurgical works and the tank farm. A flare goes up, red to signal a barrage, and shortly afterward, the shells are howling overhead into the attacking enemy. Our heavy mortars start firing, too, only farther to the right—too far. It is not long before the fire is corrected and falls exactly into the terrain which the Bolsheviks have to cross and which our infantry weapons are able to reach only with difficulty. At night, it becomes quieter again; our own losses for the moment—God be thanked—are only slight, if one does not count the many lightly wounded.

On November 13, the Wehrmacht communiqué tersely reports: "Romanian troops south of Stalingrad beat off enemy attacks of battalion strength. At Stalingrad the ground gained during the morning was cleaned of scattered enemy groups." The OKW war diary remarks: "South of Stalingrad, the enemy succeeded with two battalions to break into the positions held by Romanian troops. In a counterattack, the penetration was eliminated. In Stalingrad the mopping up of ground gained was continued with success. Enemy attacks in battalion strength from the chemical works were beaten off everywhere."

The enemy first has to recuperate from yesterday's vain attack efforts. At least that's the way things look. Therefore, I decide to pay a visit to the battalion command post in order to orient myself. From cover to cover, I work my way to the 2nd Battalion staff. Things are whistling and cracking dangerously close to me; often, I have to take cover for extended periods of time. The shells that are coming in and smashing into the machinery and walls of metal make a dreadful noise, which forces one to crouch. I finally make it and report to the battalion commander. He patiently listens to my report, pats me on the shoulder, and says: "So, Stempel, let's have a look at the terrain from an observation tower!"

We go up to the daylight, jump behind parts of the gun foundry, climb across a few pipes, and stand in front of the command armored personnel carrier. With this, we roll through the ruins and rubble, past housing and wall façades, to a block of flats that are still more or less in one piece. We mount some steps and ascend to the roof. Here we look out into a wide-open space through panels and large holes that have been torn by shells. We can see the entire field of rubble and ruin through which the main line of defense runs and in which we lie opposite the Soviets at hand-grenade distance. It's an unbelievable view. Here and there are impacts of the Soviet artillery, and then there's the wide stream, the silvery glistening Volga, gigantic in its size. We see the islands branching out in it—where the Russian logistic effort, their entire flow of supplies and reserves, is supposed to be taking place. There is their rear headquarters, which oversees all Soviet troops fighting on the west bank. During daytime, Russian movements can't be seen, and if they are, our artillery and air force catch and destroy anything that moves. But at night, the movement across the stream begins, in both directions. The view one gets here is impressive. After this "briefing," we both climb down again and, with the armored personnel carrier, roll back to the battalion command post. I take my leave and work my way forward again to the company.

On November 14, the Wehrmacht communiqué reports: "South of Stalingrad, local Bolshevik attacks remained pinned down in the defensive fire of Romanian troops. At Stalingrad, groups of assault troops took further housing blocks in hard fighting. Enemy counterattacks were repulsed and shot to pieces by concentrated fire from artillery and antiaircraft guns and by dive bombers." The OKW war diary remarks: "At Stalingrad, groups of assault troops east of 'Red Barricade' took two housing blocks and the commissar's house. An enemy attack of 150 men was repulsed."

Enemy attacks in assault troop detachment strength take place constantly. At one time, the Soviets managed to penetrate into our left trench. As they're orienting and collecting themselves, the platoon operating there has surprised them with a counterattack and taken them all out. None of the Bolsheviks got away. Sadly, we suffer four dead and seven wounded. Our trench is now completely in our hands again. No one will get us away from here. We just need to remain devilishly alert. At any moment, the next attackers—again without being observed—could stand in front of us. What will happen next? When do we finally attack again? Where are the engineers that were reported? Where are the replacements that were reported? If our company was filled up and we had support, we should be able to do it. In this way, we vegetate in this Hades and stick our heads out of piles of earth when we hear the Russians approaching—or think and suppose this. We can feel it, even without being able to see and make out anything. It is in the air; there are tensions that point to the "right" sign. If only these damned snipers weren't there! Now they're even hitting us in the darkness. Just when we're thinking that we can slip out of cover unnoticed, a rifle snaps from somewhere. Nobody will believe us if we ever make it out alive.

On November 15, the Wehrmacht communiqué reports: "In the city area of Stalingrad, enemy counterattacks were thrown back. The air force supported the battle effectively by attacks on artillery positions and airfield of the Soviets east of the Volga." The OKW war diary reports: "South of Stalingrad, an assembly area of the enemy was destroyed by Romanian artillery. At Kuprosnoje and Stalingrad several, enemy attacks were repulsed, partially by counterattacks."

On November 16, the Wehrmacht communiqué includes only one line about our battles over here: "At Stalingrad, several housing blocks were taken in commando operations and enemy counterattacks were thrown back." In the OKW war diary, this is confirmed with the same words.

Since the early-morning hours, the dive-bombers are circling overhead again and attacking the enemy. The noise of battle is coming from the right of us. We are attacking—probably in the metallurgical works and the Lasur Chemical Works. We have no orders to attack. Tense and prepared for battle, we have to observe how things are developing with our neighbors. By afternoon, as the sun is warming us again nicely, the Russians attack us. I request a defensive barrage, and all infantry weapons hose down the enemy and inflict high losses. The first salvoes of our artillery come hurtling in. They're lying well; the artillery fire strikes in the middle of the attacking Bolsheviks. But now it also comes down on us. The Soviet artillery is answering, mixed with the eerie fire of the heavy mortars. A miserable feeling of helplessness envelops us. We are used to it, and we stay in cover and are completely dependent on our observers.

Führer Order Concerning "Continuation of the Conquest."
On November 17, the Wehrmacht communiqué contains no data on the events in our sector of the front. The OKW war diary points to us with two sentences: "South of Stalingrad (at Kuporosnoje), our own artillery destroyed several enemy attacks. In Stalingrad several enemy attacks, some of battalion strength, were repulsed."

In the evening, a Führer Order arrives at the 6th Army. It contains the following text:

Führer order of November 17, 1942, about the continuation of the conquest of Stalingrad by the 6th Army.

Army Supreme Command 6 A.H.Q., November 17, 1942 Abt. Ia SECRET!

The following Führer order is to be read verbally to all commanders down to regimental commander fighting in Stalingrad:

"The difficulties of the Battle for Stalingrad and the lowered combat strengths are known to me. The problems of the Russians with the current ice forming on the Volga are even greater. So when we use this span of time, we'll save a great deal of blood later. Therefore I expect, that the leadership, with all previously demonstrated energy, and the troops, with often proven determination, will once again give their all in action to break through to the Volga, at least near the gun foundry and the metallurgical works, and take these parts of the city. The Luftwaffe and artillery are to do everything in their power to prepare and support this attack."

The Führer

signed/Adolf Hitler

"I'm sure, that these orders will give a new impulse to our brave troops".

signed/Paulus
AOK 6 Ia 4640/42 g.

That's the way the situation in Stalingrad looks. We're the focal point of the Führer's mandated attack, Panzergrenadier Regiments 103 and 108 as well as Motorcycle Rifle Regiment 64. To the right of us is the 100th Jäger Division. Well, now we are awaiting orders to attack and preparing ourselves for this journey. Does my father know how things look for us and what awaits us tomorrow? If only I could talk to him once more! How will the 371st Infantry Division survive the heavy battles south of Stalingrad? Who knows when, how, and whether we will see each other again?

On November 18, there are no reports on the Stalingrad Front in the Wehrmacht communiqué. In the OKW war diary, it is recorded: "The enemy forces encircled at the leather factory were destroyed save for two officers and some soldiers, who were taken prisoner. The enemy attacks in company strength supported by strong artillery and rocket fire against the tank farm were partially repulsed, partially the battles are still continuing. On the other front of the Army group there were no notable combat actions."

So the last little bit in front of us must be taken. We were almost completely out in front once already, but we had to withdraw because we couldn't hold against the flanking fire. Now we are to renew the attack through this hell of a labyrinthine settlement. None "up there" can imagine what this means for us. When we've made it, then we'll be standing on the Volga in earthen bunkers and extensive positions. No Russian will be able to get across this wide stream—not even in the winter when the Volga is frozen solid. But will we be able to do it tomorrow? The unbelievable efforts until now and the continuous attacking have attrited, but not broken us. We only need support. A Russian saying goes, "Russia can only be defeated when an enemy crosses the Volga." Will this become our doom?

On November 19, the Wehrmacht communiqué tersely notes: "At Stalingrad, fighting with small assault groups." The OKW war diary noted additionally: "At Stalingrad, small assault troops east of the 'Gun Foundry' on the bank of the Volga gained another 200 meters of ground. Enemy assault troops were thrown back. In Rynok (north of Stalingrad), other groups of houses could be taken."

It is already 0730 hours. We are standing by tensely, concentrated on the attack. But no orders to prepare for the attack come. No support—whether from the air force or our artillery—is noticeable. And the engineers that had been promised to us for this attack do not arrive. On the other hand, there is much excitement and hurrying among the battalion staff. But no explanations and information get through to us, only indications of a situation that has changed completely. What's the meaning of all this? What has happened that our attack cannot be launched? We continue to stand by in our extended holes in the earth and positions and look toward the east into the unknown. Even now, when darkness falls, we know nothing.

ENCIRCLEMENT OF THE 6TH ARMY AND FIGHTING IN THE CAULDRON.

November 21, 1942. Abandonment of the Volga Positions and the Move to the New Operations Area in the West.

On November 20, 1942, the Wehrmacht communiqué has only this to say: "At Stalingrad, our own assault troops took some housing blocks. On the Don front, Romanian and German troops are embroiled in hard battles against strong enemy infantry and tank attacks." The OKW war diary reports: "South of Stalingrad, an enemy attack of two companies was repulsed by Romanian troops. In Stalingrad itself assault troops of the 305th Infantry Division took two large housing blocks. Enemy attacks against the tank farm were repulsed."

As before, the company is standing by in its positions, ready to attack. But early today, it remains relatively quiet. Now and then there is harassing fire from both sides. Something extraordinary must have taken place to prevent us from assembling for the attack. But we do not have the opportunity to think about it; we have enough to do with ourselves.

All of a sudden I am ordered to battalion command post. I leave the command here to the second in command of the company, the tested and experienced sergeant major. Then I hurry back through the rubble, ruins, and craters to the headquarters of the 2nd Battalion, Panzergrenadier Regiment 103. Here I report to the commander, Captain Domaschk, who is expecting me already. The orders are flying around; chaos rules; nobody knows the larger situation around us. Only one fact is clear: the Russians are attacking the Italians, Romanians, and Hungarians in order to cut us off out here in front.

We jump into the command armored personnel carrier and drive to the rear through this lunar landscape—I cannot orient myself—and arrive at the command post of an infantry regiment of the 305th Infantry Division. We run past sentries down the stairs into the subterranean cellars, and drowning out other conversations, we loudly ask for the regimental commander. Along the walls of the long cellar corridors, infantrymen are squatting, sitting, and leaning around. One can tell what efforts they've made and how they've been affected by the altered and threatening situation. The conversation with the regimental commander is short; everyone already knows what's going on. In preparation for handing over our sector, we give the infantry maps and operational sketches. After being relieved by this infantry regiment, we are to move east, which is simply incomprehensible!

We quickly drive back to the battalion command post in the armored personnel carrier. Here I take my leave and hurry forward to the company, where they're expecting my "news." I immediately order all measures in preparation for handing over this sector to the unit of the 305th Infantry Division. All of this has to be done noiselessly, and our withdrawal must go unnoticed by the enemy. We have to get out without losses. We are now gripped by the frightening question of what has happened over there to cause us to be pulled out of the main front.

On November 21, the Wehrmacht communiqué reports: "South of Stalingrad and in the Kalmuck Steppe, the enemy launched strong attacks supported by tanks. A group of motorized enemy forces was destroyed in this. Also on the lower Don the bitter defensive battles of German and Romanian troops continue. A reinforced Soviet cavalry regiment that had broken through our positions was encircled and destroyed." The OKW war diary notes:

> Encircling enemy attacks with strong forces against Chalchuta could largely be repulsed in heavy fighting, partially they are still continuing. The enemy attacked the entire front of the 4th Panzer Army with strong forces and numerous tanks. While on the southern part of the Army they succeeded in beating off several attacks, the enemy at several locations managed to penetrate the Romanian positions between Tundutowo and the Don-Volga canal. Situation partially unclear. Tanks and the assault gun battalion of the 29th Infantry Division (mot.) could partially push the enemy back in the northern part. In Stalingrad a generally quiet day. Two attacks with about sixty men against the tanks farm were thrown back.

Furthermore: "Strong motorized and assault gun battalions have been moved from Stalingrad to deal with the situation."

We're waiting for the relief. We have prepared everything to carry out this operation quickly and without any hitches. Now they're coming, the men of the 305th Infantry Division. The hand-over and relief of positions takes place without any enemy action. Under cover of darkness and in dense snowdrifts, we move back, until we are behind the battalion command post. The Russians have seen nothing; it remains relatively quiet as before—just artillery harassing fire, as during

the last nights. Behind the remains of the halls and the walls of
the gun foundry, we assemble in order to march to the positions of our rearward services. They're on the western edge of
the city in Balkas. In the early-morning hours, we arrive there.

During a pause to tend to our armored personnel carriers,
I decide to quickly drive down to the headquarters of the 371st
Infantry Division to see my father once more. I take a motorcycle with sidecar and arrive there in short order. My father is
very surprised to see me standing in front of him all of a sudden. He is happy to meet under such extraordinary circumstances, but he doesn't seem optimistic about the situation. He
knows more than those of us who just pulled out of battle. Still,
he thinks that with a concentration of all forces and a reduc-
tion in other situations, the situation can still be resolved. We
say good-bye and shake hands, and I had back to the battalion.

While I was gone, the preparations for the move were finished. "Mount up!" All armored personnel carriers and ter-
rain-capable vehicles roll off. The snow continues to fall, and
an icy wind is blowing. The march is to the west, as expected,
on snowed-in roads that muffle the rattle of the half-tracks.
Our orders are to take up positions in the bend of the Don
behind the Romanians, who are said to be sorely pressed. But
we don't even make it there. Before we reach Karpowka, we
are stopped. In front of us—to the west, that is—echoes the
noise of battle. The armored personnel carriers remain in the
village, the panzergrenadiers take up positions along the
embankment of the railroad that leads to Stalingrad with the
front to the south. Everything goes very quickly. And so in a
short while, a main line of resistance has been built, which is
densely occupied by panzergrenadiers. On the left and right
are neighboring units, and therefore, we cannot be flanked.

November 22, 1942. We Are Encircled by the Russians.
The remains of the Regiments 103 and 108 now are known as
Kampfgruppe [Battle Group] Seydel. Apart from that, it is difficult to orient ourselves at this time because new troop movements are taking place everywhere. Everything happens too

hastily and too rapidly. Everyone probably fears that the Russians would beat us to the new area of operations. We don't know whether we'll see Stalingrad again. Is that now behind us? That's a frightening question in this oppressive, stressful, and paralyzing situation. Will the Russians really succeed in cutting us off, encircling and possibly destroying us? It cannot be ruled out.

On November 22, the Wehrmacht communiqué reports:

In the area south of Stalingrad and in the large Don bend, the bitter defensive battles continue. German and Romanian troops in a counterattack captured 600 prisoners and destroyed twenty-five tanks. Another thirty-six Soviet tanks were destroyed on November 20 and 21 by a panzer division. German and Romanian air forces supported their own troops and in continuous attacks against tank assemblies, infantry units, disembarkation points and truck columns inflicted high losses on the enemy. In Stalingrad in assault operations further strongly fortified strong points were taken and in another location attacks by the Soviets were thrown back.

In the OKW war diary, it is noted:

West of the Stalingrad-Abganerowo railroad the enemy has succeeded in advancing further to the west and southwest. Between Malije-Derbety and Aksai a new defensive front was formed by German and Romanian troops. In Stalingrad several attacks were repelled with artillery support. On the northern front of Don-Volga, enemy concentrations indicate an imminent attack. In the big loop of the Don east of Kletskaja, several fierce attacks by the enemy were repulsed. South of Kletskaja, the enemy succeeded in breaking through to the south and southeast between our tank strongpoints. Northwest of Kalach a defensive front was built.

On the night of November 22–23, the following radio message was sent from Hitler to the commander of the 6th Army: "The 6th Army is encircled for the time being. I know the 6th Army and its commander and know that they will hold bravely in this situation. The 6th Army is to know that I am doing everything to help and relieve them. I will give it my orders in time."

We are standing in Karpowka. We expand our positions; earthen bunkers are constructed, warm hideouts. In our sector, it is relatively quiet at the time. Everything is now in order; we are feeling secure. On the right and left are other units, and we have artillery support. A number of officers have been placed at the disposal of the battalion, and that is why, after having been engaged in house-to-house fighting in Stalingrad for several weeks, I now find work at the battalion staff. Lieutenant Moritz also is present again; he is with the remnants of the 108th. Our battalion command post is housed in a group of hovels in the middle of Karpowka, right on the thoroughfare that leads from east to west.

How did this threatening situation arise? Of course, the Russians have seen where our vulnerabilities were. I have experienced the Romanians on Lake Zaza; I have seen the Italians during the summer in Stalino. In the attritional and casualty-heavy battles in and around Stalingrad, we—the 6th Army—have been gutted and worn down completely. In the neighboring theaters, the wide open flanks, our allies were not able to halt the Bolsheviks. Now we are supposed to help, support, and clean up . . . but with what? Is the state of our regiments and battalions not known to the higher command? I spend nearly all day in the positions with the men of the 103rd and the 108th. It is still possible to go half of the way from Karpowka to the front standing up. Then, for the other half, one must use the terrain carefully and work his way to the covers of the main line of resistance.

Defense South of Karpowka along the Stalingrad-Chir-Kalach Railroad Line from November 23, 1942.

On November 23, the Wehrmacht communiqué has only one sentence about our situation: "In the area south of Stalingrad and in the great bend of the Don, the German and Romanian troops in cooperation with strong close support of the air force continue to wage heavy defensive battles." The OKW war diary reveals little: "From the 4th Panzer Army and the 6th Army, no reports today due to break in communications." We don't know much about the big picture.

Rumors are making the rounds; one should believe nothing. We do know that we have been encircled by the Russians. The knowledge of this fact has spread like a wildfire. How should the Russians manage to destroy us? Now and then, we spot an enemy reconnaissance troop, and once, we had a powerful attack. They obviously want to make sure that the positions here, south of Karpowka, are occupied. We won't be defending here for long, as we count on breaking out and attacking the enemy to establish a new front to the southwest.

On November 24, the Wehrmacht communiqué mentions:

Southwest of Stalingrad and in the great bend of the Don, the Soviets in operation, without regard of men and material, have penetrated the defensive front on the Don. Countermeasures are taking place. In the hard and fluctuating battles of the last two days several hundred enemy tanks were destroyed. Units of the German and Romanian Air Force continuously intervened in the ground battles despite the unfavorable flying weather. In Stalingrad itself, only local fighting.

The OKW war diary reports:

The northern front of the VII Romanian Army Corps was pushed back to the heights of Sadowoje by a strong enemy. The fighting strenght of the VI Romanian Army Corps has shrunk to zero. The units are routing. Collection points have been established, which should help to collect the retreating parts. Weak German security detachments are embroiled in heavy battles on the southern bank of the Jeszaulowski sector from Aksai to the west. 6th Army: no report. 3rd Romanian Army:

weak enemy attacks on the positions on the river Chir
were repulsed. The build-up of the security line in the
Chir sector was continued on the railroad line adjoining existing security positions. On the rest of the front
no special fighting.

The situation in our sector south of Karpowka is unchanged. Early on, I go forward to the command post of Lieutenant Moritz (108th) and tensely try to spot movement on
the enemy side. But nothing is happening there. With longer
breaks, artillery bombardments take place, mainly targeting
the hamlet of Karpowka. In the afternoon, as I return to the
battalion command post, I learn that a Führer Order has
arrived. This now finally makes clear what we are to do here:
"The 6th Army temporarily has been encircled by Russian
troops. I plan to concentrate the army in the area of north
Stalingrad–Kotluban–Hill 137–Marinovka–Zybenko–south Stalingrad. The army is to be convinced that I am doing everything to keep them supplied accordingly and to relieve them
at the right time. I know the brave 6th Army and its commander and know that it will do its duty."

I also learn that from November 26, Field Marshal Erich
von Manstein is in charge of everything. All this brings us great
comfort, and we are of the opinion that nothing is lost here.
The commander, Captain Domaschk, also brings very positive
reports from the command post of Kampfgruppe Seydel. The
armored units of the 14th Panzer Division are kept at the disposal of the army in order to mount counterattacks where penetrations occur. Apart from that, everything now depends on
how we are continuously to be supplied by air and when the
troops begin our liberation. First Lieutenant Meisel, First
Lieutenant Riemenschneider, and I, after the briefing with
Captain Domaschk, discuss for a long time which measures are
to be taken in order to lengthen and lighten our efforts to
hold on. The big problems are with the resupply of food and
ammunition and with getting the best possible treatment for
the wounded.

On November 25, the Wehrmacht communiqué reports:

Southwest of Stalingrad, as well as in the large bend of the Don, the enemy continued his attacks with strong tank and infantry formations. The own defenses were supported effectively by strong close support units and German and Romanian ground attack planes in continuous operations. The Soviet troops again suffered high losses in men and material. Simultaneous enemy attacks between Volga and Don were thrown back in bitter fighting by German and Romanian troops with high bloody losses for the enemy, and fifty-four tanks were knocked out in this. In Stalingrad itself also enemy attacks failed.

Meanwhile, the OKW war diary notes:

As has only become known now, the Romanian VII Corps, after an enemy attack on November 23, has withdrawn its positions along the road Chara Buluk–Obelnoje. From here, the position curves backward to the northwest, as the enemy pressure was very strong here and Umanzewo has been occupied by the enemy. Between the left wing of the VII Romanian Army Corps and the right wing of the VI Romanian Army Corps, the situation is unclear. Alert battalions of the 18th and 1st Romanian Infantry Divisions have arrived in the vicinity of Shutow railroad station and south of it, in order to take up the retreating parts of the VI Romanian Corps.

6th Army: X Corps is withdrawn to the heights behind the Don while leaving a bridgehead like position on west of the Don. Strong attacks on the withdrawing units were repelled. The 3rd Motorized Infantry Division north-northwest of Spartakowa is pulled out of the frontline in order to be engaged in operation on the front east of Kalach. The front at

Spartakowa is pulled back to the edge of the town accordingly. All attacks south of Stalingrad on the IV Corps were repulsed. Aerial reconnaissance made out enemy columns approaching from the southeast on the road to Businowka and from the northwest on the road to the Tschir railroad station.

I spend the entire day with Lt. Hans Moritz in the trenches. The same theme lies at the heart of everything: do we break out, or will relief come to reestablish communications with our own troops? We let a scout patrol of the Russians approach our positions quite closely in order to take them prisoner. We manage to cut them off. They are taken by surprise and captured—by us "encircled troops." They know nothing and seem to be glad that the war is over for them.

On November 26, the Wehrmacht communiqué reports: "In between the Volga and the Don and in the great bend in the Don, the strong enemy infantry and tank attacks continue. They were repulsed in bitter fighting. Again, the enemy lost many tanks. Our own aerial attacks inflicted high losses in men, heavy weapons, and all kinds of vehicles on the enemy. At Stalingrad yesterday, attempted enemy attacks also collapsed." And in the OKW war diary, it is noted:

The enemy tried to break through the hole between the Romanian VII and VI Corps with strong tank and cavalry forces. The attack was repulsed. In the 6th Army area from Stalingrad down to the Don bend, combat is being fought with a bitter intensity. The partially newly gained positions were attacked by the enemy with the utmost fierceness. By moving reserves, the attacks could be thrown back nearly everywhere. South of the Chir railroad station, enemy elements attacked with tanks and were thrown back in a counterattack. The German security forces standing east of the Chir railroad station down to Gromalslawka in the south were withdrawn to the area north and south of the Chir railroad station after throwing back enemy attacks, in order to reinforce the security here. Aerial reconnaissance reported strong columns of tanks and cavalry between Chir railroad station and Stalingrad, marching north.

Like before, we maintain our positions south of Karpowka along the railroad from Stalingrad to Marinovka and Kalach. The Russians are not attacking seriously in our sector. They advance only with reinforced reconnaissance parties, and when we open fire with all weapons, they yield straightaway and disappear into the snowy emptiness that reaches to the horizon to the south. This is repeated daily.

Much more uncomfortable are the surprise artillery bombardments. Since we are located directly in the east-west link, the artillery fire increases and increases. The Russians know exactly how crammed Karpowka is now. Staffs, rear-area troops, and reserves have all found shelter from the cold here—though not so much from the artillery fire. The casualties are sometimes high, and so we have constructed large dugouts to provide cover. This work is done in the house, hovels, and huts that are still standing, making Karpowka seem like a supply center. Everything is organized here: the defensive measures, the partition of the ammunition and foodstuffs. However, the nourishment is completely insufficient. We fear that if it continues like this, the troops will be physically broken. It is difficult to believe how quickly one's strength diminishes. We need food urgently. Warm food! Meat, fat, sugar!

By evening, our battalion—and the entire 6th Army—is given an exhortation by the Führer:

The Battle for Stalingrad is reaching its climax. The enemy has broken through in the back of the German forces and is now trying desperately to regain possession of this determining bulwark on the Volga. In these difficult hours my thoughts and those of the entire German people are with you! You're to hold the position

Stalingrad, that you have taken with so much blood under the leadership of such capable generals, under all circumstances. It is to be our unshakable determination, that like in Charkow this spring, this Russian penetration will lead to its destruction, due to the measures already taken. What is in my power is being done in order to support you in your heroic struggle!

These are words that strengthen us psychologically, that drive away the doubts that assail us in many situations. These are words that allow us to bear the indescribable suffering and horrible circumstances. In this campaign, there have always been difficulties to overcome. We think of the encirclement of Demjansk, of the holding of the encirclement of Cholm. Why should we, the 6th Army, victorious until now, perish here?

On November 27, the Wehrmacht communiqué says: "All tank and infantry attacks of the enemy in the Volga-Don area yesterday again failed in the face of the excellent fighting spirit of the troops. Fifty-five Soviet tanks were destroyed. Attacks by dive-bombers struck the enemy with destructive effect. Army troops on the Volga near Stalingrad sank two enemy motorized ships." In the OKW war diary, the situation is described as follows:

On the left flank of the VII Romanian Army Corps, the enemy attained a penetration of the 4th Romanian Division. A repeated effort of the enemy to penetrate the gap between the VII and VI Romanian Army Corps failed. A cavalry regiment was destroyed. In order to fill the gap between the two corps, remaining elements of the 18th Romanian Division and an ad hoc march battalion are on the move. On the left flank of Army Group Hoth the enemy succeeded in taking a village. At the 3rd Romanian Army several enemy attacks on the positions on the Chir. East of Chir the Loshi railroad station was occupied by the enemy. At Group Hollidt the enemy tried in vain to attack the newly arrived

62nd and 294th Infantry Divisions with the strongest forces possible. The remains of the 1st Romanian Panzer Division (twenty tanks, one battalion, and the majority of the artillery) have arrived at Group Hollidt. The 22nd Panzer Division could also be pulled back behind the Chir. On the rest of the front, apart from the left wing at Liwny, where a small enemy attack was thrown back, no fighting.

There follows an addendum that clarifies the situation with the 6th Army:

Enemy attack against the northeast front of the 94th Infantry Division. Heavy fighting at the point of penetration four kilometers southwest and two kilometers northeast of Orlowka, as well as at Point 145.1. Seven T-34s were destroyed. Situation not completely clear yet. The remains of the 24th Panzer Division have been shoved into the line west of Rynok. VII Corps: enemy breakthrough of about forty tanks; some of these were knocked out. Heavy battles are in progress. Don bridgehead kept. Defense of Marinovka and the southeast successful. Thirty-two destroyed Russian tanks, eleven immobilized tanks, and numerous destroyed trucks were sighted during pursuit into enemy territory. With this, the southwest front was closed, even if only with weak forces.

An attack against the south front of the IV Army Corps south of Marinovka is in progress; south of Zybenko-Wargotaniki, it was thrown back. The reinforcement of enemy assembly positions southwest of Staroff was spotted. On 26 November, twenty-seven Ju52 transport aircraft landed. Fuel situation extremely critical, which soon will threaten to paralyze every movement.

LI Army Corps: penetration location west of Rynok was reduced by half by the 24th Panzer Division. Two motorboats on the Volga were sunk. Situation of 76th Division unchanged. Today twelve tanks destroyed. Withdrawal of the XI Corps from the Don bridgehead started as planned; the 16th Panzer Division was relieved and put at the disposal of the army. Situation at 14th Panzer Division and IV Army Corps unchanged. Penetration at Marinovka cleaned up after heavy battles. At IV Army Corps, four tanks were knocked out.

In front of our positions, it is quiet, apart from enemy scouting parties. On the other hand, a great deal of battle noise can be heard from our left and right, where the Bolsheviks are attacking without pause. We can see the impacts of the Russian artillery. Our village, Karpowka, is fired at from time to time in harassing fire. Out here in front with Lieutenant Moritz, I can scan the open ground before us without any hindrance. From here, no movement goes unnoticed. Even at night, everything can be seen on the bright snowy plain. By midnight, the Russian ground-attack aircraft, the "sewing machines," are again overhead. They continuously fly over Karpowka and drop their bombs and other ordnance on us. As always, they come gliding in noiselessly, and after dropping their loads, they disappear suddenly with engines howling into the night. This is bad, since one cannot take cover against it. Amidst the sudden impacts, one has no opportunity to take cover or protect oneself.

On November 28, the Wehrmacht communiqué reports:

Between the Volga and the Don, in the great bend of the Don and in Stalingrad heavy enemy attacks again failed in determined battles. Antiaircraft artillery and ground-attack aircraft intervened effectively in the ground battles and destroyed thirty-four Soviet tanks. According to reports the enemy between the Volga and the Don has until now lost 319 tanks. Apart from that, twenty-six guns were destroyed, and more than 2000 prisoners were captured.

And in the OKW war diary, it is reported about both army groups, the German 6th Army and the Romanians:

Army Group Hoth: Romanian security detachments are yielding to the enemy pursuing from the Jessulowskij sector to the southwest. A group of German forces were encircled at the railroad station of Shutow. Attacks on Kotelnikowo by enemy cavalry were repelled. 6th Army: no reports have been received. On account of snow storms there have been few supply fights.

Romanian III Army Corps: Futile enemy attacks on the positions near Chir and on the railroad west of it. In the Chir-sector activity only by scouting parties. Group Hollidt: Romanian 1st Panzer Division in an attack to the east. Details as yet unknown. Enemy attack against 22nd Panzer Division repulsed. 62nd Infantry Division on the left flank of Group Hollidt reached the Krjuschan sector in the face of strong enemy pressure.

An addendum about the 6th Army continues:

Continuation of strong tank-supported attacks against the northern and northeastern front. The break-through on the northern front was cleared up after heavy fighting. Fierce fighting continues to the west. At the VIII Army Corps strong enemy attacks are in progress. Twenty tanks have broken into our positions on the left wing. The Don bridgehead of the XI Army Corps was pulled back as planned. All bridges blown. On the southern front the IV Army Corps beat back enemy attacks with infantry and tanks inflicting heavy losses on the enemy.

The enemy is feeling his way forward in our sector. Only now and then is Karpowka subjected to artillery fire, but then it mostly is from heavy-caliber guns. From the west, strong sounds of fighting continue to be heard. That's coming from Kalach and promises nothing good. The ring has been closed around us, and now the Soviets are trying to bottle us up in a shrinking space. We know what it's like to be the encircling force, which we were in the big battles of last year and May of this year. What happened to the Russians then is happening to us now.

If we manage to hold out here, if support from the west comes in time, things will look quite different; we'll correct the situation and control what happens on the battlefield. The continuing snow storms and falling temperatures will make the Russians suffer like us. In the fighting positions, it is hardly bearable. Every group has built a bunker-like shelter for itself in which men can take turns warming themselves. The cases of frostbite are increasing , but dysentery is also reported more and more. I'm beginning to show symptoms that remind me of the jaundice I suffered last year. But what does that matter? One cannot take things like that into account here. We have little food, nothing really filling— watery soup, horsemeat, some sausages, and some bread. That's all that can be found. Everything else has been blundered, primarily by "homeless" Romanians whose units had been gutted and no longer existed.

On November 29, the part of the Wehrmacht communiqué about our sector reads as follows:

> Yesterday, German and Romanian troops again thew back all attacks by numerically superior enemy forces between Don and Volga. Thirty-five tanks were destroyed. In the great bend of the Don a counterattack threw back the Soviets across a sector of river. Strong aerial forces, amongst them Romanian ground-attack aircraft, supported our Army troops with good success. A large number of vehicles were destroyed.

Rail lines on the lower Volga were attacked with success during the night. Fast Italian bombers on the middle Don attacked motorized enemy columns and troop shelters.

The OKW war diary reports from the 6th Army: "The focus of yesterday's attacks was the southern front south of Stalingrad; all attacks, which were mounted with strong tank support, were repulsed. On the northeastern front, there was an enemy penetration with tanks, which was contained; countermeasures have been put in motion, aerial resupply improved."

In a dense snowdrift and icy winds, I work my way forward to the fighting position of Hans Moritz. Once there, we visit all the positions in order to see for ourselves the situation in the sector assigned to us. We speak with the men assigned to security. Great confidence still rules, even with the meager supplies and decreasing ammunition. With the icy cold, cases of frostbite and other disease are bad—and these circumstances get worse day by day. By evening, I make my way to the battalion command post. There I witness a Russian artillery bombardment on Karpowka. There are many wounded and damaged vehicles and material. That doesn't stop me from finally sending a message home:

Karpowka, 29 November 1942—1st Advent
Whether this letter will ever reach you, I do not know. You'll certainly have heard that we have been encircled by Russian troops around Stalingrad. Yes, that's bad luck! But it probably is only a temporary situation. The Führer has promised us help. And the Führer keeps his promises! This letter is to wind its way to you own via a Ju52. I hope it works! It is not a very good feeling to have been cut off completely from our own troops out here. Dad's also here in the bag. What will he have to say about this!?! Recently, a week ago, when we were pulled out of Stalingrad, I paid him a quick visit. With the miserable remains of

our grenadiers we were to go to the northern bend in
the Don in order to help out there. But we never got
there!

Even when we reached Karpowka, the road was
blocked by the damned Russians! What they have
managed to get from the German Wehrmacht! Vehicles, tanks, ammunition, fuel, supply dumps, postal
trains! One can become so angry about this! Of
course they've broken through in the north, as well as
in the south (Kalmuck steppe) with the Romanians.
Only in that way could they encircle us. We, who have
been bled white in Stalingrad. Pitiful! My arm has
improved again, only my stomach is not good. Have
lost a damned lot of weight. We're unlikely to get mail
for a long time! But . . .

On November 30, the "situation on the Stalingrad front" is
described in only a few sentences in the Wehrmacht communiqué, painting a similar picture as in the days before. In the
OKW war diary, the report on the 6th Army reads as follows:

On the westfront the withdrawal of our lines from the
position on high ground (roughly running from
Kotluban to Marinovka) was carried out according to
plan. The enemy followed gingerly. By the 29th
(Motorized) Infantry Division, the enemy withdrew
about three kilometers and is digging in. Enemy
attacks on the southern point southwest of Stalingrad
were largely repulsed. A smaller penetration was contained and eradicated in a counterattack. On the right
wing of the Romanian 3rd Army, enemy attacks were
thrown back in an easterly direction and to the east of
the Chir rail station. On the left wing, an attack of our
own was made against a still existing enemy bridgehead. The transport of the 6th and 11th Panzer Divisions, 15th Anti-Aircraft Division and the 336th and
318th Infantry Divisions is in progress.

Captain Erich Domaschk brings positive news about our situation. Everything is being done in order to quickly bring about a change here. Of course, we'll have to wait until our own forces can come up. The only important thing is that the army remains alive. Danger begins to loom when the aerial resupply cannot be increased. Daily the ring of Soviet antiaircraft guns increases; daily we can observe that the Soviet pilots are ruling the skies. Our Ju52s—those that come to us—perform unheard-of labors in these weather conditions, with the Russian defenses and the miserable circumstances of landing. But the commander of the 2nd Battalion of Panzergrenadier Regiment 103 shows himself to be an optimist and radiates confidence. Another few words with the officers, and then everybody hastens back to his place. And yet dark thoughts creep up on me when I explore the situation further and take in account all negative aspects that possibly could arise.

In the Wehrmacht communiqué of December 1, only the second part contains a brief account of the battle for Stalingrad, and it offers not much that is new. The OKW war diary records for the day:

> 6th Army: During the past day, the army achieved a big defensive success. Today all enemy attacks that were carried out with strong forces against the northwestern and southern fronts were beaten off with high losses for the enemy. Numbers of enemy prisoners and captured equioment still have to come in. As a result of an improvement in the weather the aerial resupply could take place as planned. All enemey attacks on the rail lines west of the Chir rail station could generally be beaten off. Only on the northeastern front did the enemy succeed in taking a hamlet; countermeasures have begun. On the remaining front of Army Group B no remarkable fighting took place.

With us, the panzergrenadiers of the 103rd, the situation is unchanged. We defend the Stalingrad-Kalach railroad in a southerly direction, from which no Russian attack has yet come. To our left and right, the noise of battle can be heard constantly; in front of us, there continues to be no movement. I observe out here in front for hours. From time to time, one thinks he recognizes something in the open ground. But soon it becomes clear that nothing has changed; it is the same dark spots that look like Russians working themselves forward. Even reconnaissance parties are not spotted anymore; apparently, they are no longer working their way forward. The conversations all concentrate on the theme of relief attack. Will the attacking troops make it? Can they hold and throw back the Russian divisions that are advancing farther to the west?

On December 2, nothing can be found in the Wehrmacht communiqué that leads to the conclusion that a change in the current bad situation is imminent. The OKW war diary concludes:

> On the northeast front of Army Group Hoth, enemy reconnaissance troop action; weak attacks were repulsed here. Our own advance east of Kotelnikowo to the northeast is in progress. Details are still lacking. 6th Army: weaker attacks against the north and south font were repulsed. Resupply had to be stopped at 1400 hours due to danger of icing and low clouds. At Group Hollidt, parts of the 22nd Panzer Division took a village in their attack north.

On December 3, the Wehrmacht communiqué reports: "Yesterday, as before, renewed enemy attacks of strong infantry and tank units in the Volga-Don area failed in the face of determined resistance of German and Romanian troops. In cooperation with strong German and Romanian air support, huge losses were inflicted on the enemy, and just between the Volga and Don, sixty tanks were knocked out."

Since we have no contact with the enemy at this time—apart from the constant artillery shelling of Karpowka—we have time to establish and improve the combat strength of the troops of the 14th Panzer Division assembled in Kampfgruppe Seydel. The panzergrenadiers and the motorcycle riflemen await an enemy attack coming from a southerly direction. On the other hand, we are prepared to reestablish the situation with immediate counterattacks should the enemy penetrate our right and left neighbors. For that purpose, there are tracked units standing by here in Karpowka that can intervene straightaway. The commander of the armored personnel carriers is First Lieutenant Riemenschneider. During the evening, I once again write home since we are all allowed to write one letter today; the Ju52s are to bring the mail out of the pocket. What is there to report? We hold on and wait for the "liberation" by relieving attacks from our comrades coming from the west. That probably is the primary theme with the others as well.

On December 4, the OKW war diary reports: "At the 6th Army, the Russian attacked on the south front and, with strong forces, on the northwest front. All attacks were without success. Due to the danger of icing, no aerial resupply took place. Yesterday on the entire Chir front, the enemy attacked our positions. All attacks were repulsed with losses to the enemy. The enemy had to yield Krasnokutskaja to the attack by parts of Group Hollidt."

Once again, the noise of battle is coming from our neighbors to the left and right. The Soviets try to break through there in order to split the pocket, cut off of the "nose" at Marinovka, and get at Pitomnik airfield. With that, they would have the main supply point of the encircled army in their hands. That is not to be allowed under any circumstances; it would be the end of us all. I once again I pay a visit to Lieutenant Moritz in the positions of the 108th, and afterward, I stay with parts of the 103rd until dusk. In front of us, nothing happens. It is a nerve-wracking wait.

On December 5, the report about our sector in the Wehrmacht communiqué sounds quite positive: "In vain, the Soviets also attacked on December 4th in between the Don and Volga using a large number of tanks. Seventy-five tanks were destroyed; thirteen were rendered immobile and huge losses in men and equipment were inflicted on the enemy. A powerful attack of our own tank troops eliminated enemy tank and cavalry forces, in which 2,000 prisoners and fourteen guns were captured."

Today we learn that the Führer has ordered an increase in our aerial resupply. All transport aircraft are to be used here in order to supply the army. Yesterday witnessed a high number of resupply flights. More than fifty Jus and fifteen He111s are supposed to have been flown in. The distance our machines have to fly, however, increases constantly with the continued advance of the Russians to the southwest. Again and again, we are wondering why our boys have not yet attacked effectively. We only know that they have assembled and are standing by.

On December 6, the Wehrmacht communiqué reports: "In fluctuating battles between the Volga and Don, a Soviet battalion was destroyed, twenty-six tanks were knocked out, and numerous enemy guns and infantry weapons were captured. Despite the most difficult weather conditions, transports units of the Luftwaffe supplied the fighting troops." In the OKW war diary, it is briefly noted: "At the VII and VI Romanian Army Corps, nothing special to report. No reports have arrived yet about the battle in the Kotelnikowo area. 6th Army: In a counterattack, the enemy penetrations attained on December 4th were cleared up. According to reports, twenty-six resupply Jus have arrived up until now. On the other front of the Army no fighting to note."

On December 7, neither the Wehrmacht communiqué nor the OKW war diary provide any further information about the continuation of the operations here at Stalingrad or in the area southwest or northwest of it.

On December 8, the Wehrmacht communiqué reports: "In the great bend of the Don, the Soviets yesterday resumed their fierce attacks with strong tank forces. They collapsed in the face of the defenses of our troops, which were supported by German and Romanian ground-attack aircraft."

On December 9, the Wehrmacht communiqué reports:

Mass enemy attacks by infantry and tank forces between the Volga and Don led to very hard fighting in which our troops were successful. Prisoners and booty were collected; fifty-four tanks were destroyed. In the great bend of the Don, German panzergrenadiers threw the enemy out of our positions in a counterattack and destroyed forty-six Soviet tanks without suffering tank losses of our own. German, Italian, and Hungarian air forces on the Don front attacked enemy advances and troop billets.

On December 10, the Wehrmacht communiqué has this to say about the situation on the Stalingrad front:

In between the Volga and Don, enemy forces that had succeeded in breaking in were encircled and destroyed. In other areas, the Soviets again suffered high losses in the continuation of their futile attacks. On December 8 and 9, they lost 104 tanks in this sector alone. Despite fierce resistance, infantry and tank forces threw back the enemy in the great bend of the Don, repulsed counterattacks and destroyed sixteen Soviet tanks.

And the OKW war dairy reports:

Along the Kotelnikowo-Stalingrad railroad east of the rail line, enemy attacks were thrown back; west of the railroad, an enemy attack is in progress at the time of writing. On the railroad front west of the Chir station, an enemy attack was repulsed by the attacking 11th Panzer Division. West of it, a vain enemy attack failed. In the 6th Army area, the attacks were weaker than in the preceding days. A temporary penetration on the northern front was eliminated in a counterattack. On the northwest front, multiple enemy attacks in battalion strength were beaten off. On the southeast front, a renewed enemy attack is in progress. The aerial transport of supplies was less than in the preceding days.

At the battalion—at Kampfgruppe Seydel—the situation is unchanged. No larger operations are taking place yet. But they'll come. From the louder and louder noise of fighting from the west, it becomes clear that the Russians are compressing us more and more and want to roll us up against Stalingrad. They want to gain control of Pitomnik airfield, which is essential for landing our urgently needed supplies of food and munitions and evacuating our many wounded. Pitomnik airfield is supposed to look horrible; it's filled to capacity, and the wounded are lying around, partially without care, in this icy cold. Now it all depends on whether the relief forces will get here soon.

Once more, I write a letter home:

This evening, I want to send you a few lines, as tomorrow the airplane that takes the mail is supposed to fly out. How are you doing at home? How beautiful Christmas must be with you! To sit in a chair, listen to the radio, read—delightful! Well, these times will return for us as well one day! One does not need to sleep in bed. Sleeping on a tapestry is quite sufficient. That would be a feudal bedstead compared to what we've got here. Yes, Christmas! We cannot think of stuff like that over here. We don't want to anyway. It is useless anyhow, even more so as the food becomes less and less, as we are encircled by the Russians. Four slices of bread, a little fat, some meat, and three cigarettes a day. During the afternoon, some watery soup. That's all! We now have captured a horse that will be slaughtered during the coming days. 240 grams of this horse meat per man! Now we have to get drunk; that way, one can survive these festive days better. We have enough to drink—vodka, rum, schnapps, and red wine. When the combat situation allows it, we let our radio play. Then we listen to jazz music from home. Jazz! It is to die laughing! Jazz here in the steppe! One has more than enough room to dance over here if one

has the inclination to do so! For us, the daily dance
with the Russians is sufficient. Yes, yes, my dears, if
only mail from you got through! But that cannot be.
That is completely out of the question! Damn it all
once more. These damned Russians! Well, we'll show
these lads!

On December 11, the Wehrmacht communiqué is very
reserved about our sector. Only the normal actions are taking
place here. In the OKW war diary, we find the following report:

On the north front of the Romanian VII Corps, enemy
attacks failed because of counterattacks of German
units. North of Kotelnikowo, enemy reconnaissance
activity. On the bridgehead east of the Chir, enemy
posts were thrown back. While the 11th Panzer Division gained some ground to the northeast, strong
enemy counterattacks with tanks collapsed in the same
region. Seventy-five tanks were knocked out. Behind
the front east of the 11th Panzer Division, the enemy
has been encircled with a strength of twenty tanks and
100–200 men. On the railroad, all other enemy attacks
failed. On the northwest front of the 6th Army, only
weaker enemy attacks. The old penetration location on
the northeastern front was wiped out in a counterattack. Strong pressure on the southern front.

On December 12, the Wehrmacht communiqué offers
only one sentence, which mentions nothing about what is taking place with us. The OKW war diary records:

While the day passed relatively quietly for Army Group
Hoth, the enemy attacked the railroad positions and
the Chir front of the 3rd Romanian Army with strong
forces. In two locations, he succeeded in breaking
through the positions with elements of his forces, these
being west of the Chir, where he advanced with some

tanks in a southerly direction through our own positions, and at Jurowikino, where two battalions with tanks
broke into our positions and advanced about six kilometers in a southerly direction in the Back valley. Elements
of the XXXXVIII Panzer Corps have been put into
action against this. The enemy attacked the 6th Army
with strong forces from southwest of the Volga. Apart
from a temporary penetration that could be dealt with
quickly, all attacks were thrown back. On the southern
front an enemy attack is in progress. On the other fronts
of the army, only local fighting was reported.

I've gone off to see Lieutenant Moritz in his dug-out. The
morale here is high. We all hope that we'll soon be freed from
this situation. But we're nothing anymore—one has to admit
that. We have established our defenses for this sector very well
indeed and are well prepared for any Russian attack. But it is
not the same unit that advanced to the Mius position last year
and broke one Russian resistance after another. No, today we
are run down and burned out. Ultimately, we need to catch
our breath and relax once more; we need to freshen up; we
cannot continue like this, for sure. We need new men, new
weapons, and new vehicles. The men here give their all; we
can completely depend on them; they share all with us. We
have to continue under these difficult and extraordinary circumstances. Just now, a Russian deserter is brought in. It is difficult to believe that the Russians are still deserting.

By evening, I send off another letter to the folks at home.
Who knows how long this will remain possible?

Tomorrow is the third advent. And as tomorrow the
mail leaves by air mail again, I want to write a letter
tonight. I have remained one of the 108th. That is to
say, it has finally come down from the division that I
am to be a company commander in the 108th. For the
time being, I am to remain with the 103rd, however.
All the panzergrenadiers and motorcycle riflemen, the

engineers—all are commanded by Captain Domaschk. They are only about 150 men anyway. In these heavy defensive battles, regrettably First Lieutenant Seidel has been killed, after he had been wounded eight times. First Lieutenant Krug has also been killed. My friend, Lieutenant Moritz, is still there. He joined us only in October. . . . Write soon! Always to field post number 11444. Think of us out here from time to time! Sieg heil!

December 13, 1942. Waiting for the Relief Attack by Army Group Don.

On December 13, the Wehrmacht communiqué reports:

Local Soviet attacks in the Volga-Don area were shattered by the defense of the German and Italian troops. Hungarian assault troops on the eastern bank of the Don destroyed enemy fighting positions. Prisoners and equipment were collected. German, Romanian, Italian, and Hungarian air forces were used at the focal points of the battle in supporting the army. In aerial battles and by antiaircraft defenses, thirty-seven enemy aircraft were shot down. Seven of our own aircraft were reported missing.

Meanwhile, the OKW war diary reports:

In its advance northeast yesterday afternoon, the attack of the LVII Panzer Corps on both sided of the Kotelnikowo-Stalingrad ralroad reached the villages of Chilakoff and Jablotchni, about twenty kilometers south of the Aksai River. The XXXXVIII Panzer Corps eliminated a breakthrough in an attack west of the Chir rail station. The second penetration west of Surowikino was also eliminated by elements of the Corps. At the 6th Army, the enemy attacked without success on the southern wing east of the Don canal.

West of the Volga, they succeeded in penetrating our
lines. A counterattack to eliminate this penetration is
in progress.

A great start to the day! We've just heard that our relief is
coming. Word of this spreads like wildfire. Everyone is in the
highest of spirits. Now it won't be long before we can hear
them, our comrades, that want to free us. Who'd have thought
that things would come around like this? Hopefully, we can
hold on until they've gotten through, until the pocket has
opened up somewhere. But now it really comes down to it.
What will the Russians do? How will they react now that we are
behind them?

On December 14, the Wehrmacht communiqué reports:
"Our own tank forces, which advanced from the area southwest of Stalingrad, destroyed the strong enemy, whose counterattacks failed with a loss of more than twenty tanks." The
OKW war diary notes:

According to the latest reports, LVII Panzer Corps,
which had begun its attack to the northeast from the
Kotelnikowo area, has reached the road from
Samochin to Chitakoff and crossed it (23rd Panzer
Division). The Russian 254th Tank Brigade on the
right wing did not accept battle, but withdrew to the
northeast. North of the Kotelnikowo-Stalingrad railway,
major elements of the 6th Panzer Division crossed the
Aksai on an intact bridge and, with the left wing,
advanced to Werchnij-Kumskii. Elements turned away
to the west. An attack on the advancing left flank of the
panzer division with thirty Russian tanks was thrown
back. Ten tanks were destroyed.

On the bridgehead east of the Chir, the enemy managed a penetration. West of it, there was hard fighting
at the old breakthrough points. Apart from an attack
against the left wing of the 297th Infantry Division,
which is standing in the southern sector, only unsuc-

cessful enemy attacks took place against the 6th Army yesterday. No reports have arrived yet about the supply situation. On the front of the Romanian 3rd Army, fortifications could be made out. An enemy attack with tanks on the center of the Romanian 3rd Army was repulsed.

Today the Bolsheviks are attacking our positions. Assault parties of platoon strength are attacking the entire front of Kampfgruppe Seydel. But they don't get far; they are pinned down far from our positions in our defensive fire. Our artillery is also laying some salvoes on the attacking Russians, who quickly withdraw. We remain on alert status, however. They'll certainly try again to gain control of this important strongpoint.

On December 15, the Wehrmacht communiqué contains nothing new about the relief attack, but the OKW war diaries notes:

The enemy repeatedly attacked the point units of the advancing panzer divisions of the LVII Panzer Corps with strong forces, but was unable to stop the advance. On the right wing they lost forty tanks. The elements advancing along the railway found an undamaged railroad bridge at Shutow station and formed a bridgehead north of the river. Our troops that had crossed the river west of it yesterday were attacked in the north and on the flanks in vain. The enemy that had managed to penetrate the Chir bridgehead yesterday has advanced further south. The emergency bridge is still held by our troops. From the south as well the enemy is trying to penetrate our lines, in order to cut off this advanced salient in our positions. At the 6th Army: advances on the Volga front. On the northeast front the enemy attacked several locations. Temporary breakthroughs were eliminated with counterattacks.

Again today, the Soviets felt their way forward against our positions on the Stalingrad-Kalach railway, but they are no longer attacking with the usual support. Perhaps they are more busy delaying our comrades who are coming to help us. It is clear that they can end up in a difficult situation themselves: be encircled and eliminated when our fresh troops arrive. That would be our reward for holding on here for so long with no way out.

If only the aerial resupply could be increased! Slowly, we in the pocket are growing weak in the knees. The physical exertion becomes a burden that cannot be eased. The cold temperatures add to it, and the breakdown of strength becomes clearly visible. I always feel weak and miserable, which might have something to do with my constant stomach ailments. After liberation, something has to be done to improve it.

On December 16, the Wehrmacht communiqué is silent on events southwest of and in Stalingrad. The OKW war diary reports:

> Groups of the LVII Panzer Corps repulsed strong enemy attacks from their positions. Fighting is still continuing on the left wing of the most forward elements of the 6th Panzer Division. Weaker attacks from the flanks were thrown back. The bridgehead south of the Chir rail station was withdrawn according to plan and the position straightened out. At the 6th Army, no remarkable actions. No reports have arrived yet regarding Assault Group Hollidt on the left flank of Army Group Don.

While it starts off quietly enough in our sector, loud sounds of battle can be heard from the west from the direction of the "nose" that juts out of the salient at Marinovka. Is that already our comrades coming to relieve us from this bad situation? Have they come up already? From the regiment, we have heard nothing yet about the way the situation has developed or the progress of the liberation offensive. Why are there no reports? All are waiting for new messages, for confirmation of their own hopes and expectations. Or don't they want to let us have any bad news? It cannot be ruled out that the Russians would manage to stop this relief attack. We don't want to think about that! We cannot perish here! Why don't we attack and meet up with our comrades? We cannot continue this vegetating existence for long. We're fought out and physically run down—dung, dirt, simply disgusting circumstances, completely beset with lice, constant hunger. The hunger increases everyday. Added to that are the frostbite cases, which are the order of the day with this icy cold. They cannot imagine this back home. They certainly cannot; the imagination does not suffice. But we trust our leadership, we build on Field Marshal von Manstein. To write off an entire army is simply unthinkable. They'll do anything to prevent such an end.

On December 17, the Wehrmacht communiqué reports:

> German and Romanian troops, supported by ground attack units, threw back the enemy in an attack between the Don and Volga, and in the Greater Bend of the Don repulsed repeated attacks by strong forces, partially in counterattacks. Thirty Soviet tanks were destroyed. Using strong infantry and tank forces the Soviets continued their attacks in the sector of the Italian troops on the Don. In cooperation with German units of the Army and the Air Force huge losses were inflicted on the enemy. The battle continues.

The OKW war diary reports:

> A defensive front is being built up on the northern flank of the VI Army Corps and the VII Romanian Army Corps that leads to the northwest via Werchnij Sal and is to cover the flanks of the advancing panzer divisions. Yesterday, the panzer divisions of the LVII Panzer Corps repulsed enemy attacks that were especially strong on both sides of the railway north of the

Aksai River and on the left flank on both sides of the river. According to preliminary reports, thirteen Russian tanks were destroyed. Exact reports about the objectives attained have not arrived yet. On the Chir bridgehead weaker enemy attacks were repulsed.

At the 6th Army: No special activities. The enemy attacks on the railroad positions were weaker than in the preceding days. The enemy pressure was especially strong on the northern part of Army Group Don. Enemy attacks of battalion strength were thrown back for all intents and purposes. In the center of Group Hollidt, the enemy managed a penetration that could be sealed off. Apart from that, the enemy attacked the positions on an infantry division on the Don and advanced in a southerly direction. Exact reports are lacking.

Waiting for news about the advance of our own forces from the west is painful. We all look to the west, especially during the night. Is anything visible? Can something be made out that indicates our own guns, cannons, or tanks? In front of us, it is more quiet than ever, apart from the Russian artillery fire and the damned "sewing machines," which plague us every night. The damage they do is—God be thanked—light. But wherever it hits—dug-outs, dumps, and workshops—there are always bad losses. We've gotten used to it.

On December 18, the Wehrmacht communiqué notes: "Enemy attacks in the Terek area, in the Stalingrad area, and in the great bend of the Don failed with high losses to the opponent. More than twenty tanks were destroyed. In between the Volga and the Don, German divisions penetrated strongly manned positions of the enemy on a controlling ridge and in the attack gained further ground." The OKW war diary describes the new situation on the northern flank very plainly: "The big Russian offensive against the 8th Italian Army has begun yesterday morning and has led to deep penetrations in the front of the army. At Army Detachment Hollidt on the

Chir, the enemy also managed to penetrate." That is the important point in the current situation report at headquarters. The war diary also reports:

> Multiple enemy attacks on both sides of the railway against the bridgehead of the 23rd Panzer Division were beaten off and the bridgehead was expanded. West of it at the 6th Panzer Division successful tank battles. The 17th Panzer Division, which had been brought up from the south, in its advance north reached the Aksai and here, east of the Don, formed a bridgehead.
>
> At the 6th Army, several enemy attacks on the northwest front, of which one led to a penetration. A counterattack is in progress. On the right wing of the railway front west of Chir railroad station, there were multiple enemy attacks which could be stopped shortly before our positions. Enemy elements which had penetrated temporarily were driven back north. On the left wing a weak enemy advance was driven back.
>
> At Group Hollidt: About 35 kilometers south of the Don the enemy, after having beaten off at one location, attacked our own positions with one or two rifle divisions and 80–100 tanks. A counterattack is to take place on December 18 against those elements which managed to penetrate. The penetration just south of the Don on the northern front has not been eliminated yet.

Today the commander of the 2nd Battalion of Panzergrenadier Regiment 103, Captain Domaschk, entered the room of our miserable hovel which is used for meetings, discussions of the situation, and dissemination of orders with the words: "Shit, a new mess has happened!" As he goes to sit down, there is a howling in the immediate vicinity, and with a deafening explosion, a shell of a new Soviet bombardment explodes on Karpowka.

"Damn it, close the window here! One could be hit in a shack like this!"

That's true, and subsequently, the captain briefs us on the situation, which impresses us deeply. In the southwest, our comrades are advancing quite well apparently, while in the northwest, the Russians have launched a new offensive against the Italians. From where do they get these troops? And now it all boils down—as it probably does everywhere—to whether we should attack in order to join up with Army Group Hoth. We have too little fuel, too little ammunition for such a risky effort. But I remain of the opinion, as many other front officers do, that it would offend any soldierly morality and any comradely duty and be despicably dishonorable to leave thousands of wounded behind in this hellish situation and leave them to the tender mercies of the Russians in their helplessness. That is impossible. As long as we can fight and defend ourselves, they all are under our protection.

On December 19, the Wehrmacht communiqué reports about our situation around Stalingrad:

> German and Romanian troops threw back the enemy further to the northeast between the Volga and Don despite fierce resistance. In counterattacks the Soviets lost twenty-two tanks. At Stalingrad and in the great bend of the Don, enemy attacks were repulsed. On the Don front the Soviets continued their attacks with strong forces. German and Italian troops inflicted heavy losses on the enemy in cooperation with air forces and antiaircraft batteries. In this cramped area alone the Soviets lost over fifty tanks.

In the OKW war diary, the big Russian offensive and their deep penetrations against the Italian 8th Army are discussed in the situation report. Furthermore, it explains:

> The Romanian 5th Cavalry Division advanced pickets to the northeast in a general line from Shutov–Werchnij

Sal. Enemy attacks along the Stalingrad-Kotelnikowo railway were beaten off, and in pursuit some ground was gained. After a tank battle, the 6th Panzer Division was able to advance to the east of Werchnij-Kumskij. The 17th Panzer Division reached the area west of it. West of the Chir railroad station, the old main line of resistance was retaken. At the Romanian 3rd Army, the enemy succeeded in advancing across the Chir east of Obliwskaja and taking a village. Countermeasures have commenced. Northwest of it, a weaker enemy attack was repulsed. At Group Hollidt, the enemy took Bokowskaja. An attack across the Don at the old location of the penetration against the Romanian 7th Infantry Division was beaten off. At 6th Army no real fighting.

It is quiet in our entire sector. The Russians must have other worries. Trust and optimism rule here. "Our comrades" are actually closing in more and more. Soon they can be heard, but the Italians up there—like the Romanians—are not capable of keeping the Bolsheviks from our necks. If we had sufficient supplies, ample ammunition, enough fuel, and adequate winter clothing—my God!—we would free ourselves from this bad situation. We all think like that over here. This idle waiting in a situation that worsens daily paralyzes the troops.

On December 20, the Wehrmacht communiqué reports:

In cooperation with Romanian forces German Panzer Divisions gained an important sector of river in an attacke against a determinedly defending enemy between the Volga and Don. Strong enemy attacks in the great bend of the Don and the Stalingrad area were repulsed after bitter fighting, partially by counterattacks. In these battles, the Soviets lost 164 tanks. Ground-attack squadrons attacked enemy reserves, artillery positions and tank assembly points. On the Don front, German and Italian troops remain in difficult defensive battles against strong Soviet infantry and tank forces. Units of the Army and the Luftwaffe destroyed another twenty tanks. In the southern sector, twenty-six Soviet aircraft were destroyed with five losses of our own.

The OKW war diary reports:

On both sides of the Kotelnikowo-Stalingrad railroad several enemy attacks were beaten off. The 6th Panzer Division took Werchnij Kumsky. The 17th Panzer Division advanced northeast to Mischkowa and there (as there was no river crossing present) turned to the east. Southwest of Surowkino, a panzer division eliminated a breakthrough. According to unconfirmed reports sixty enemy tanks have been destroyed. Apart for some smaller penetrations which could be cleared up, several enemy attacks against the west front of the 6th Army were repelled. Aerial resupply carried out with thirty-eight Heinkels and ten Junkers. At Group Hollidt, the enemy managed to advance from the east to the Chernaja sector.

At the battalion, the tension has risen to a climax: all rumors about the progress of the "relief attack" by our comrades coming from the west surpass each other. Everyone wants to know that it is merely a question of days. It is reported that our own artillery is already audible, and at night, the sky is lighted by a brightness to the southwest. The hope that rules here is growing, giving us the strength to hold on and overcome all the unbelievable difficulties. We will get out of here! We simply believe that all will be well in the end. Until now, we have always succeeded in getting out of difficult and hopeless situations.

I spent the entire day in the positions with Lieutenant Moritz. Although the eyes of the men are gleaming, we are all run down. Some very clearly suffer from it; others tuck it away somewhere. They are hard toward others and especially toward themselves. There are many moving examples of bravery, boldness, discipline, and the will to fight.

On December 21, the Wehrmacht communiqué reports:

In the Volga-Don area, heavy fighting continues. In bitter tank and infantry battles, the Soviets in general once more suffered high losses in men and material. Yesterday in the Don area, more than seventy enemy tanks were destroyed, according to reports received up to now. On the middle Don, the enemy, after having attacked for days with the strongest massing of forces, succeeded in breaking through the defensive front located there. This was paid for with unbelievable Bolshevik losses. In order to face a threat on the flanks, German divisions that were on the march occupied positions in the rear that had been prepared according to plan and prevented an exploitation of the initial enemy successes. The battles rage with continued intensity.

The OKW war diary notes:

The attack of the LVII Panzer Corps could win only a little ground. Strong enemy pressure on the bridgehead gained by the 17th Panzer Division at Nishne-Kumskii. At the Romanian 3rd Army, the strong enemy pressure in the bend of the Chir continues. A village was lost. Enemy attacks against the southwest front of the 6th Army were beaten off for all intents and purposes. A penetration is being eliminated at this time. The enemy gained further ground to the west and southwest of the breakthrough at Bokowskaja and north of it across the Chir and is standing in the area north and south of Nishne-Astachow. By withdrawing troops, a new defensive line is to be erected there.

Since the early hours of the morning, the very loud sound of fighting can be heard from the direction of Marinowka. I am in our positions, and I cannot make out any movements by

Soviet attackers in front of us. The usual Russian artillery effort at Karpowka occurs at the usual intervals. That's nothing new; we've known it for a few weeks and now anticipate it. But the noise of battle from the west increases all the time. At battalion, I hear that the Russians are attacking everywhere. With superior forces, they throw themselves on the panzer divisions that are thrusting to meet us in order to bar the road to Stalingrad. Our own attack is said to have been halted and developed into a bitter defensive battle, the commander tells us in today's situation report. And in the northwest, a catastrophic situation is said to have developed. The Russians are advancing farther and farther. Army Group Hoth will soon be cut off. Disappointed but still full of hope, we return to the order of the day and to carrying out our duties.

On December 22, the Wehrmacht communiqué reports:

At Stalingrad, the enemy tried to gain a foothold while attacking across the Volga. He was thrown back in bitter hand-to-hand fighting. The defensive battle on the middle Don continues with the same intensity. German divisions and battle groups offered a determined resistance against continued enemy attacks and inflicted heavy losses on the Soviets in cooperation with the Luftwaffe. In the last ten days, 404 Soviet tanks were destroyed in the sector of two German panzer corps alone.

The OKW war diary for the same day reports:

In front of the left wing of the Romanian VII Army Corps, strong enemy movement took place, tanks among them. At the LVII Panzer Corps, the attack of the 23rd Panzer Division gained ground to the north and reached the area of Gnili-Aksaiskaja. Despite strong enemy attacks, the 6th Panzer Division formed a bridgehead across the Myshkova. At Stalingrad, strong enemy attacks on the banks of the Volga with a local enemy penetration. Fighting is still in progress. Attacks on the railway west of the Chir were thrown back. On the left wing of Army Group Don, the flanking division stands curved back at about forty kilometers south of the Don. The Italian Divisions have withdrawn south from their positions on the Jablonaja and extend to the 62nd Infantry Division to the west.

Now it seems to be starting. Beginning early in the morning, the sounds of heaving fighting come from the Marinowka area. Artillery and mortars are firing incessantly; one gains the impression that the action is slowly moving to Karpowka. We are standing by, ready for battle, and have principally reinforced our right wing to prevent us from being taken from the rear at any cost. Artillery fire can also be heard from Stalingrad itself.

On December 23, the Wehrmacht communiqué says: "The Soviets again suffered high losses in renewed attacks between the Volga and Don and in Stalingrad. On the middle Don, the battle continues." The OKW war diary has nothing really important to note: "Heavy defensive battles on the right wing of the LVII Panzer Corps. At the 6th Army, strong enemy attacks in the Stalingrad city area were thrown back. On the Chir front, no special fighting. The situation at Group Hollidt on the right wing of the penetration site is still unclear."

Christmas in the Stalingrad Pocket: The Liberation of 6th Army Is Cancelled on December 24, 1942.

Tomorrow is Christmas. Christmas in "the Pocket of Stalingrad"! We had all hoped that by now a decisive battle would have relieved us of all worries, exertion, suffering, and catastrophic circumstances. But in all likehood, this cannot be expected anymore. We don't even know exactly how close these relief forces have approached and where they're standing at this time. Perhaps today there will be word from them in the situation report. Today the commander was at the 14th Panzer Division and discussed operational possibilities and

procedures for the armored parts of the 2nd Battalion of
Panzergrenadier Regiment 103. First Lieutenant Riemenschneider accompanied him since he is commander of this
operational group.

On December 24, the Wehrmacht communiqué only
briefly reports about this area: "In an attack between the Volga
and Don, 600 prisoners were captured, and fifteen tanks were
destroyed. Counterattacks by the Soviets collapsed. In the Don
area, the defensive battle continues in fluctuating fighting."
The OKW war diary notes:

> The attack of the LVII Panzer Corps could not be con-
> tinued because of strong enemy pressure. While the
> attacks at the 6th Panzer Division were beaten off, the
> Russians succeeded in breaking through at the 17th
> Panzer Division with a simultaneous attack on the
> northwestern flank. At the 6th Army, strong enemy
> attacks against the metallurgical works and south of it
> led to multiple penetrations, which could be con-
> tained. Weaker attacks on the northwest front were
> repulsed. South of Artemov in the Chir river bend
> strong enemy pressure continues. The enemy
> advanced south of the Don on the road south in the
> direction of Miljutchinskaja and was stopped there by
> assembled reserves and beaten back.

Tonight is Christmas Eve. At the battalion, there was no real
fighting. On the other hand, fighting can be heard from the
northern and middle parts of Stalingrad. Nevertheless, Christmas is celebrated in all positions where the situation allows it—
dug-outs, bunkers, and other shelters. While this goes on, the
usual artillery harassment fire, which is coming down on Karpowka just now, does not cease. With its fighting positions, supply dumps, and crossroads, Karpowka remains a worthwhile
target for the Russian gunners. We are well prepared for such
sudden bombardments, having taken all precautions to disappear into trenches and manholes immediately. Even so, several

direct hits have inflicted evil losses. Tonight it is a little different, with the "sewing machines" unloading their blessings on us. They're flying so low that they are clearly visible overhead in the bright moonlight.

To the extent that we can free ourselves, we officers have been ordered to the the regimental command post of Panzer-grenadier Regiment 103 of Kampfgruppe Seydel. We are the old "fire eaters," the remaining officers of the panzer-grenadiers and the motorcycle riflemen of the 14th Panzer Division. We shake hands and then Lieutenant Colonel Seydel greets us. He reports to us about the situation meeting, from which he has just returned.

> The relief efforts of Army Group Hoth and Army Detachment Hollidt have failed definitively; they had to be abandoned. These forces are at this moment turning away from us in order to avoid a new encirclement and to throw themselves at new offensive armies of the Soviets. The chances for a liberation of the 6th Army through other means have been reduced rapidly by this. A breakout by the remains of the 6th Army cannot be undertaken either, as the individual and larger units are not mobile enough and do not have enough fighting power to carry out such an undertaking with success. That is the situation; that is what I had to tell you today, gentlemen.

In response, only shocked silence rules. So that's what things look like. We say our good-byes at the command post and give reports of departure, and then everybody hurries to his troops, to his post.

No mail from home arrives; we've had none for weeks. We had a vague hope that they would surprise us with some today for Christmas. Only the radio links us with home now. Morale has sunk to new lows. But we're accustomed to the most primitive circumstances—which cannot get any more so—and we survive the lack of mail, which has hit everyone at the deepest level.

We're living through a unique Christmas here; it's an experience no one can take away from us. It is a pity that I am not a writer, or I would have recorded in moving words how Christmas 1942 took place in the snowy desert of Stalingrad and in the ruins of the former city. Christmas! Flares in the sky. The tracer aimed at enemy positions flies its course and makes a bright path in this dark and icy night. It is not very difficult to see these images as glittering decorations of a Christmas tree. "Silent night, holy night!" We look at each other silently and look southwest into the endless dark of this night. It is probably clear to every German soldier that there is hardly any hope that we can break the ring that encircles us. We are 250,000 men who can't be saved anymore. Perhaps a few hundred wounded can still be evacuated by the Jus.

The tanks of Army Group Hoth had reached forty-eight kilometers from us, which Lieutenant Colonel Seydel explained to us. Many had been able to see the fire of our own artillery, which had brightened up the nighttime skies in the south, from Marinowka. Now all is covered again by darkness, and from now on, we have to deal with everything ourselves. And so we go from one difficulty to the next crisis. Of course, our leadership tries to get a grip on the situation with all means possible. But our means are so diminished that we cannot fight actively for our own liberation.

On December 25, the Wehrmacht communiqué includes the following report: "In the Don area, our heroically fighting troops, supported by operations of newly arrived units, launched counterattacks at several locations in the course of the day. In determined battles, they destroyed enemy motorized and tank forces which were trying to penetrate in to the rear areas through holes in the newly erected front." And in the OKW war diary, it is now plain and clear: "The defensive battles continue along the northern front of the LVII Panzer Corps. Elements of the 6th Panzer Division are disengaging and marching away to the west. 6th Army: stronger attacks on Stalingrad and weaker attacks on the north front were beaten off. Aerial resupply was impossible due to snow storm. The disengagement of Group Hollidt south in the Gnilaja sector took place as planned."

Now we understand what has been going on to the west of us. It is completely clear to us that nobody is capable of freeing us from this devilish encirclement anymore. Many still believe that "miracles" can happen; they are unable to comprehend that the Führer cannot beat us a path out of here. And yet we have to keep a clear head and endure everything—hunger, the icy cold, and the impotent rage of being delivered to the enemy, of not being capable of defending oneself anymore. But first tonight we write home. They should know how the situation really stands.

And so I write on December 25, 1942, Christmas Day:

Now Christmas 1942 is past. Short and without pain! I really wanted to write you yesterday evening, but I was not able to do it. This Christmas I will not forget for the rest of my life. Christmas in the Stalingrad pocket! Can you back home imagine what that means—not only far distant from one's home, but completely cut off, encircled by the Russians, no mail since November 5, no Christmas packages, nothing to eat? But principally, what we experience here is unique. First, the hell of Stalingrad; now this difficult situation.

Yesterday at 1400 hours, I wished our good father a "merry Christmas" over the telephone. From the southwest corner of the pocket, where I'm stuck, over some connections to the southeast corner, where Dad is. It worked . . . I also congratulated him on his promotion to lieutenant general. The weather was "Russian"—snowstorms, icy cold, then again a clear frosty sky full of stars.

At 1500 hours, there was a "Christmas celebration" by our commander for all officers of the battalion. A home-built advent wreath and an accordion and a

violin. Every man was staring in front of himself.
Where were our thoughts? We had hoped for mail,
but none came. At 1600 hours, we said our good-byes
since everybody had to return to his post.

From 1700 to 18.00 hours, the Russians launched a
shameless surprise bombardment at our village with
heavy artillery that howled and exploded. It was our
"Christmas organ." The Russians had wished us "all
that is good" for Christmas in leaflets that descended
on us. Furthermore, they have erected speakers in
front of our positions, through which they call all sorts
of nice things to us. They want to give us a Christmas
that we'll remember for the rest of our lives. Well, go
at it then. . . .

Have you perhaps listened to the "circular broadcast" on the radio? Have you heard "Greetings from
Stalingrad"? How good some of the others have it!
France, Norway, the Crimea, the Channel coast,
Mediterranean coast, Crete, and so forth. Well, all has
its positive side. We at least have lived through something unbelievable. While listening to the radio, I have
eaten a schnitzel of horsemeat with a slice of dried
bread. My Christmas roast! Then coffee with a home
baked "cookie" from water and rye meal. Great!

Now I am sitting here in a dark corner and writing
you on Christmas Day! Perhaps the next Christmas
will look somewhat different. Earlier, Dad called me
to see whether I could join him for Boxing Day. Of
course, I'll go to him if the situation allows it. That is
my "Christmas present" then. That was my first Christmas outside the elderly home. And straightaway
something like that! By the way, I have been listed for
a mention in the "honor roll"! Perhaps you don't
know that at all. Well, I'll tell you about that later. . . .
Of the officers of the 108th, only First Lieutenant
Schuster, Second Lieutenant Moritz, and I remain in
the pocket.

With best wishes for the new year, I conclude this letter and hope that it will get home. Somewhere and somehow, perhaps it will read by a drunken Bolshevik.

Supply Situation in the Pocket Is Completely Insufficient on December 26, 1942.

On December 26, the Wehrmacht communiqué contains no new information about our sector of the front. Nor does the OKW war diary offer much about the progress of the fighting: "Strong enemy pressure principally against the forces of the LVII Panzer Corps. In the afternoon, the army had been without aerial resupply for forty-six hours."

We feel the effects of this more day by day. The supplies are used up, and only little is coming to us in the pocket due to different causes. Sometimes, the weather over the airfield of departure prevents planes from taking off; sometimes, the weather here on Pitomnik airfield prevents them from landing. Other times, the strong Russian antiaircraft defense and the lack of our own fighters hinder the supply planes. Whatever the cause, somebody should be responsible for this. We need 946 tons per day. They cannot demand that we hold on and then not give us the necessities to do so. The supplies that reach us are insufficient. My God! How are we supposed to fight and hold on here? We do not blame the airmen, who perform unbelievably. That's what our supply personnel at Pitomnik and the other landing areas at Gumrak and Stalingradsky tell us. The air crews are giving their all.

By afternoon, I take my leave to drive to the command post of the 371st Infantry Division. But I don't get there. We get stuck in deep snowdrifts, the Kübelwagen cannot pull through. We just can't make it through this snow in the icy storm that roars over the wide-open fields. We'll have to try with another vehicle tomorrow.

On December 27, the Wehrmacht communiqué reports:

Enemy attacks in between the Volga and Don and in the Stalingrad area were thrown back. In the great bend of the Don infantry and tank units threw back the Bolsheviks to the north and took a number of villages in a progressive counterattack. A strong concentration of enemy forces with tanks was encircled. German, Italian and Romanian air units intervened effectively at focal points in the ground battles.

The OKW war diary notes:

Near the Romanian 5th Cavalry Division, the enemy broke through our own positions and managed to penetrate to Charmutowski. There was also strong enemy pressure on the left wing between the 5th Romanian Cavalry Division and the 23rd Panzer Division. On the north front of the LVII Panzer Corps, the enemy broke through at several locations. Situation still unclear here. The enemy that had managed to penetrate to Height 103 was thrown back again by the corps reserve of the LVII Panzer Corps. Despite this, the enemy succeeded in penetrating to an area twenty-five kilometers north-northwest of Kotelnikowo. At the 6th Army, there was nothing special to report apart from assault party operations on the Volga. The penetration on the northeastern front could not be eliminated yet. Aerial reconnaissance spotted eighty-five enemy tanks on the march from Chir railroad station to the northwest. Reports are lacking about the movement of the 22nd Panzer Division. Elements of the 6th Panzer Division threw enemy tank forces out of Grusinow back to the northwest. In the Byskaja Valley to the south, elements of the 11th Panzer Division advanced in a southerly and southwesterly direction, flattened an enemy bridgehead and threw the enemy back to Tazinskaja.

On this day, Army Group Don received a Führer Order for the continuation of the battle on the southern wing of the Eastern Front:

The aim of all decisive action and the fundamental operational command must remain the liberation of the 6th Army. Army Group Don is therefore to receive all consideration for preparing to be the starting point for the continued supply of the 6th Army. Therefore, Army Group B is to prevent the northern flank of Army Group Don from being threatened. Army Group A must give up the railroad running through Rostow for supply purposes in favor of Army Group Don and reroute its supply lines over the Kertsch Strait.

It is also ordered in detail that Army Group Don has to hold the Kotelnikowo area at all costs as the starting point for the liberation of the 6th Army. Army Group Don offers the only possibility of freeing the 6th Army. The tanks of the 7th SS Panzer Division *Wiking*, as well as the tanks already en route to this point and a Tiger battalion, are earmarked for this purpose. Furthermore, the airfields of Morozowski and Tazinskaja should be retaken.

December 27, 1942. Last Talk with My Father?

There aren't any remarkable operations or events today. Early in the morning, I try again to drive down to see my father at the command post of the 371st Infantry Division, and we actually succeed in reaching it. The joy of meeting each other again is great, but we are saddened by the depressing situation and the dreariness in which all are stuck. Attentively, I listen to the situation report my father gives me. It is sober and very realistic. Without gilding the lily, he ends his explanation by saying, "We won't be able to put up resistance as long as is necessary to organize everything until the weather is in favor of as large an operation as is needed here." I don't ask any questions, and I don't tell him the obvious conclusions I've drawn. Before it grows dark, I say good-bye and return to Karpowka. I report about this conversation to Captain Domaschk, and this evening, I think a great deal about what lies ahead.

On December 28, the Wehrmacht communiqué does not mention the battles in and around Stalingrad. Like before, it mentions defensive successes between the Volga and Don. The OKW war diary records:

> Pimen Tscherny had to be given up in the face of the heavy enemy attacks on the border between the Romanian VII Corps and the LVII Panzer Corps south of the Stalingrad-Kotelnikowo railroad. North of the railroad, attacks by enemy tank forces were beaten off. At the 6th Army, there was no real change apart from local fighting. In the Chir valley the enemy advanced south and reached the area north of Siwolobow. The enemy encircled at Tazinskaja is compressed further from all sides.

A new supplementary operational order from the Führer arrives at Army Group Don: "My intentions continue to be as before: to maintain the 6th Army in its fortress and to put in place the measures needed for its liberation. Furthermore, at individual locations, the Russians are to have the initiative taken from them by mobile operations, and in this way, the superiority of the German leadership is to make itself felt once again."

Detailed orderes are also given to the army groups. Army Group Don's orders begin with the following conditions: "Army Group Don, as before, has the duty to do everything necessary to make possible the liberation of the 6th Army. Therefore, it can only withdraw its units to the west when it is really necessary, and then only in continuous battle, in order to inflict as many losses as possible on the enemy, and hold or create room and time for the advance of reinforcements that are coming up."

Among the members of Kampfgruppe Seydel, each day presents the same picture, the same passing of night and day. We accept the rumours of what is happening. Today, the Russians are attacking our neighbors to the right, who give them a "warm reception," and the Russians disappear into their starting positions. We are waiting for them to attack here. We can see the Russians advance across the big snow plain in front of us. Artillery fire is called in, and then we open fire with our rifles. The Russians can do little except halt their attack.

It was relatively easy for us to control the situation here and hold this important point, the village of Karpowka. Our neighbors have also succeeded, until now, in stopping the Russians from changing their main line of resistance. It is said that there have been several breakthroughs on the northeastern front of the pocket, where the Soviets have flattened everything with tanks and heavy weapons. We can always clear that up with counterattacks by our own tanks, but how long can this last?

It is already late at night, and I want to write home again.

Today I want to write a letter once more. The last one I wrote on December 25. I mention only in passing that I've received nothing from you yet. Caring for the troops! A mad pig's mess! For over six weeks, we've received no mail! Who do we thank for this? On December 26, I wanted to pay Dad a visit. I traveled more than half the distance and then got stuck in the high snow and the snowdrifts. I nearly froze my hands in this! Damn it! Twenty-five or thirty degrees! That's what we're having now. It is good that we have our warming winter equipment. It keeps some of the cold away from us.

Dead Romanians and Russians lie in the streets. Weakened by hunger, they've let themselves drop into the snow. They of course were frozen straightaway. Mad images! A human life is nothing in this world anyway! And here in the war? Here it is not only nothing, but nothing but "shit and entrails"—unnecessary! Please forgive me for this talk. But it really is so! You simply cannot imagine it. Even wolves are walking around here, which are tearing up the bodies and the cadavers of the horses.

At night we—First Lieutenant Meisel, First Lieutenant Riemenschneider, First Lieutenant Daehn, and I—have sat here in our bunker until 0700 in the morning with two bottles of schnapps. At 0800, we were at it again, and I drove down to see Dad. Sometimes, Father and I have not uttered a single word for a long time, then we've discussed old times, more beautiful times. We don't have to count on mails. The Ju52s are only to carry fuel and ammunition. Well, then we'll go without!

My dear mother! Do you sometimes think of your men that are fighting here at the most dangerous position of the front? I believe that most men simply cannot imagine what we are doing and going through here. I end this letter with the conclusion that we have to win here in order to survive, and with my best wishes for the new year.

New Year in Karpowka in the Stalingrad Pocket on December 31, 1942

On December 31, there is no mention of the progress in our front sector in the Wehrmacht communiqués and only little mention in the OKW war diary—only numbers of destroyed tanks, weapons, and other things.

Tonight we once more make our rounds. We are not to fire in order to conserve ammunition since we don't know when or even whether we'll receive more supplies. At about 2100 hours, it grows quiet in our sector—only a few flares here and there, some bursts from infantry weapons. The year 1942 will soon say good-bye to us in an atmosphere marked by tension, disappointment, and even despair. At midnight, we would like to mount a hail of fire to prove that we still stand here. Everywhere around us is an island of fire in this desert of snow and ruins. The Bolsheviks must concede that German soldiers still stand and fight here.

Finally, it is time: midnight! 0000 hours, 0001 hours! A wild "fire show" begins. The entire front becomes a sea of light that reaches as far as the eye can see. If someone could witness this spectacle from the air, he would see exactly how the front line runs, how this pocket is formed. After a short time, the phantom passes; it was only a show of anger, a flare up. The darkness and icy cold again cover everything that had just been illuminated in the brightest of lights. "Hang on, the Führer will get us out of here!" the brave soldiers cry in the bunkers and dug-outs.

On January 1, 1943, the Wehrmacht communiqué and the OKW war diary contain no detailed reports about the fighting here in the Stalingrad area. They make clear, however, that the Russians are slowly but steadily advancing west. The new year brings us no good news. The front line of the units that have assembled to liberate us seems to grow more distant all the time. For days, we have not heard any exact reports although many rumors are making the rounds. My God! Is there no way out anymore? Why are the tanks and assault guns not getting closer? Why don't they send paratroopers into the pocket?

Misery slowly destroys our resitance. Ammunition, especially that of the artillery, is rary, very rare. Our Jus simply cannot fly in the necessary and urgently needed supplies. The Russian barrier of antiaircraft artillery has been built up to such an extent that our aircraft can reach the pocket only with great difficulties and losses. The Russians shoot many of our planes down en route and immediately after takeoff. For us, watching our aircraft crash into the snowy planes after being show down is a sad and unaccustomed sight. The skies are full of Soviet fighters, ground-attack aircraft, and bombers. And our fighters? None are to be seen here anymore.

DESTRUCTION IN THE RUINS OF STALINGRAD

January 5, 1943. Relief Forces Give Way Farther to the West.
On January 5, the Wehrmacht communiqué reports only this: "The heavy defensive battles in the Don area continue." The OKW war diary summarizes everything briefly: "The withdrawal of the 1st Panzer Army continued to be carried out as planned. Around Stalingrad, attacks were thrown back."

Now the Soviets are trying to cut the pocket in half and squeeze it out; apparently, the battle has lasted too long for them. Wherever they attack—whether to our right or left—we chase them back. Up at headquarters, whoever is writing things like "attacks were beaten off" cannot imagine what the men suffer here and how things look in reality. We put up bitter resistance and contest every meter of ground. Those who are forced to give up their positions or evacuate are in a bad situation: they'll have to lie in the snowy wastes in temperatures of thirty degrees below zero without cover or protection—to say nothing of the superior Russian, who immediately catch them and mow them down. We are fighting; we want to hang on.

On January 6, the Wehrmacht communiqué reports:

In the Don area yesterday, the heavy defensive battles continued with the same intensity. Soviet attacks were beaten off with high enemy losses. A panzer division destroyed thirty-one tanks. In a counterattack, a motorized grenadier regiment destroyed another twenty-five Soviet tanks as well as two batteries and twenty-two anti-tank guns. At another location, a German counterblow destroyed two battalions. The Luftwaffe attacked the supply traffic and troop assemblies of the enemy.

The armored parts of the 2nd Battalion of Panzergrenadier Regiment 103 consist only of ten armored personnel carriers (APCs), which are led by First Lieutenant Riemenschneider in "special operations." His main task is to shore up weaknesses or clear up a situation somewhere. The counterattacks he has to carry out as divisional reserve are always very costly. Most of the time, they are unsuccessful, too, since fuel, ammunition, and the necessary strength are lacking. Everything perishes in the face of massive Soviet superiority.

On January 7, the Wehrmacht communiqué brings no real news. On the other hand, the OKW war diary gives more information about the progress of operations:

The 1st Panzer Army withdrew its right wing. The 6th Army was able to bar penetrations with the 16th Panzer Division and the 29th Infantry Division (Motorized), but was not able to eliminate them. New attacks were thrown back. The 4th Panzer Division threw back the enemy at Stavropol (north of the Manytch) and repulsed further enemy attacks. Terrain was lost in doing so. Army Group Hollidt repelled strong attacks against Corps Mieth and the XVII Army Corps. The enemy that had advanced across the Don was thrown back, the situation on the left flank was reestablished by a counterattack. Withdrawals took place according to plan.

Now it has become clear to all of us that there will be no salvation from destruction by the Soviets. From our superior command, all we hear is "hang on." Each day that we are able to offer resistance to the Soviets is important. We must keep them occupied here so that a new front—far away from Stalingrad—can be constructed to prevent Soviet advances elsewhere.

On January 9, the Wehrmacht communiqué is very terse about the progress of operations between the Don and the Volga. The OKW war diary is similar. We hear that during the afternoon, the Russians have made an offer of capitulation to the 6th Army. Not comprehending, we stand in the face of this new situation. The enemy is coming from all sides, and from overhead, we get bombs and shells, no food. We get leaflets, many leaflets, written by the communists Ulbricht and Weinert, which exhort us to stop the fighting and surrender: "You are sitting in the pocket like condemned men. Manstein's army, which was to advance up to you, was beaten at Kotelnikowo." The Soviets' last great offensive comes next, and we all know what that means. Worn out, hungry, and without hope, we lie by our weapons in ice and snow and wait for the attack to come. I have no expectations about the results. If only I could talk with my father one more time, before everything comes to an end!

On January 9, there is no mention of the situation in and around the Stalingrad pocket in either the Wehrmacht communiqué or the OKW war diary. But the Russians are preparing their attack right in front of our eyes. By day and at the night in the bright searchlights, they move their artillery and Stalin organs to firing positions close by. Apparently, they don't care about camouflage and cover anymore. We're not allowed to attack them because ammunition is being rationed and must be held in preparation for the coming offensive. It is horrible to have to watch this. I learn at the battalion command post that the surrender offer has been rejected. Fate must run its course.

Beginning of the Russian Offensive, January 10, 1943.
On January 10, the Wehrmacht communiqué reports:

> The defensive battle in the south of the Eastern Front continues with unabating intensity. All enemy attacks were thrown back. During the fighting and in counterattacks by German forces, twenty-six enemy tanks were destroyed. Infantry and tank units in cooperation with strong air support threw the enemy out of several villages and at one location destroyed an enemy regiment. In Stalingrad, local assault parties were active.

The OKW war diary adds: "The 1st Panzer Army has withdrawn even farther. The enemy increased his artillery fire against Stalingrad. By the 4th Panzer Army and Army Group Hollidt, individual counterattacks and several enemy attacks, in which some villages were lost."

In our battalion, losses result less from enemy actions than from frostbite and general loss of physical strength. The operational readiness of the remaining elements of Panzergrenadier Regiment 103 sinks more and more. With daily rations of 75 grams of bread, 200 grams of meat (horse meat with bones), 12 grams of fat, 11 grams of sugar, and one cigarette per man, there is little we can do. And so the men ask more loudly and more urgently: "Have we been forgotten? Have we already been written off? Have the steady promises been so much empty air? Will the great counterblow still come?" The Führer promised us it would, and everyone fights on and sells his skin dearly. Every step has now become an exertion; the smallest of activities has become difficult. The icy cold penetrates torn uniforms like they were paper. There is no possibility of getting warm anymore. "They cannot give up an army," the men say. "They will certainly get us out of here. It is simply a matter of time."

All of a sudden, at about 1000, a raging fire opens up from enemy artillery, mortars, and Stalin organs. It will last for two whole hours. Cover! Down into the positions! Observe! After this, they're sure to attack, but first, they transfer the fire forward, and then back again. Everything is ploughed over and destroyed. The main effort of the barrage is located to our right in the Marinowka area, which must be held. There is no yielding here because then we'll be on the open snow plains. Our artillery returns fire, but the Soviets manage to penetrate in the south and north and also to the west of us in Marinowka.

"First Lieutenant Riemenschneider, immediate assembly! The enemy that penetrated 1,000 meters from us is to be attacked straight away and destroyed, and the old main line of resistance is to be reestablished!"

The engines of the armored personnel carriers howl into action. The crews are mounted up, wrapped like mummies against the biting cold, and then they move off slowly, using the slope in front of us to close with the enemy that has managed to penetrate. From our positions, we cannot see anything anymore because of the onset of dusk. We no longer hear anything either. It is quiet in front of us. We await the enemy. First Lieutenant Riemenschneider and his men do not return.

On January 11, the Wehrmacht communiqué reports: "In the North Caucasus, near Stalingrad, and in the Don area, the continued attacks of the numerically superior Soviet infantry and tank forces were repulsed in bloody fighting. The Luftwaffe intervened with strong forces in the fighting." The OKW war diary notes: "In front of Stalingrad, the enemy resumed his attacks against the northeastern, western, and southern fronts and created a penetration eight kilometers deep and five kilometers wide."

January 12, 1943. Karpowka Is Given Up, Pitomnik Airfield Is Defended.

On January 12, the Wehrmacht communiqué reports:

> In between the Caucasus and the Don, in the Stalingrad area, and in the Don area, the enemy with assaulted thepreviously attacked focal points with a renewed effort by strong forces. In bitter fighting, partially in counterattacks, he was thrown back and lost sixty-three tanks, of which forty-five alone were lost near Stalingrad. The Soviet losses conform to the massed effort of infantry. In a counterattack, an enemy rifle division was encircled destroyed. More than 1,000 prisoners were taken. A German panzer corps in the great bend of the Don has destroyed 511 Soviet tanks since December 5. Hungarian troops on the Don repulsed the attacking enemy with losses.

The OKW war diary notes: "The concentrated attacks against Stalingrad were stopped, or, where the enemy had managed to penetrate, sealed off. The location of yesterday's breakthrough was reduced again."

Now it is our turn. Kampfgruppe Seydel is to give up the positions south of Karpowka. The enemy is attacking everywhere, and we must get out of here quickly or the Russians will have passed us by already. We have orders to yield about four kilometers and then establish our defenses again. Pitomnik airfield must be kept open, and we have a look at it when we reach the new main line of resistance. Innumerable wrecked aircraft are scattered around on the snow-covered field. If we lose the field, any hopes of resupply would be completely gone.

That day will come more quickly than we can imagine. We try not to think of that. Just now, a plane dropped supplies down to us from a very low altitude. A Ju52 just went down on the enemy side right in front of us, crashing in the deep snow. The Russians were grateful for the cargo and promised the crew good treatment. The things that are happening here are simply unbelievable. As food is getting more and more scarce and hard to find; even dogs and cats are now hunted and slaughtered. A soup is made with rye meal, which we wolf down while it's still hot—it does us good.

On January 13, the Wehrmacht communiqué contains nothing about our difficult situation. In the OKW war diary, on the other hand, one sentence now spells it out clearly and without mistakes: "The 6th Army, whose resupply is troubled by snowdrifts, defended itself against heavy, tank-supported attacks in which the enemy managed to attain new penetrations."

On January 14, the Wehrmacht communiqué reports: "In the Stalingrad area, the German troops repelled strong infantry and tank attacks in heroic heavy fighting." The OKW war diary notes: "Around Stalingrad, concentric attacks again took place. After fluctuating battles, a new, but thin security line was erected on the southern front."

The losses of our battalion have increased constantly in the daily bitter fighting. Each day brings new gaps that cannot be filled anymore. Soviet artillery fire continues to fall on Pitomnik airfield, and despite everything, our aircraft land and take off in the middle of the detonating shells. But the Russians keep up the pressure; they want to knock out the airfield. Captain Domaschk personally, with the few remaining armored personnel carriers, holds off the attacking Russian infantry at the threatened locations. It has become an unequal fight, and no one doubts the outcome anymore. We lack food and other supplies; the barbaric cold covers us, as it has since Christmas. Boundless loneliness descends on us all, and we sense the darkening prospects for the future.

Suddenly, our troops—those that have managed to avoid Soviet encirclement—move past us toward Stalingrad.

January 15, 1943. New Defenses on the Western Edge of Stalingrad.

On January 15, the Wehrmacht communiqué records: "In the Stalingrad area, German troops defended themselves in bitter fighting against the continuing heavy attacks of the enemy." And in the OKW war diary, the situation is described as follows: "In Stalingrad, where troops partially are forced to fight with sidearms due to lack of ammunition, the front in the line from Bolchaja Rassochka to five kilometers southeast of Nowo Rogatchnik was pulled back during the night of January 14–15."

We withdraw farther. Kampfgruppe Domaschk is leaving the positions west of Pitomnik and taking up new positions on the western edge of Stalingrad. We use the few remaining armored personnel carriers and some other vehicles to transport the men to their new positions. We go past Pitomnik airfield. I have never seen anything like this before. It is now a ghostly scene, with aircraft wrecks as far as the eye can see. Since yesterday, aircraft can no longer touch down on this snowed-over field of wrecks. But there is still the auxiliary airfield at Gumrak; hopefully, it can be held.

Where are we supposed to enter the new positions? The area assigned to us is a ploughed-over and burrowed field, frozen solid and covered in deep snow. It is level and wide, allowing us to spot any approaching enemy early. In this bone-hard soil, we establish our positions in such a way that we can engage and destroy any enemy force with our machine guns before they reach us. Frozen to the marrow, starved, and awaiting the next Bolshevik attacks, we try to dig in and prepare our defenses. By evening, I report to the battalion command post, which has been established in an abandoned hamlet. It is amazing that everything continues to run its well-ordered course. Everybody is doing his damned duty and helps each other to cope with the hopeless situation. People begin to talk about how the end will look and how we are to behave.

On January 16, we are not mentioned in the Wehrmacht communiqué, and on January 17, there is nothing at all. In the OKW war diary, it is recorded: "The mass attacks in Stalingrad continued. On the southwest front, the main line of resistance was withdrawn. And in Stalingrad, enemy attacks were repulsed in front of the new lines of resistance. The supply situation of the 6th Army is completely beyond control. Continued enemy dive bomber attacks could not be prevented anymore by antiaircraft defenses."

On January 18, the Wehrmacht communiqué reports on the defensive battle that has been raging for two months and continues in unabated intensity: "The German troops that are fighting in Stalingrad faced further attacks, under the most difficult circumstances with endurance and determined will to fight." The OKW war diary adds: "In Stalingrad, the northeastern, western, and southwestern front had to be retaken."

In the southern sector of Stalingrad, the remains of our battalion—together with the remnants of the infantry divisions that were operating here—are defending strongpoints in groups of houses, ruins, ravines, and rubble heaps; cellars offer the possibility of warming oneself. The staff of the 2nd Battalion of Panzergrenadier Regiment 103 are located in well-defended cellars. Everyone predicts the situation can last only a few more nights and days.

From a bright, icy, and frosty sky, the Soviet bombers dive down on us again and again, dropping bombs and firing on us with their automatic cannons. We defend ourselves with anti-aircraft weapons, and the soldiers aim their rifles high and fire at the chains of enemy aircraft. Just now, another four Russians are coming at us, flying at low level. I order the men to raise their rifles and fire.

"Take off your gloves!" I cry to a corporal first class who is incapable of firing his rifle in the thick winter gloves he is wearing. He looks at me and slowly removes the glove from his right hand. A bloody black mess of flesh emerges, partially sticking to the glove. My God! Can nobody here help? It is unbelievable what our men are still doing. Ruined and ragged, unwashed and unshaven, we don't recognize each other anymore while we suffer and rot together. Yet each new day bring combat, and everybody has a mission to complete. Like before, the leaders and troops form a single iron fighting community, but the ranks get thinner and thinner. Those who want to warm themselves disappear into the cellars and do not get back on their feet again, partially from lack of strength and exhaustion; they remain lying somewhere down there.

How are things wit hteh 371st Infantry Division? All hell must be loose there as well. Yesterday, I tried to reach my father through the radio but without success. It is depressing to know that one's father is out there in the inferno on the Zariza and that one can do little to help him. I fear we won't see each other ever again.

January 19, 1943. I Am There. The Commander of the 6th Army, Colonel General Paulus, Talks to My Father.

On January 19, the Wehrmacht communiqué once again offers only one sentence about the events in our sector of the front: "The troops in the Stalingrad area steadily defend themselves in hard battles against new attacks by the enemy." The OKW war diary elaborates: "In Stalingrad, food distribution has been paralyzed due to insufficient supplies. Nevertheless, attacks and penetrations could still be thrown back. On the northeastern front, the main line of resistance was retaken."

I finally succeed in getting through to the 371st Infantry Division on a radio link. My father is talking on the other end and asks whether I can come once more when the situation allows it and I won't be missed here. I immediately got permission from Captain Domaschk, jumped into a Kübelwagen, and straightaway drove off in the direction of Werchne Jelchanka. The command post, like the positions, has been built up for winter operations. I meet my father in his bunker. After a short greeting, I quickly conclude that he has been thinking about the end of this battle in Stalingrad for a long time.

"My boy," he says, "we won't see home and our family again. That is very hard, but cannot be changed anymore. They did not keep their promises to us. We could still defend ourselves;

we were ordered to remain here. Now it is too late to get out of this grip. We're being sacrificed to help prevent an even greater catastrophe far away from our own lines and bases—which we cannot reach anymore and from which the others cannot advance to us anymore. Well, there's nothing we can do except follow orders and hang on as long as possible and tie up Soviet forces while doing so. That's also exactly the same way the commanders of the neighboring divisions see it."

Then the door of the bunker opens and the commander of the 6th Army, Col. Gen. Friedrich von Paulus, comes in. He looks tired, bitter, and full of despair. He is tall and slender and is forced to stoop in this bunker; his face is pale. He no longer exudes authority, even though he appears determined. I'm permitted to remain and hear the entire conversation. My father gives a situation report, after which Paulus speaks.

"My proud 6th Army—it is approaching its inevitable destruction, experiencing a fate it didn't deserve; it cannot be helped anymore. Yes, Stempel, it has all turned out differently from what we expected last autumn. And in the end, we face a difficult course of events. Stempel, you know what you have to do as the last act of a German general. Myself, I will defend the Silo [the grain elevator] with my staff. And when the Russians will attack it, it will be blown up with us."

After a final handshake and good-byes between Paulus and my father, the supreme commander of the 6th Army bids me farewell, too, and then walks outside, accompanied by my father. My throat feels constricted, and I can find no words to start a conversation with my father when he comes back. While the remains of his 371st Infantry Division defend their positions here in the south of Stalingrad, we the remnants of Kampfgruppe Seydel have set up defenses in the middle of the city, lessening the distasnce between us. Therefore, I hope that in the next few days—before the end comes—I can report to my father one more time. For now, though, my father and I exchange a heart-felt good-bye, and I drive back to the battalion command post, where I report the conversation with Paulus to Captain Domaschk.

First Lieutenant Meisel listens to my report with a stony face. But we cannot think about it any further since we are in battle with the last remaining men and must try to carry on the battle. We make it very difficult for the Soviets to advance on us, firing on them every time they attack, yet we still know the end is near. We discuss when it will come and how we are to act. Capture is beyond the pale, and so is letting ourselves be shot. So we must break out! We must attempt to reach our own lines somewhere to the west and meet up with the German counterattacks that are surely taking place there. Lieutenant Moritz and some sergeants of the 108th agree, and the preparations for such a breakout attempt are developed.

January 20, 1943. The Battle in the Ruins of Stalingrad Continues.

On January 20, the Wehrmacht communiqué reports briefly and tersely: "Despite heavy privations, the defenders in the Stalingrad area beat off all Soviet attacks unfazed." The OKW war diary has only one line: "Around Stalingrad, all attacks were beaten off."

That is all that is written down about an event that surpasses everything that we have seen before and next to which all other comparisons pale. This murderous sacrifice, this languishing fight, this apathetic holding on, this desperate stand on ice and iron—none of that is mentioned in the official reports, not one word. No person in the rear, no strategist standing by a map in a warm bunker, can imagine what the men of the 6th Army are achieving, shouldering, and suffering here, without food, nearly without ammunition, without sufficient winter equipment—and without hope. Nobody can imagine the state of the wounded and those who are incapacitated by severe frostbite; some do not receive any care. And the Russians continue to attack, advancing slowly and very carefully, purposefully and systematically.

On January 21, the Wehrmacht communique reports: "With their ultimate defense, the German troops in the Stalingrad area meet the continuing efforts of the enemy trying to squeeze the defensive front and throw back mass attacks in bitter fighting." The OKW war diary records: "The 6th Army on the northwest front, despite the losses of men and material this entailed, began a shortening of the front, occasioned by a penetration."

This situation becomes more and more unbearable. One can't describe it anymore; it's as if everything is in a dream. In front of us, the Soviet infantrymen who were attacking have withdrawn under our fire. Now the bombers are again overhead while artillery fire shatters the walls and facades of the houses that still stand. Everything is collapsing. The Russians want to soften us up for capitulation.

There are now a number of cases of dysentery, which is a torment for the sufferers. Ice and snow have to be thawed for water, which is not enough to wash our clothes. Malnutrition and freezing are widespread. The men lie and lean in their positions and holes; they do not move anymore. The battle continues. It must continue. Bursts of fire whip everywhere.

On January 22, the Wehrmacht communique reports about our situation:

> Yesterday, the German forces in Stalingrad that are encircled and resisting enemy pressure also had to face enemy attacks from the far superior forces of the Soviets. Despite a heroic defense, the defenders of Stalingrad were incapable of preventing an enemy penetration in the west, which forced a withdrawal of several kilometers. A large number of Soviet tanks were destroyed in hand-to-hand fighting.

The OKW war diary again has only one sentence about the events in Stalingrad: "The battle for Stalingrad took place mostly on the western front. The enemy took Gontschara."

And then January 23 comes, and the Wehrmacht communiqué describes the situation in our sector of the front as follows: "During the entire previous day, the defenders of Stalingrad offered strong resistance to the enemy in a heroic fight. Twenty tanks were destroyed in close combat. A deep enemy penetration of the defensive front was contained by assembling all available forces." The OKW war diary concludes: "In Stalingrad, the ammunition is running out. Despite this, we still succeeded in repulsing enemy attacks or containing them by shortening the front."

By now, we have withdrawn completely and crawled into the cellars of the ruins of houses around Red Square in Stalingrad. Although there is nothing to defend here anymore, we still form groups that find cover upstairs between the ruins of buildings. From these positions, we can engage the approaching enemy and stop him with machine-gun and rifle fire. We continue to prepare for our breakout attempt. Going into captivity should not be the conclusion of any military career.

On January 24, the Wehrmacht communiqué reports: "At Stalingrad, the situation has worsened because of another penetration of strong enemy masses coming from the west. Despite everything, the defenders still hold the more and more compressed ring around the city as a shining example of the best German military tradition. Their heroic efforts tied up strong enemy forces and for months now have prevented the enemy supply effort at one of its most important points." The OKW war diary concludes: "In Stalingrad, attacks on the northern front were thrown back; in the only weakly manned defensive line to the west, the enemy attained new penetrations. The space between the northern and southern corps cannot be closed anymore due to lack of strength, and the last airfield northwest of the city area can no longer be used."

ATTEMPTED BREAKOUT FROM THE POCKET

January 25, 1943. Dismissal by the Regimental Commander of Panzergrenadier Regiment 103, Lieutenant Colonel Seydel, and "Freedom of Action."

The same bleak situation still prevails. From time to time, we take shelter in the cellars of ruined buildings in the southern part of the city and find at least a little protection from the bar-

barous cold. Soldiers are scattered everywhere, many of them belonging to units that don't exist anymore. They exhibit a failure of fighting morale. Wherever strong and cool leadership is present, however, discipline and operational readiness remain solid. Only in this way is it possible to build up resistance again and slow down the Russian advance.

I've just been at the divisional command post of the 14th Panzer Division and witnessed our signals station listening in on Russian radio conversations. From their words, it becomes clear that they don't really believe we are crumbling. They think ambushes, mine barriers, and raids are everywhere. If only we had our normal strength, these Russians would be right. As it stands, they are very wrong. I learn that more than 18,000 wounded are rotting in the cellars without any medicine or bandages. The 44th, 76th, 100th, 305th, and 384th Infantry Divisions have been destroyed; they don't exist anymore. My father's 371st still exists, maintaining its positions in the extreme south of the city on the Zariza. When I have returned and joined my comrades, we discuss the possibilities of a breakout. With no time to lose, we begin our preparations. Sergeant Major Eckman gets the backpacks, pistol ammunition, maps, compasses, and felt soles to put in our army boots (the thick winter boots could not be used in this case).

On January 25, the Wehrmacht communiqué reports: "In Stalingrad, the 6th Army has attached an immortal honor to its colors in heroic and sacrificial battles against a suffocating superiority. Units of the Romanian 20th Infantry Division and 1st Cavalry Division together with their German comrades resist to the last and partake fully in this glory." The OKW war diary records:

> In Stalingrad, the elements standing around Goroditsche were able to fight themselves through to the northern part. In the southern part the west front could still be held. The army command radioed: Under command of capable generals that are fighting at the front, and officers that have maintained a grip

on the situation, around whom the few remaining men
still capable of fighting have grouped themselves, on
January 25 the last resistance on the edge of town in
the southern part of Stalingrad will be offered. The
tractor works in the northern part of the city can possibly be held a little bit longer.

In the afternoon, all officers belonging to Panzergrenadier
Regiment 103 and those officers serving under the regiment
are ordered to the regimental command post. It has already
become dark, and the ruined building that shelters the staff
has little light. The commander, Lieutenant Colonel Seydel, is
sitting on an ammunition box surrounded by the officers who
remain after all the hellish days, weeks, and months of fighting. We all look old and decrepit, with bearded, unshaven
faces, unwashed, dirtied, torn, and tattered. We have hollow
cheeks and bitter faces and a fixed look in our disappointed
and saddened eyes. This is probably the last "orders group"
that we will experience in our military life. The regimental
commander, who stands out in the surroundings in his black
tank uniform with green collar tabs, looks each of us in the
eyes and says a few words of thanks. Thereafter, he describes
the hopeless situation and announces: "From 0000 hours,
everyone is free to act as he pleases." We are no longer bound
by orders, and we now will have the opportunity to give oneself
up to the Russians or try to break through the Soviet ring and
make it to the troops to the west.

All sorts of possibilities run through my head when I am
ordered to the regimental commander. "Stempel, Lieutenant
Stempel, please go over to the 371st Infantry Division and
hand your father these corps orders!" After that, there's
silence in the room, stony faces. So this is how the end looks?
The end of Panzergrenadier Regiment 103, the 14th Panzer
Division, the 371st Infantry Division, the corps, the army? We
shake hands, report our departure, and exchange a few more
words. Then without orders, we leave this regimental command post and hurry to where we were last. The units are wait-

ing, the remains of platoons and groups. What will happen now? I tell my friend Lt. Hans Moritz, "I will carry out the orders I just got, say my goodbyes to my father, and then we piss off tonight and try it." Everything has been discussed already; everything has been prepared.

I leave the cellar. I jump from one piece of cover to the other, across mountains of rubble through ruins and masses of remains, across rails, and through deep snow into more open terrain. I already see the Balka with a few small huts and many earthen dug-outs, the last of which stretch from the slope into the valley. Here is the command post of the 371st Infantry Division, not too far from the Zariza. I run into the main bunker and meet my father, who is among his officers. Immediately, I see that all military and personal goods are being burned and destroyed. It feels like the end of the world, just like it does at the 103rd.

My father greets me briefly and takes me into an adjoining room, which has been his living room for the past few weeks. Everything here is prepared for destruction, too—data, maps, manuals, papers, documents, notes, photographs, letters, sacks, suitcases, packages. I sit down next to him while a corporal collects all the items and takes them outside to be burned.

Last Good-Byes of My Father in the Zariza Ravine before the End in Stalingrad.

So now father and son sit opposite each other. We look at each other and first do not say a word. Then I begin with the transfer of the corps orders and subsequently ask: "What now, father?"

Overburdened, tired, and deeply disappointed, he slowly and very quietly says: "In a very short time, things will end. We have been let down here. And yet it is no use to look for culpable persons. They who are responsible for this are dilettantes. We have been sacrificed here in order to at least save some others. And yet the definitive defeat cannot be staved off anymore. Losses such as the army and air force have suffered here are too large to make up. We bit off more than we could chew.

We'll never see home and our family again. Hopefully, they can cope without us.

"You should try to make your way through to our own lines, which are, however, growing more distant day by day. The officers on my staff have asked me to try a similar break-out in order to avoid Russian captivity. But I will not do that. I will not be a burden to my staff officers in such an undertaking, nor will I imperil the effort. Physically, I'm at my end, and I'll do nothing to give the Russian an opportunity to capture me alive or possibly wounded. I'll sooner shoot myself since capture is not an option for a German general. My division has been destroyed, and I will act like the captain who does not abandon a sinking vessel, but rather goes down with it. I belong to my fallen soldiers, who all died for me doing their duty to the utmost. Captivity is out of the question, Soviet captivity all the more so. Unto the last moment, behave like a decent soldier should!"

We embrace one last time, and then the staff officers and divisional chaplain enter the room to partake in a final meeting with the division's commander. I rise once more, collect my strength, stand at attention, and say, "Father, I thank you for everything that you have given me in my life—for the education and safety in my dear home, for your love and care, for your advice and actions regarding my choice and aim of profession. Now all will end here, and I cannot express how much I despair."

At this, my father lays his hand on my shoulder and says, "It's all right, my boy! Shortly, we'll meet again up there, where all brave soldiers find their peace and quiet. Go with God!"

Slowly, I put my hat on, stand, and salute. I report my departure and amble out, stricken, conscious of the fact that I've just seen my father for the last time. The looks of the officers follow me until I'm in the dark of the night.

January 25, 1943. First Attempt to Break Out of Stalingrad South.

I don't know how, but all of a sudden, I am standing in front of the old cellar and rejoin my awaiting comrades. Lt. Hans Moritz and both sergeants have prepared everything in the meantime. We collect our meager belongings, stow it all in our backpacks, and holster our two pistols, with the magazines on the outer pockets of the jackets. Then we rise. Together with us, several noncommissioned officers and men also rise to join our group. We climb the few steps and then walk south in the icy night. From time to time, the surroundings are illuminated brightly, and everybody freezes. Rifle and heavy-weapons fire often force us to take cover. Suddenly, we notice in the light of the flares that about three dozen figures are following us. This wrecks our plans. We had wanted to make our way out in a group of three to five men, not in a formation of platoon strength.

It's too late to do anything about it. Just as we're crossing a brightly lit field, there is an ambush from the front, left, and right. "Down! Cover!" We cannot get any farther here; we're walking straight into the Russian positions. So we turn and go back. When it is pitch dark again, Lieutenant Moritz and three corporals jump up with me to get into cover across the open terrain. As we jump, we shout to everybody to follow us. The bursts of Soviet infantrymen, who are controlling everything with their flanking fire, tear into us again. Then there is a tearing feeling in my right hand. I'm hit! Damn! Luckily, it's only a grazing shot. But there are other shouts from men who've been hit worse. "Take me with you! Don't let me lie here!" cries a private first class who has been hit in the chest.

We take all of them along, and after a few hours, we return to the cellar. While my hand is being treated, we confer about what to do next. The soldiers who followed us have once again assembled all around us. They believe that only with us a breakout could succeed. We had led them for more than a year in every kind of situation, and they trusted us now. They think there's a chance with us alone.

We continue discussing the situation with the officers and sergeants and conclude that the only chance of success is to sneak through the Soviet lines in groups that are as small as possible. We must try to cross the steppe heading west in order to reach German positions, perhaps near Rostow, without being noticed. We form small groups—Lieutenant Moritz, the adjutant, Sergeant Bellmann, Lieutenant Bonz, and I are in one—and decide that another action might allow us to break through. We'll march down to the Volga, where we'll try to break through the barricades of the infantry positions and then march on the ice to the south until we've gotten behind the Russian positions. Then we'll make a right turn onto the bank and continue to the southwest. We'll do it like that; it could succeed. We're convinced of it. In the coming afternoon, we'll break camp and reconnoiter the positions through which we'll pass to the Volga, straight through mines and other blockades. Nobody has foreseen this situation.

January 26, 1943. Renewed Attempt through the Minefields at the 71st Infantry Division.

On January 26, the Wehrmacht communiqué reports: "In Stalingrad the defenders, among whom apart from Romanian divisions also a small Croatian unit is present, have closed in on each other in the middle and southern parts of the ruins of the city. There, under the command of their generals, they continue to put up heroic resistance, supported as far as possible by the Luftwaffe under the most difficult operational circumstances." The OKW war diary records: "In Stalingrad, the Minia suburb was lost. In the Zariza sector, a new front was established. The enemy attacked the entire city in one continuous attack from the air."

We are sitting in the cellar with the "dismissed" soldiers of Panzergrenadier Regiment 103, while Soviet airmen pummel the position with bombs and machine-gun fire. We're preparing our next move. We must hurry because the Russians have managed to split the pocket into two parts. Our goal is simply to get out of here, out of this inferno. The situation is unbearable. All around us, in the cellars and subterranean halls, the stragglers, these "homeless and leaderless" soldiers whose units have long since been destroyed, are assembling. They camp here without food and wait for the end, for the Russians to come. No! We don't want to wait for the Bolsheviks to enter the cellar and drive us out with hands raised and take us into captivity or shoot against some wall. We want to try to get out of here and reach the German troops to the southwest.

We prepare ourselves in the early afternoon and march to the 71st Infantry Division, which is supposed to be directly in front of us on the Volga. The route goes through fields of ruins and a shattered landscape of unknown scope. Again and again, we have to take cover from artillery fire and bombs. In the early evening hours, we reach the 71st Infantry Division, which is well situated in positions the extend down to the Volga and face east. As everywhere, an end-of-the-world atmosphere rules. The divisional commander, Lieutenant General Hartmann, has been killed. Many officers and men have shot themselves. Alcohol is flowing, martial songs are sung, and constant shots are heard in between. We have to get out of here.

For the time being, we remain in a company command post, discuss our plans, and then asked to be briefed on the sketches and maps of the minefields and other blockades that have been erected in front of the main line of resistance. It has become dark, and so the briefing is delayed until the following morning. We let ourselves drop onto some empty cots, which are more comfortable than anything we've had in a long time.

January 27, 1943. Flight to the South on the Ice of the Volga.
On January 27, 1943, the Wehrmacht communiqué brings the following report about the events in this city: "The parts of the 6th Army that are still capable of fighting hang on to the ruins of the city of Stalingrad. Giving their utmost in all defensive situations in the face of incessant Soviet attacks on the ground as well as from the air, they tie up the forces of several Soviet armies. A group of enemy forces that had penetrated into the city was destroyed in bitter fighting." In the OKW war diary, it is written: "In Stalingrad, the enemy occupied the southern part of the city down to the Zariza. On the western front, attacks were beaten off. The supplies in the city have been exhausted. Capable commanders still are trying to form defensive groups from the stragglers, whose number, with that of the wounded, has risen to 30,000 or 40,000."

Throughout the entire night, we can hear the noise of fighting, which increases to the north. Sometimes, we can hear machine-gun fire and tracer rounds whistling down to the Volga. Up here, we stand in our bunker and look out into the night, which is icy and bright with stars. Suddenly, we hear aircraft again, and then we see them coming. They are He111s looking for German troops at low level. They drop supply bombs. Some of them must have landed nearby behind us, but the majority, however, land in Russian territory. A few come around again at very low altitude. We can clearly make out the crosses on the wings. Begging, we look up at them: "Guys! Get us out of here! Before we croak! You'll be back and in safety in a few hours!" But they fly away in the illumination of the burning city to the west and very quickly vanish from our sight.

When daylight comes, an engineer sergeant shows us the positions. We look down on the gigantic white desert, the wide stream of the Volga. It's an imposing view. Apart from that, though, nothing can be made out in the bright haze that covers everything to the east. There are a few dark spots that have been caused by bombs and shells. There's no movement out there, just the roar of artillery fire. All the positions here are occupied. The infantrymen of the 71st Infantry Division are standing everywhere, ready to beat off Soviet attacks. Under normal circumstances, no attacker could reach the banks here; they'd be mowed down while closing in. It's just a matter of time, though, before this position will fall into Soviet hands without any fighting; they'll simply come from the west and suddenly appear behind the infantry because nobody will be able to stop them. These are the thoughts that pass through our heads while the sergeant explains the layout of obstacles.

We quickly note recognizable points that we'll be able to see in the darkness. Then we establish the order in which we'll pass the obstacles and progress south on the ice. Lieutenant Moritz will go first, and I'll follow. Then will come Sergeant Bellmann, Staff Sergeant Eckelmann, and Lieutenant Bonz. Moritz asks a few questions, and the good engineer is dismissed. Shaking his head, he wishes us good luck, although he doesn't think much of our attempt. The men here will probably fill up with alcohol and then end it all with a pistol after listening to the national anthem once more.

Not us! We will at least try to seize the only chance of avoiding perdition. We don't want to surrender, nor do we want to let things take their course. Now we begin to question our dress. Should we take off our orders and badges? Should we take off our shoulder straps and rank insignia? No, we won't do that. If the Soviets were to catch us or shoot us, at least they would see immediately what kind of people we are—soldiers of the front lines, not rear-echelon stallions.

We discuss are advance to the Volga once again, eat some of the marching rations that remain, and lay ourselves down. Sleep is out of the question, but we doze a little and wait for the onset of darkness. Finally, it is time. We shoulder our packs, and without making any noise, we go down to where we know the Volga is. Quickly, we reach the first barbed wire and then the "alley" which the engineer sergeant showed us in great detail. We march through the obstacles, some of which we have to push away.

In front of me, there's a muffled explosion followed by a suppressed cry and loud cursing. Lieutenant Moritz has stepped on a mine. My God! He's wounded in the foot and bends over in pain, collapsing to the ground. We cannot see anything but feel the warm blood running into the snow. Sergeant Bellmann treats the foot and binds it up. With strenuous effort, we force the foot into the boot again. How long with Hans Moritz be able to hold out? He wants to continue and doesn't want to be left behind.

Now I lead the group and head straight for the middle of the Volga. But where is the middle? The river isn't a flat ice plain; there are mountains of ice shoals that have crawled on top of each other. Machine-gun fire bursts from the other bank; parachute flares brighten the scene. We throw ourselves down, and as soon as the parachute flares go down and darkness returns, we stand up and march onward. We climb across the hard, angular mountains of ice, and then another wide

plain. Flares continue to go up, and we go down. It is a murderous process that robs us of our last strength.

There are voices on the right bank, shouts and cries in
Russian. Behind it, there's the brightness of a burning Stalingrad. It is a truly horrific picture. After hour of this difficult
march, we are tried and broken. We slow down. Lieutenant
Moritz suffers great pain. We cannot carry him or support
him anymore. Again and again, we have to take cover, then
get up and begin again to gain another piece of ground.
Then it becomes more quiet on the bank, giving us time to
catch our breath.

Since we left the positions of the 71st Infantry Division, we
have been on the move for eight hours. Now we must risk getting to the bank and find a hide-out in which we can hold out
undiscovered for the day. Carefully, at great intervals we work
our way toward the bank and assemble our group in the cover
of a steep slope that rises inland. Then we follow a ravine and
reach a deserted fighting position with entrenchments, dug-
outs, and winterized earth bunkers. For the time being, we
continue. Then, amidst these positions, we find a hide-out in
which we can vanish from the earth during the bright daytime,
safe from discovery.

January 28, 1943. Last Hours of Freedom.
On January 28, the Wehrmacht communiqué reports: "In Stalingrad, the heroic defense of the defenders has been broken.
Attacks of the Soviets against the western and southern front
collapsed under heavy losses for the enemy." The OKW war
diary notes: "Despite the hopeless fight in Stalingrad, the
enemy attacks were repulsed once again."

Meanwhile, we lie exhausted, tired, and frozen in a small
earthen bunker and try to quiet down and warm ourselves
somehow. It has become day outside, and we can see the area
around us clearly. It seems to be deserted over here until Staff
Sergeant Eckelmann, who has guard duty at the moment,
excitedly whispers, "Someone's coming . . . Russians! Apparently, they are searching the bunkers and abandoned posi-

tions." Tense, we listen to further reports from Eckelmann until he has nothing more to say and tiredness has overwhelmed us. Then, all of a sudden, I'm awakened. It's 1400 hours—my turn to stand guard. Lieutenant Bonz lays himself down in my spot, and I stare at the terrain in front of us. Where's my father? What has happened to the 371st Infantry Division? Nothing is moving out there; everything is covered in white but seems gray and dirty. I don't see any Russians and only hear the noise of their artillery. At 1600, I wake the others.

We plan to eat something, prepare ourselves, and leave by 1800 hours. By 1730, it has been dark for a long time, and we leave the comfortable warmth of the bunker and step out into the icy cold. We want to get away from this miserable hell. We march in a column across fields through snow and over slopes and sunken roads. After a short time, we are already frozen in our thin clothing and cold leather boots; we are incapable of protecting ourselves from the stabbing and biting cold. Meanwhile, Lieutenant Moritz suffers even greater pains and has great difficulty continuing. But he does not quit—he cannot quit! If he did, all would be lost for us.

After marching for about two hours and gaining little ground, we take a short break and gather our strength for the journey. If we reach a road or street that leads to the southwest, we should use it in order to make better progress. That's what we do when we come to a road that has been driven flat. We orient ourselves and march toward the southwest; we're now moving significantly better and without great exertion. The hard snow crackles under our boots; our breath seems to light up in the air.

What's that over there? We slow our pace. For God's sake! We are in the midst of many earthen bunkers that are probably used to house troops. White smoke rises everywhere in contrast to the dark sky. Here and there, a bit of light flashes when a bunker is entered or left or doors are opened and closed. What do we do? Continue marching? Go around? Wait in some cover? We make a quick decision to keep going. We march quickly but like a group that is near the end of its journey.

All of a sudden, we are challenged by a guard who is making the rounds in front of a bunker. He's walking to and fro in short steps and then shouts something to us. He's about 200 meters away. What do we do next? Make a run for it on the double or continue marching quietly, very quietly? We choose the letter and remain in columns, holding the march tempo. Sergeant Bellmann shouts out, "Karacho, all the best, comrade!" The guard stops for a moment, looks in our direction, and finally disappears into a bunker. Onward! We need to get away from here. We sense that something bad is developing.

On January 29, the Wehrmacht communiqué offers the following from Stalingrad: "In Stalingrad, furious enemy attacks against the southern front are in progress, which the defenders face up to despite the hardest privations and the great superiority of the enemy." The OKW war diary adds: "In Stalingrad, the enemy penetrated the Zariza front west of the railroad. Here and on the northern front of the southern group new defensive lines had to be built. The northern group continued its resistance. Wounded and sick no longer can receive any sustenance."

CAPTURED BY THE RUSSIANS

January 29, 1943. Surprised and Shot Up.

It is already after midnight. January 29 has come. Will we make it? By now, we must have put about twenty kilometers behind us, away from the city of Stalingrad. In a wide bend, the road leads in the direction where we hope to disappear into no-man's-land. We cannot see far ahead; small hills and ravines limit our forward view. At the moment, Lieutenant Bonz is leading; behind him, Sergeant Bellmann; then me; then Lieutenant Moritz and Staff Sergeant Eckelmann in the rear. The snow is crackling under our leather soles. The wind is blowing icily in to our faces.

Suddenly, there's noise in front of us—voices and horse hooves. A wide sled is galloping toward us. Should we jump away from the road into cover? Should we fire? Before we can act, Soviet machine pistols open up. There are shouts, orders, and more bursts of fire. "Hands up!" I'm hit in the left arm and collapse to the ground. Bellmann is shouting something at the Russian. Two Soviets throw themselves at me. One is kneeling on me, and the other is aiming his pistol at me and shouting words I don't understand.

Another shot rings out, followed by a cry next to me, and then there are only four of us. With shouts and violence, we are herded together and searched. We are prisoners of war. It's over, finished. What's hit me? I don't feel anything anymore. I don't know what has happened or what I went to the ground. We have to hold our arms clasped over our heads, and with machine pistols aimed at us, we are individually marched to the bunkers—the same ones we passed a while ago. Inside is the staff of a Red Army unit.

We are shoved into a bunker and thoroughly searched again. Except from our personal belongings, everything is taken from us. We take off our camouflage jackets, and we stand there in our uniform coats with orders and medals on our chests. No one takes them; no one removes our medals, watches, or other belongings. We sit on stacked planks and wait to be interrogated, beaten, and tortured.

Early in the morning, I am led to another bunker, where I wait in a front room. Then it's time. I am shoved into an adjoining room. Behind a flat map table, a Soviet officer, a major, sits. He immediately asks, "Name, rank, unit, mission?" When I tell him nothing except for my name and rank, the major tells me, "You are from the 14th Panzer Division."

In the meantime, unnoticed by me, a puddle of blood has formed to the left of me. Blood is running from my left sleeve and dripping onto the floor. The major sees this and has me ushered out with brief instructions. What will happen now? I am led to a bunker far to the rear, whose entrance is decorated with a Red Cross flag. We enter this bunker and are in an operating room where Russian nurses and other medical personnel are present. A Red Cross nurse takes off my jacket and opens the left sleeve of my blouse and shirt. Then she starts to clean and treat the wound. After half an hour, my wound is bound up. Subsequently, I am brought to my comrades, who are squatting in the corner of a bunker and trying to cope with the experiences and the things that are still to come. Sergeant Bellmann is not among them anymore.

Prisoner of War of the Red Army from January 29, 1943.

We are in Soviet captivity—wounded, broken, physically and morally at the end of our rope. What will happen now? What will they do with us next? Will we still be able to muster the strength to face up to that which is inevitably coming for us and live through it in a decent manner? We don't know. We have no answer to these questions. Russian noncommissioned officers, whose dug-out we're sharing, try to strike up a conversation with us.

They are not scornful. No, they admire us and even regret our fate. To each of us, they explain their badges of rank and tell us about themselves and their families. The food—kacha, meat, and bread—is ample. It is given to us with the words: "Eat! Soon there'll be little food for you. When the others to the rear have taken you over, you'll be in for a damn bad time!" We are wondering about these words and the behavior of these Russian soldiers. Front soldiers probably are like that everywhere. That's how we always treated our prisoners before we sent them off to the rear. But we had not expected something like that here, and a small sprinkle of hope and confidence springs up in each of us.

But in a short time, a very short time, we will experience things that will change everything completely, the beginning of a path of suffering which most of us will not survive.

Tanks of the 14th Panzer Division move out toward Stalingrad.

A battle group prepares for battle southwest of Stalingrad,
August 1942.

Romanian soldiers on the watch, waiting for a sign to move out.

Heavy German flak and artillery fire on Russian defenses
around Stalingrad, September 1942.

German 8.8cm flak in action at Stalingrad. The city burns in the background as the result of wave after wave of Stuka attacks.

Parts of units were thrown together as "fortress battalions."

Panoramic snapshots of the quarters of the battle groups and fortress battalions.

Burying the dead in the cold ground.

The last positions are held.

Scrounging up supplies.

The grain elevator.

Romanian artillery awaiting their orders.

General Hoth at the Romanian command post.

Outskirts of Stalingrad.

The ruins of Stalingrad. Every pile of rubble is a possible
hideout for snipers.

CHAPTER 3

The Final Fight for Berlin, 1945

Albert Liesegang

I arrived in Berlin from the 329th Field Replacement Battalion, 329th Infantry Division, and was thrust into the final fight for the capital of the Third Reich. In April 1945, I had become an aide in a newly raised regiment, called "Northwest" and commanded by Colonel Seifert, who was headquartered in the police barracks at the Alexanderplatz. On April 21, 1945, the codeword "Scharnhorst" went out: highest alarm!

Our staff established its command post in the safe cellar of a bank, where we were thrown together to form a new unit with all the soldiers we could find: soldiers from storm companies; naval and air force troops who had arrived here before the ring around Berlin was closed; Hitler Youth boys who had volunteered when the alarm went out; and stragglers from all the branches of service who were constantly rounded up at collection points (no one could escape these checkpoints, and if they refused to serve anymore, they could be shot or hanged as deserters).

Fortunately, our battalion and company were led by officers who had experience at the front. They came to us from military hospitals and "leader reserve courses." We had all kinds of rifles, but it was difficult to find ammunition for them, so only a few were useable. We also had some Czech mortars.

We had a good connection with the artillery firing positions at the Berliner Zoo (*Tiergarten*). An active special leader was assigned to us; he was an expert on the telephone lines and could complete even the most complicated connections. More than once, he succeeded in contacting the Ivans who had overtaken German command posts that we still assumed to be in our hands. Because of these communications, we often had a better idea of the whole situation than our own commanders.

The aid station was set up in the cellar of the Castle, and very soon, it was already overcrowded with the many wounded who came in from the fierce battle. Suddenly, an officer from an antitank company stopped and asked me to tell him the best way to get his company to Köpenick. I told him that the Russians were already there. He didn't have any other orders, so we agreed that it would be better for him to stay here and help us defend the position. So the antitank unit took up defensive positions at the Alexanderplatz.

The fight for the center of Berlin soon began. Strong Russian artillery fire constantly fell in our area. Shells hit the top of the cathedral, the venerable Pergamon Museum, and the Castle. Despite all this, we believed that we still could win because we kept hearing on the radio the reports of the gauleiter and Propaganda Minister Goebbels that Army Wenck would be here soon; their spearhead had already reached the *Tiergarten*. Meanwhile, the *Panzerbär* ("The Tank Bear"), Berlin's front newspaper, reported that the Soviets had overextended themselves and were now abandoned by the Allies. The bombardments had also stopped.

In the meantime, the Soviets' armored spearheads had reached the Alexanderplatz. Many Russian tanks were knocked out by our antitank company and also with *panzerfausts*. The Soviets came closer very slowly, afraid of our antitank weapons.

In the underground stations, disorder prevailed. The stations were full of citizens of Berlin who were looking for protection from artillery fire and walking around in corners and angles of platforms, together with refugees from the eastern areas. Children, mothers, and old people were asking for food and drink. In only a few cases was our field kitchen able to get food to them—and then only to the poorest among them. Only with a great deal of energy and the losses of the few men we had could our companies hold the above-ground rapid-transit railway from Alexanderplatz to Börse to Friedrichstrasse. Because of heavy losses, the regiment decreased to half its original strength in only a few days. Reserves from neighboring units filled out the gaps, but only for a short while because these men were not even trained to fight.

In this difficult situation, Combat Commander Z ordered Regiment "Northwest" to be dissolved, and the command authority over the unit fell to Combat Commander A, to which Colonel Seifert was also subordinated. I went to Command Post Z, which was in the Aviation Ministry, and when I announced myself there, Colonel Seifert appointed me his first ordnance officer.

The command authorities in Z had changed. SS-Brigadeführer Krukenberg was now responsible for the protection of the Reich Chancellery and Hitler's bunker. The remainder of his units ("Nordland" and "Charlemagne") took up positions in the left section. These units fought until the bitter end. I know that these foreign volunteer untis sometimes fought harder than our own countrymen.

My task was now to lead the armed clearing up of the Potsdammerplatz and the Anhalter Bahnhof in order to halt the enemy penetration. With the support of a few Panther and Tiger tanks, we succeeded in several counterattacks and took back some house blocks. Heavy house-to-house fighting was costly, but our Tigers and Panthers did chase Ivan away at least a couple blocks, if only for a short time. Then I received the order to lead a combat patrol toward Spittelmarkt since the Soviets had succeeded in penetrating behind "Nordland" there. I was to have a company for the purpose.

This company seemed to have been very hastily formed. It consisted of naval soldiers flown into Berlin not long ago; older *Volkssturm* men; and young and even veterans soldiers rounded up as stragglers. After examining these men and their armament, I ensured that we obtained suitable ammunition for the different rifles they carried. With three machine guns and some antitank guns, we pulled out along the Leipziger Road toward Spittelmarkt.

On our way out, we took the first casualties from Russian artillery fire. We divided ourselves into small groups, and in short jumps, group after group, we finally reached the edge of our objective and observed that it was till free of the enemy. When I tried to secure the inlets of the roads, however, all hell broke loose. An enormous artillery assault forced us to find cover in nearby cellars and fight the Russians from there. Slowly but steadily, they still advanced on us. I was wounded in my left arm by an artillery shell fragment. The explosion collapsed a wall, which fell down over me, and I was disoriented. I regained my senses when medics carried me back into the cellar of the Aviation Ministry.

At the aid station in the cellar, a medic treated me, and my arm was wrapped up; further fighting seemed to be out of the question for me. Gloom prevailed in the cellar as the wounded groaned and feared that the enemy could shoot into the cellars at any time. The main line of resistance was at that time only a few hundred meters away. As soon as I gained some strength, I went back to Command Post Z, which wasn't far from where I was. There I saw that we had succeeded in holding the Spittelmarkt after our own tanks had been thrown into the battle.

Men of the *Volkssturm*.

A young soldier learns how to use the *panzerfaust*.

Alfred Regeniter.

CHAPTER 4

An Assault Gun Commander's Story

Alfred Regeniter

ALFRED REGENITER'S BACKGROUND

Alfred Regeniter was born on January 13, 1922, in Rade-vormwald in the Bergisch Land, Rhineland, the second son of schoolteacher Friedrich-Wilhelm Regeniter. The latter taught in the German colony in Buenos Aires before 1914 and, at the start of World War I, was smuggled—because of the British blockade—as a stoker on a Swedish freighter to serve with the German colors. From 1914 to 1918, the elder Regeniter served with the naval infantry near Dunkirk, at the Somme, and near Verdun, rising to the rank of lieutenant.

Alfred spent five years at the town *Rektoratschule* (middle school) in Radevormwald and then four years at the *Röntgen-Real-Gymnasium* in Remscheid-Lennep, where he graduated at the beginning of March 1939, passing his *Abitur* with a "very good" mark. Two weeks later, he was drafted into the 4th Battery of the 206th Artillery Replacement Battalion (*Artillerie-Ersatz-Abteilung 206*) in Braunsberg, East Prussia. Four weeks after that, he went to the best troop in the west, the AVT (*Artillerie-Vermeßtrupp*) with the staff of the 4th Artillery Battalion of the 255th Infantry Division at Herongen on the German-Dutch border.

At the beginning of the French campaign on May 10, 1940, he marched through the southeastern tip of Holland as a gunner, then through Belgium via Louvain, Brussels, Namur, and Cambrai in the direction of Dunkirk. After the armistice, the

255th Infantry Division was transferred to the 10th Battery near St. Gilles in Chateau de Beaumarchais, where he was promoted to lance corporal in autumn 1940 and took part in an officer cadet course (*O.A. Kursus*). Here, instead of the old, obsolete Heavy Field Howitzer 13 (*Schwere Feld-Haubitze 13*, or SFH 13), which dated back to World War I, the unit was reequipped with the modern long-barreled SFGH 18.

In January 1941, he moved to the 11th Battery in Aiguillon-sur-Vie, and in February, the unit was transferred to the east by train—first to Peilau near Reichenbach in the Eulen Mountains in Silesia. Here continuous battery exercises took place, as well as a marching exercise with firing practice on the troop training ground at Wischau in Czechoslovakia. Regeniter was promoted to corporal. Then the unit marched to the troop training ground at Radom, Poland, and in April to the Soviet-German border.

On June 22, 1941, at 3:15 A.M., the sudden storm of shelling on the villages beyond the Bug began. The Russian campaign had started. Near Wlodowa, Regeniter crossed the river and then the Pripyet marshes in an endless march through heat, mosquitos, and dust. He was in constant action, employed as leader of the ranging troop and later as forward observer in Bereza-Kartuska, Slutsk, Kobryn, Zhlobin, Bobruisk, Rogatschev, Smolensk, Vyazma, Mozhaisk, and Ghatzk, all the way to Ruza.

At Ruza, Corporal Regeniter experienced the counterattack of the fresh Siberian troops near Panovo, forty kilometers from Moscow, in a biting frost (as low as minus 54 degrees Celsius) and deep snow. In an infantry action with a handful of people he had gathered together, Regeniter defended this village until nightfall so that the heavy horse-drawn 150mm howitzers could be brought to safety. He was wounded and subsequently treated in a hospital in Vienna. After his convalescent leave, Regeniter reported to the 4th Battery of the 206th Artillery Replacement Battalion in Bautzen. Here he tried to sign up for the Afrika Korps, the Luftwaffe, and even medical studies in order to avoid being posted back to the horse-drawn artillery—but in vain.

Via the Königsbrück Training Grounds, where he was introduced to the legendary Subhas Chandra Bose and the "Legion Free India," he traveled by train back to the Eastern Front with replacement troops for the 255th Infantry Division. But first he was routed by mistake to the 225th Infantry Division near Leningrad, and then he was taken on an adventurous detour through partisan attacks and blown-up railways before finally reaching his old unit, which was stationed in Temkino on the Ugra River in the center section of the front.

Starting in September 1942, Regeniter was employed again as a forward observer, this time with the 12th Battery of the Heavy Artillery Regiment of the 255th Division, with whom he saw action on the Worja and Ugra Rivers. It was relatively quiet compared to the drama unfolding to the south at Stalingrad.

During the so-called "Buffalo movement" (*Büffelbewegung*) in March 1943—which straightened the front salient east of Vyasma in order to free twenty-two divisions—Corporal Regeniter was posted to the assault artillery during the withdrawal. He joined the 400th Assault Gun Replacement and Training Battalion in Deba-Debitza, Poland, where he took part in a training course and, after the battalion had been transferred to Frederikshavn in Denmark, was posted as one of thirty participants in the fourteenth ensigne course at the artillery school in Grossborn, Pomerania.

From Grossborn, Regeniter—now a senior ensign—went to the Assault Artillery School in Burg, near Magdeburg. With secret orders, the assault artillery men were transported to Breslau, where Regeniter was seated twenty meters from the dais in the *Jahrhunderthalle* when Adolf Hitler addressed the 10,000 lieutenants at the school. The Führer told them to lead by example and die by example—horrifying and macabre.

In March 1944, Regeniter, whose promotion to lieutenant had been backdated to December 1, 1943, joined the 276th Assault Gun Brigade (*Sturmgeschütz 276*) in the field near Burg.

After being seriously wounded at his gun on February 10, 1945, Regeniter had the luck to escape from Eastern Pomerania in a hospital train before the Soviets broke through to the Baltic. In Kronach, Upper Franconia, he witnessed the entry of the Americans after an artillery bombardment. When the Russians occupied Thuringia, he fled from the hospital, which was guarded by Poles, through a back window on the third floor, and ran across a hedge, not knowing that the Russian advance stopped fifteen kilometers away.

He began his medical studies in Bonn in the winter semester of 1945–46, still plagued by an open wound in his upper thigh. After having spent five and a half years with the army, he graduated with a degree in physics, and after six more semesters in the medical college in Düsseldorf, he passed the state examination with "good" marks. During this period, while married and raising two children, he earned his keep for his family and paid for college by working as a controller on the tramways, then a nighttime telephone operator with the British phone lines, and even an unpaid assistant at the medical college.

After working in various clinics, Dr. Regeniter settled in as a specialist in orthopedics at Düsseldorf until he retired twenty-six years later at the age of sixty-six. In 1988, his old leg wound had to be cut out completely because of a malignant tumor—a "souvenir" from the war.

OPERATIONAL REPORT OF LT. ALFRED REGENITER

This is my report of my service with the 276th Assault Gun Brigade, which was completely wiped out during 1943–44 in the encirclement of Brody and Tarnopol, although it managed to save 90 percent of its personnel.

From May 8 to October 1, 1944, the brigade was re-equipped "down to the last button" in Deutsch-Eylau (Western Prussia). I arrived here as a "freshly baked" lieutenant from the Artillery School at Grossborn in Pomerania (previously in Jüterbog) and the Assault Artillery School at Burg near Magdeburg. Together with 200 other lieutenants, I was dismissed upon graduation with a firm handshake from the school's commander, Colonel Hoffman-Schönborn, who had earned the Oak Leaves to the Knight's Cross.

At eighteen years of age, I was already a veteran of the 1940 campaign in France and the campaign in Russia from 1941 to 1943, where I served as a corporal and forward observer with the heavy battalion of the 255th Artillery Regiment. Like most assault artillerymen, I was a volunteer. Only six men from my old battalion managed to join this new arm. I was helped in this by my old friend and comrade August-Wilhelm Vogel, who had been in France with me as a lance corporal and who was now a lieutenant and battalion adjutant. During the autumn of 1944, I would meet him again in Eastern Prussia, where he was a captain and the adjutant of an artillery regiment in the 549th Volksgrenadier Division. Years later, in 1956, I would be one of two people to answer for his conduct when he was trying to be reactivated as a captain. He would go on to serve as a brigadier general and the first postwar German military attache to Moscow.

In Deutsch-Eylau, we noticed many of the events on the nearby front. In Sommerau, we had a wonderful battery party with the local population. I went on marriage leave to Solingen and had a honeymoon without any problem in the coastal resort of Zoppot. In the officers' mess in Deutsch-Eylau, our adjutant, Lieutenant 1st Class Semke, approached me and handed me my transfer papers to the student company in Bonn, which I had wanted to enter two years previously so that I could study medicine. Without much doubt or debate, I told him to trash the telegram; I would stay with the unit because I was with the right "mob." This was no time to study. Today I think I made the right decision because it's possible that I would have been "wasted" with a student company in the Eifel Mountains or "kicked the bucket" in one of the American hunger [POW] camps near Remagen or Bad Kreuznach.

In Deutsch-Eylau, I noticed that during battery exercises, it was possible to talk by radio from gun to gun only by taking off one's steel helmet since the broad, jutting rim of the helmet made it impossible to wear headphones. Since it would be dangerous for the gun chief not to wear a helmet in the gun turret, I proposed to my commander that we obtain paratrooper helmets, which didn't have the rim. But where could we find some? Berlin was a possibility, so I was ordered to drive there with five men. At the Luftwaffe Supply Office in Berlin-Tempelhof, I called on all the authorities, from the *Generalluftzeugmeister* down to the *Generalintendant*, and I had to use all my persuausive skills to get 100 steel helmets. Helmets were a privilege and the pride of the entire Luftwaffe. Finally, we were given permission to drive down to Brandenburg, where we received 100 steel helmets (sizes 52 to 62) from the paratroopers' clothing store. We filled the six sacks we brought with us, and off we went with the sacks on our backs. The assault gun crews received the helmets enthusiastically. The 276th Assault Gun Brigade was the only army unit equipped with paratrooper steel helmets!

The veterans of the 3rd Battery first put me with a 10.5cm howitzer, which "was also fit for tank-destroying work." But soon I learned that loading a separate round and cartridge was very time consuming, and at the first opportunity, I switched to a 7.5cm gun. The following experiences in combat have been reconstructed from my diary, which I managed to preserve. It is the only written source regarding the 276th Assault Gun Brigade.

On August 4, 1944, we counterattacked northeast of Zwirgdaizai, Lithuania. Until seven o'clock, we managed to advance well, always through the corn fields from one tree-lined hamlet to the next. Even before we reached the old main line of resistance, we came under massive fire from enemy antitank and field guns firing over open sights. Three hundred meters ahead of me, I saw a Russian antitank gun; I could see the crew loading the gun. A high-explosive shell swept them away. Then about one kilometer away, I saw several Russians watching from a hill with binoculars. Almost immediately thereafter, an 8cm mortar shell burst 50 meters in front of our gun, followed by a second impact 50 meters behind the gun. Now the situation became dicey. "They're bracketing us," I thought.

I went down into the turret to give the order to move when the third shell impacted with an ear-splitting explosion right next to the flat turret. Everyone screamed with horror and shock. The 1.5-centimeter-thick covering plate was ripped and bent, but no one was wounded. If I'd still been looking out or if the shell had landed in the turret, it would have been curtains for me. We quickly changed position. Next to the shattered antitank gun were three dead Russians; their urn-shaped foxholes were empty. Soon afterward, we saw the destructive power of the Russian mortars with infantry Captain Merten, whose upper thighs were ripped away, probably by the same mortar. We bandaged his stumps. To this day, I can hear his East Prussian voice: "Please, lieutenant, take me back. I've got a wife and two little kids." We loaded him onto the gun. The next day, I learned that he had died.

We carried out counterattacks daily, including one on August 5 in conjunction with Panther tanks and infantry halftracks. I was always glad not to be in such a high tank, which offered a much better target than our low-slung assault gun without a turret. On August 6, 1944, the brigade destroyed five tanks.

On August 7, we began a renewed attack from Zwirgdaizai eastward. In a small wood about 200 meters in front of us, I saw a group of Russian infantry milling around. No antitanks guns were visible. Therefore, we would fire dispersing rounds. I gave the commands, "High-explosive shells with delayed action!" and "Aim at the open space 50 meters in front of the woods!" My loader quickly set each shell at a delay of 0.015 seconds, and off went the first one. In rapid succession, ten rounds were fired. The results of the 10.5cm ammunition exploding in the trees were truly horrifying. Then as we closed with the Russians at maximum speed, fifty men came toward us with their hands up, looking like giants in their long, earth-brown overcoats. Nevertheless, we remained careful. There were dead lying everywhere under the trees, even in their foxholes; some were killed by shrapnel penetrating their steel helmets. Their *kascha* (a stew of barley with bits of meat) was still

standing there uneaten; they must have been completely surprised. We let the prisoners pass to the rear and continued to
advance. While doing that, I saw First Sergeant Kampmann
fire at a fat Russian with his 7.5cm gun at a distance of sixty or
seventy meters: a direct hit! Only a few bits of the overcoat flew
up ten meters high (a beautiful soldier's death). It was like this
from 8:00 A.M. to 3:00 P.M. without pause, and the following
days were no different.

The situation became especially critical starting on August
15, 1944, when the Soviets launched a massive attack from Ver-
siai to Neustadt. We were attached to the 1097th Grenadier
Regiment of the 549th Volksgrenadier Division. During a
reconnaissance drive with the amphibious Volkswagen near
Totorcinai on August 16, our battery chief, Captain Stück,
encountered Russian infantry lying in the gutter on both sides
of the road. Here his driver Obergefreiter Naschenweng (I
always called him *Nasch-ein-wenig*—"Eat-a-little"—in jest) was
killed by a hand grenade and burned in the car.

On August 17, the Russians were one kilometer from the
seventy-ton bridge at Brämerhusen, which was completely without any cover. I made sure that the bridge was covered by the
2nd Company of the 277th, with five guns and thirty-five
infantrymen, and reported the situation to division headquarters. Accompanied by Battle Group von Werthern (under Freiherr Thilo von Werthen, who received the Knight's Cross on
Septebmer 8, 1941) and led by Capt. Edmund Francois, we
began an attack south toward Rockai ("Fir Height"), in which
we knocked out two tanks. The commander of the 3rd Battery
of the 276th, First Lieutenant Stück, is wounded in this action.
Lieutenant Sehrt—who, like me, is a platoon commander in
the 3rd Battery—takes charge of the battery.

On August 18, I attended a large O group. Major General
von Krosigk, commander of the 1st East Prussian Infantry Division, and Lieutenant Colonel Quentin of the 6th Panzer Division, 4th Rifle Regiment ordered an attack south of the
seventy-ton bridge at Brämerhusen in an easterly direction—
whatever the cost might be. We had to hold our lines until the

1st Infantry Division arrived, which could be brought into play only over the bridge. General von Krosigk was a magnificent organizer. He got us everything we needed, from munitions for the 2cm antiaircraft guns and 7.5cm munitions for the tank guns to 10.5cm ammo for the howitzers.

On August 19, our three guns—in the end, only Sergeant Major Kampmann was at Point 43 (Totorcinai)—beat off all attacks, together with Battalion Wollgemuth (under Maj. Karl Wollgemuth). Daily attacks and counterattacks followed one another.

On August 21, our battalion commander, Maj. Norbert Braun, was killed by a hit from an antitank rifle in the turret of his gun. The brigade buried him with full military honors in Ebenrode (Stallupöhnen).

From August 25 to October 11, 1944, a lull set in. Ivan had had enough for the time being and had failed in his objective of conquering Eastern Prussia as part of his great summer offensive. We really had put the wind up him.

Not until October 11, in cooperation with the 1090th Grenadier Regiment under Lt. Col. Karl-August von Bülow, did we have to beat off a strong Soviet reconnaissance in force east of Rutkiskai—some 100 meters south of the rail line Wirballen-Wilkowischen, as well as north of it. A murderous fire from both artillery and antitank guns lay upon our positions, and then the Russians broke through. At the battalion headquarters of the 1st Battalion, Captain Horstmar Menke showed us our positions. One platoon advanced left of the railway, and my platoon advanced to the right of it. With the 1st Company, we regained our own trenches. Hardly had I gained a flat slope twenty meters on the other side of the trench that enemy antitank guns opened up at a distance of 12 to 1,500 meters; we had many near misses. Fighting this many targets would have meant suicide. We quickly backed down the slope, still lying under murderous antitank fire. The old front line had been reestablished.

At Captain Menke's battalion headquarters, we were given schnapps and cigarettes. The Russians left 120 dead, 13 prisoners, a large number of machine pistols, one light machine gun, and three sniping rifles with telescopes. The young prisoners were full of brawn and naivete; they told us that they had been in their positions only since early that morning and had been sent forward by their officers.

By 5:30 A.M. on October 12, another local attack of the Soviets with 100 men is beaten off. After that, there was lively artillery activity from the Russians (acquiring their targets?) all day long, and they even used captured "DoGeräte."

On October 16, the magic starts: a massive Russian attack toward the west on both sides of the railway line. Our preparation area, the estates of Saugoniskai, is subjected to a very heavy drumfire barrage. A personnel bunker next to ours recives a direct hit, but the 1.5-meter-thick roof of the bunker holds. One man comes tumbling down the steps of our bunker, jittering all over his body with very heavy nerve shock, and he couldn't be quieted down. (I was reminded of the stories my father told about World War I at Verdun.) Two of the dug-in guns received direct hits; two others are towed away. On both sides of the railway, the Russians have broken through toward the west, exactly on the boundaries of the 1st Infantry Division and the 549th Volksgrenadier Division.

After the drumfire barrage died down, we immediately got into our guns. In a counterattack with the 1099th Assault Company, we advanced fighting for three kilometers to Boblaukis, but we met only Russian infantry, while three kilometers to our left, we saw fifteen enemy tanks and masses of Russian infantry flooding to the west; we could do nothing about it. Yes, the Russians exactly knew where our assault guns were positioned—and avoided them like the plague. When we drove past a Lithuanian cottage on our left, two comrades of a howitzer (my old one, number 331) came walking toward us. This howitzer had carelessly forced a way into the hedge-lined cottage without accompanying infantry and had run into enemy infantry who had immobilized the gun. When the crew abandoned the gun, my former driver, Gunner Mescher, had his head torn off by a hand grenade.

We immediately turned left and cleared up the situation. My driver, who had been a school friend of Mescher's, was shooting through the driver's eye slit with the machine pistol. Eight or ten Russians came out of the bushes, laid down, and hesitantly held their hands up. Perhaps there were still others sitting in the bushes waiting for us to come out of our gun.

It was horrible to see Mescher lying beside the howitzer without his head. Later, we put him on top and towed the gun away. Using paths and driving through wheat fields (which were full of Russians), we advanced to Boblaukis, destroying many antitank guns and machine guns along the way. It was a pyrrhic victory, however; in the evening, we had to evacuate our front salient again. The new front line lay east of Wirballen, where the bridge over the river Ost had been destroyed by bombs, so we had to look for a ford.

On October 17, we carried out an attack without infantry north of Bilderweiten toward Sandau in conjunction with five tank destroyers of the 1131st Tank Destroyer Battalion under Lt. Col. Freiherr von Schaumberger, during which ten antitank guns, one SU-85 assault gun, and one T-34 were knocked out. Together with the Leibstandarte Adolf Hitler, we advanced in the direction of Stanaiciai and Bajorai. While at the Zenthof estates, the 1099th Grenadier Regiment was subjected to a fierce Russian aerial attack, which caused serious casualties.

When we secured the area northeast of Sodargen on October 18, we suffered horrible bombardments from Stalin organs, and everyone fled back in a southwestern direction. Therefore, we were ordered to advance in conjunction with the Leibstandarte Adolf Hitler via Sommerkrug to Wabbeln. During this advance, an unbelievable shower of artillery bombardments and ground-support aircraft poured over us. We could barely see the neighboring guns for all the gun smoke and the mud splashed up by the impacts of shells. A 15cm grenade exploded in the meadow right in front my gun. The whole gun shook.

Once in Wabbeln, in front of the high plateau from which the Russians could spot all our actions, a lonely infantry captain, who was happy to see us, showed us to our positions from his slit trench. On the other side of Wabbeln, there were already Soviet tanks. I carefully drove through the village and took up an ambush position behind a hedge. Then I saw three large silhouettes of tanks on the horizon at a distance of 1,000 meters. My heart is jumping with joy; this is like being at the firing ranges. The Ivans don't suspect anything. I should be able to take them with three rounds. But it's not to be; no rounds hit. It's like we're cursed. The last shot we fire explodes in an apple tree 50 meters in front of us. The gun is completely out of order.

Now another 15cm grenade explodes in front of us. Our position has been spotted. We are rocked by near-misses. Now we throw the gun into reverse and take cover behind the houses. It is enough to make one cry. Although we are completely buttoned up, the young loader, Nickert, gets a shell splinter in his arm. Sergeant Amberg receives a direct hit, and his driver, Koscher, is killed.

On October 19, our brigade headquarters was located in Königseichen near Trakehnen. The stables of the famous Trakehner stud were empty. We received eight new guns.

In the afternoon of October 21, we undertook an attack with eight guns from Kleinschellendorf (three kilometers southeast of Hainau on the road from Schlossberg or Pillkallen) to Ebenrode (Stallüpöhnen) to the northeast. We completely lacked elan and barely got beyond the starting line in front of the gardens. Noone ventured out into the open terrain behind the village. We were glued to our houses because a massive fire from antitank and tank guns set in as soon as one of us showed himself. In the gully to our left, the Russians were milling around, and I shelled them with high-explosive rounds. Then I recognized in my binoculars, at a distance of 2,000 meters, a JS-122 assault gun standing without cover. Each of our six armor-piercing shells hit exactly on the mark; we saw the tracer curve toward the target—slower and slower—six times; all bounced off! No wonder: the turret alone had an armor of 30 centimeters. Only with luck did we manage to pierce it between the turret and the fuselage; otherwise, we would have to close in to under 400 meters.

When dusk set in around 4:30, we assembled east of Kleinschellendorf in an open field. My boss, First Lieutenant Stück, stood next to me and from his turret reproached me for not advancing. But he himself had also remained standing in the foremost gardens! It had been a rather clueless advance anyway, without any tactical planning. I swore to myself that I would act differently next time. Stück's reproaches upset me, and when he ordered me to attack the village "bie Abbau" to our left, I made a furious left turn with my gun and nearly got stuck in a deep Stuka bomb hole that we had not spotted in the darkness. We drove toward the brightly burning fire in front of us on the flat slope. The bridge over the gully, where I had fought Russian infantry in the afternoon, is still intact, God be praised. Both my loader and I loudly shout "Hurra!" over the humming of the engines and fire our machine pistols into the bushes on our left and right in order to keep the Russians and their hand grenades away from us. I still could see the torn-off head of my first driver, Mescher, in my mind.

We drove blindly into the dark, into unknown terrain, upslope on a dirt track. When we were about 200 meters from the burning haystack—which is illuminating everything in its vicinity—I saw Russian infantry running from left to right toward the houses. In front of us, everything became uncannily quiet. The haystack crackled and glowed. I did not want drive into the illuminated area for fear of giving a tank or antitank gun a target to ambush. Since the Russians fled to the right, there positions had to be there, too. Therefore, I drove off the road to the left and around the illuminated area, all the while peering into the darkness in front of me. After about 100 meters, I turned to face the village.

Then First Lieutenant Stück came up with the other boxes. I fired a star shell and saw a knocked-out German assault gun in front of me. We had to be careful. Who knew what was creeping up on us in the dark? Between two long sheds, I spotted an alleyway with a dark mass. What was it? A pile of manure? A vehicle? A truck or tank? I gave the order: "Distance 100 meters, armor-piercing shell. Let me do the aiming." I pushed the head of the gunner out of the way. "Now do you see what I'm looking at? Fire!" And a T-34 exploded in flames.

With my heart still beating for joy, I made out an even bigger mass to the right of the exploding tank. "Man, it's a Josef Stalin! Same distance, armor-piercing shell. Fire!" And . . . bounce! The tracer, fiercely shaken, continued it trajectory in a different direction. Four shells ended up like that. Damn shit! All those hits and no result! Although I presumed that the Soviets had abandoned the tank in the meantime, one never knows.

I was shaking with excitement as I pressed my eyes to the gunsight and tried to aim the point of the targeting triangle at the spot where I thought I saw the joint between the turret and the fuselage. "Fire!" The tracer hit the tank and went straight through, but it didn't explode. A small flame licked the bottom of the fuselage, which I was now able to make out clearly as a black stripe. First Lieutenant Stück called out from behind, "We're going back!" What were we doing here in the dark without infantry? Two minutes later, the Stalin exploded in a giant fiery mushroom with flames shooting 100 meters in the air. What a sight! (The next morning, it was the talk of the entire front.)

We felt our way back with map and compass. At the crossing of a deep gully, we warned each other by shouting, and we elevated the guns to the maximum height so that they did not stick in the mud. Three kilometers to the rear, we reported to the regimental headquarters, ate, and topped off our fuel tanks and ammunition stocks. We slept in the cold vehicle.

On October 22, we were awakened from leaden tiredness after only an hour of sleep. It was 2:00 A.M. We were to launch another attack. This time, we would have 120 men, an entire 44 battalion. The infantrymen climbed on top of our guns, and we roared off into the darkness, over a narrow stone bridge in the meadows. Then we hung a left and saw a burning farmstead on a long ridge. That was our objective.

I drove toward that point at walking tempo because ten or twelve infantrymen were hanging from my gun like bundles of grapes. Then I realized that this farm had already been noted as occupied by the Russians several hours ago when we drove back. We were able to make out two long sheds in front of us; between them was an alleyway that was illuminated by the fires burning behind it. Judging from the previous incident, I suspected that the Russians placed their tanks in such alleyways during the night, and I saw that this alley could hide a tank. So I ordered, "Stop! Distance 800, armor-piercing shell, target . . . Now let me aim . . . Fire!" A T-34 exploded with a loud bang and bright fireworks.

What did my comrades in the other guns think of me now? Could they see in the dark? What did the Russians think? Enthusiastically, I shouted to Stück: "That's the third tonight!" I didn't know whether he could understand me over the noise of the engines and rifle fire. I continued to advance to the left in front of the house-covered hill, then stopped and fired a star shell, which lit up everything as clear as day. There! Close in front of us were three monsters, three Russian tanks. We stood about sixty meters in front of them. No orders were necessary now; the guns were already roaring. The first exploded. A new star shell went up. Then the second blew up, then the third. We were shouting with joy and relief, and I slapped Sergeant Strohbach, my gunner, so hard on his shoulder that it hurt.

Three burning torches stood in front of us, glowing and hissing and rattling in all directions; then their ammunition exploded. The Russians must be depressed about this. They had to think we had magic or a new night-sighting device—their positions had been so beautiful. The Russians withdrew, and at dawn, we retook the village without opposition. Our infantry took up covering positions in the direction of the enemy, and with our tracks, we ground up three light 3.7cm antitank guns and towed away a 7.5cm gun, a so-called *ratschbumm*. Five tanks in one night—not bad for a start. The "old sweats" now looked at their new lieutenant with different eyes.

At ten in the morning on October 22—after an exhausted sleep of three or four hours—we renewed the assault with seven guns at Kleinschellendorf, which has been occupied by the Russians. First Lieutenant Stück was relieved, and I took over. We mob of infantry accompanied us. We got mired in a massive Russian assault launched from Kleinschellendorf toward the southeastern point of the woods near Hainau. The Russians wanted to get into the woods. We spoiled that for him because he had not counted on an attack from our side.

In the gully to the left, Sergeant First Class Seelbach killed two self-propelled 7.62cm guns, and some Ivans ran away from their burning guns. We fired what we could, and Ivan halted. On the left, the Russians retreated to Kleinschellendorf, but right in front of us, they dug in on a flat hill, where they put up a fierce resistance. Not even fifty meters in front of us, there were three Russians lying behind their Maxim machine gun in a hastily dug trench, and even at close quarters, they were firing at us in a tough and determined manner. Before our gun blotted them out, the extremely young forward observer from the 549th Artillery Regiment fell dead from our gun. I had just been talking to him, and I'm pained by his death. He had been so cheerful and spirited. We took him and his backpack radio with us when we left.

The Russians continued their fierce defensive fire. Our infantry, about 100 men, ran backward down the hill, and we stood in maddening artillery and antitank fire. The infantry lieutenant tried to rally his men, but in vain; they wouldn't go forward again. What else could we do but return to the starting positions on the southern edge of the woods?

North of "bei Abbau," ten to twelve Russian tanks drove to the right toward Kleinschellendorf; from time to time, they fired at us and damaged us. The distance of 1,800 meters was too great for us to do much, but we pinned them down nonetheless. When the other half of our guns returned from being resupplied with ammunition, we were able to withdraw as well. But the Russian tanks at "bei Abbau" should get what's coming to them. After all, we still have armor-piercing shells.

Therefore, together with sergeant Banaskiwitz's gun, I turned off to the right in an eastern direction from the long road through the woods leading to Hainau. I drove down a narrow road and took up a position beneath the trees at the edge of the woods. I saw how the Russians here have aimed their tanks for the woods. With two guns forced one behind the other on the narrow road through the woods, I killed two Russian KV-85 tanks at a distance of 1,400 meters. Two Russians baled out from one of them and disappeared behind the houses.

It became clearer to me that the Soviets wanted to enter our woods and then take the nearby town of Hainau. If their infantry reached the woods, Hainau would be lost, including the important communications route that ran through it from Schlossberg in the north to Ebenrode in the south. All of a sudden, we came under fire. The Russians saw my muzzle flashes! There were explosions in the tops of the trees, splinters whirred around, and branches fell on top of us. I wanted to withdraw, but Banaskiwitz stood right behind me, buttoned up. He didn't hear my shouting, and we had no radio communications. My loader had to get out, climb on top of the gun behind us, and tell them that way. It was a horrible situation to be under fire from the front and not be able to reverse. Thank God we were in the dark shadow of the trees. Finally, Banaskiwitz reversed, and we were able to do so ourselves.

At brigade headquarters in Hainau, where we took on new fuel and ammunition, our report and opinion on the situation were immediately passed on to the division. From the brigade commander, Captain Sewera, I got a few glasses of schnapps—and the Iron Cross, First Class. When I stressed the threat to the southern edge of the woods, my views were taken very seriously because, once the Russians trickled into the woods, they would have Hainau.

After eating, it was time to move forward once more. I had the last operational gun in the brigade. In the meantime, without assault guns as a backbone, our infantry had given up the southern edge of the woods. Hainau was under severe artillery fire. On the main crossroads, Gerlach's gun stood with a shot-off track. In the midst of fire, we helped repair the track, and we pulled it back onto the gun. Gerlach drove back to supply, and I told him to send reinforcements toward the eastern edge of the woods, which I now followed carefully in a southern direction. I did not like to go through the woods on my own anymore. Along the way, I picked up five withdrawing infantrymen who were pleased to follow me with their machine gun.

While aiming to the south, I saw how the Russians had already marched with tanks and antitank guns into the southernmost point of the Hainau Forest, which was already in Russian hands. I took up firing positions, destroyed three heavy antitank guns, and disabled a T-34 in front of the southeastern point of the woods. Now I had to watch out for the woods on the right. I sent two of the infantrymen with the machine gun to the edge of the woods on the right as close-in defense. I kept the other three near the gun. We were all alone and left to our own devices. Then one of the infantrymen climbsed on top and shouted, "Lieutenant, sir, tank noises in front of us!" I shut down the engine . . . silence. Then I heard it, too, the typical crackling noise of a Russian tank diesel in front of us, but I was not able to see it since it was apparently driving down a sunken gully. However, this gully ran out to the left, and the tank would have to pass down there. Quickly, I took up firing positions under a cherry tree next to a small house. And I was right: there came the tank—without infantry! "Fire!" The tank stopped and started smoking. One Russain crawled from the turret hatch. My ninth tank kill since last night.

We turned and drove back while keeping the edge of the woods at a safe distance. Not far from Hainau, we encountered reinforcements: three Hetzer tank destroyers that were sent in after me by Gerlach's gun as ordered. About twenty infantrymen have also assembled here. On the left, on the other side of the valley near Seidlershöhe, the Russians were advancing over open fields in large masses. I broke off the point by rapid fire, but I saw how the commissars drove their herds forward. Then the Hetzers opened fire at Iwan. We caused a blood bath. At last, the Russian masses began to retreat. Two tanks quickly disappeared behind the sheds. The advance was stopped.

Now I checked out the woods behind us. In my periscope, I saw some Russians crawling around in the bushes and setting up a machine gun. I was now completely out of ammunition. I shouted at the others and pointed to the edge of the woods to make them aware of the danger. Then I drove back. This was about 3:30 P.M. By 4:30, the Russians were in Hainau, which was burning like a torch. Our brigade headquarters was now located west of Hainau in Strehlau.

After being resupplied at 5:00, I secured the new front line west of Hainau, together with Sergeant Frech and Sergeant Banaskowitz. My gun fell into an infantry trench that ran straight through the fields. By midnight, we have repaired the gun and towed it away in the light of the fires in Hainau, which was only 300 meters away. Once again, we had three operation guns on the front (No. 331, 332, and 152, under Bartsch).

While in the infantry trench, something special happened to me. In the dark, I heard a loud voice with an Eastern Prussian accent over the noise of the spades and the shouting. I was stunned: it was Corporal First Class Schalk! In 1942–43, he was forward observer with the 12th Battery of the 255th Artillery Regiment in the sector of Army Group Center near Samytskoje-Bereski on the banks of the Ugra-Worja! I shouted, "Schalk!" A voice answered, "Here!" It was indeed Schalk. He was still a telephone operation, now with the 349th Volksgrenadier Divison.

Finally, I was relieved. At brigade headquarters, after seventy-two hours of continuous operations I fell asleep three times over a bowl of chicken soup, and our brigade's medical officer, Dr. Cordes from Cologne, had to wake me each time to continue eating. I slept for fourteen hours until my batman awoke me.

On October 24, Captain Sewera and First Lieutenant Stück took the old front line west of Hainau. I had to go back on account of gun damage. Subsequently, I was ordered to see Colonel Kötz, commander of the 349th Volksgrenadier Division. He drank a cognac with me, and his chief of staff, First

Lieutenant Reifen, offere me a "peacetime cigar." I was put up for the "mentioned in dispatches" clasp. (In 1986, I found out I was turned down.)

On October 25, the battle group of Colonel Kötz was mentioned in the Wehrmacht Report.

When I went to brigade headquarters at nine o'clock on the morning of October 26, Dr. Cordes and Lieutenant Schmidt, the adjutant, told me that Lt. Rudi Sehrt was killed earlier that morning. I wasn't able to cry, so great was my grief. I talked to his driver, who told me they ran over a mine in front of Strehlau and had to bale out. While doing that, Rudi was hit by a machine-gun salvo. One bullet went straight through his heart. He had recently borrowed the box for my Iron Cross, which he kept in his left chest pocket, along with his paybook and letters. The box was shot straight through the middle. Poor Rudi! He had suspected he would get killed. He had a girlfriend from Deutsch-Eylau, Käthe Pschak, who was pregnant with his child. He wanted to marry her as soon as possible. If he were killed, he asked me to tell her. What a sad duty! He had just relieved me and was in my gun. Why not me? My joy about the nine tank kills vanished. My best friend in the brigade was dead.

On November 17, we stood by in Burgkampen estate, the former camp of the Reich Labor Service. The front had quieted down and stabilized, and the Soviets had not succeeded in overrunning Eastern Prussia. We had played a considerable part in that. During the entire operation, the patented linked-up suspension mounting for periscopes in the turret worked extremely well, and all gun commanders had one fixed in their turrets. The guns came equipped with a short mounting fixed in the twelve o'clock position, which allowed observation only straight ahead; to look elsewhere was impossible without hitting one's head. Therefore, I constructed a second swinging mount with plugs for the periscope, which was mounted on the plugs of the existing mount in such a way that almost an entire 360-degree view was possible. Only an assault gun commander can judge what this meant in terms of security and observation, especially in operations without infantry in unknown territory. Most of the time, the so-called "round-view mirrors" on the turret were muddy or dusty and did not enlarge the view as the periscope did. In many cases, it was impossible to check the sides and rear with binoculars since it was too dangerous.

On November 25, north of Schlossberg, we were ordered to mount an attack on a high hill from which the Russians were able to see deep into our rear areas. They had had four weeks of "quiet" to dig in. Just before the attack, I received a telegram from my in-laws in Solingen: "Bomb damage." Certainly, any leave would have to wait until after the attack. It was an open question whether Captain Sewera or Colone Kötz would allow the leave.

On November 26, after standing by in Alderswalde during a terrain recce, I asked whether I could take a three-day leave. Sewera immediately approved it, but I told him that I first wanted to take part in the attack the next morning. Surely, he had not expect otherwise. In the woods that evening, Corporal First Class Tischler, my loyal Upper Silesian driver, told me, "Lieutenant, sir, I'd like to be as stupid as you one day. Instead of taking leave, you participate in this attack! Perhaps we'll all kick the bucket tomorrow." That was the way we comrades talked, thought, and acted.

At seven o'clock in the morning on November 27, we moved from our stand-by positions with ten guns—the complete battery—to the starting positions for the attack. One gun drove into a bomb crater on the way—a bad omen. Only hours later, with the help of two eighteen-ton prime movers, could it be pulled out. One gun had to be given up to the brigade commander, whose gun broke down. Another gun had broken its gear box while pulling out. Four guns, including my own, ran over mines in front of the Russian trenches. No one had given any thought to the Russian wooden box mines that had been buried twenty-five or thirty meters in front of their positions. Several of these cigar boxes could be seen lying on the surface after it rained. One gun was killed and burned out. Two guns

(First Lieutenant Stück and Sergeant Richter) gained the heights but could not hold them on their own under the massive defensive fire.

Twenty meters in front of the barbed wire, I was forced to halt by a torn track. The gun next to mine on the other side of the trench received a direct hit and burned out; the crew got out. With my crew, I was lying beneath the gun in murderous artillery, antitank, and mortar fire, which was so massive that both Strohbach, my gunner, and Nickert, my loader, were wounded—the latter with a round in the upper thigh. My driver, Corporal First Class Tischler, held out with me. It was a good thing that our "box" didn't get another direct hit and explode. At dusk, the shelling decreased and eventually stopped. Sergeant Major Pahlke towed us off in the dark, during which we were subjected to a Stalin organ barrage.

The attack showed that we were not able to do much anymore. Afterwards, I took my leave. After all I had been through, I could barely comprehend that I was about to see my hometown again. On December 13, I returned to my unit after an adventurous train ride. The 3rd Battery was positioned in Tannsee. Stück was promoted to captain and awarded the "fried egg" (German Cross in Gold). Five percent of the men were given leave.

On December 20, we were loaded onto trains in Gumbinnen. I was in charge of loading. Via Ortelsburg, we were to travel to Chorzele, deep in the south of "darkest" Poland. On December 21, we were unloaded at Chorzelle and marched fifty kilometers to Polozk, where we celebrated Christmas with speeches from the battery commander. Promotions and gifts were handed out. I received a bottle of wine, a bottle of Calisay, a bottle of apple juice, a crumbly cake, a raisin bread, a cake with cheese, a bar of chocolate, a Coca-Cola, fifty cigarettes, tobacco, liquorice, and other things. I was given richer presents than ever. In the evening, Sergeant Major Hufnagel and I inspected the quarters.

On December 28, we made night marches via Chorzele, Fraschnitz, and Zichenau to Grucin, about 100 kilometers. On

December 31, we made another night march through Zichenau toward Grudusk, about forty kilometers. Until six the next morning, we celebrated the New Year here after listening to a speech by Hitler.

January 13, 1945, was my twenty-third birthday. I celebrated with twelve officers of the brigade in Grudusk. We were all nicely blue. We skated on the village pond. When I saw a hare race over the snowed over fields at a distance of 100 yards, I shot him with one round from my carbine and later roasted him—a fine meal. In the evening, there was another celebration with the staff, because Lt. Erich Stüwe also had his birthday today.

On January 15, the expected Soviet offensive with four armies began from the Narew bridgehead—ten Russian divisions against one German division. We had no illusions. The front collapsed. Everything flooded back toward the northwest. There was half a meter of snow, and the temperature dipped 20 degrees below zero. In the evening, we took up withdrawal positions at Zichenau, which heavy bomber attacks have turned into a smoking rubble. Broken telephone masts, fires, and collapsed houses made passage virtually impossible.

On January 17, we change positions toward Bielsk. On the eighteenth, I transported the battery wagons to Gilino in snow and frost. I heard that we lost all guns. What will become of us now? The next day, the corps wanted to use us as infantry. Captain Sewera went to army headquarters to get new guns, and we wondered whether he'd be successful?

By January 20, we had no fuel or maps. Lieutenant Stüwe radioed in from corps: "Get the hell out of there as quickly as you can!" We marched in the direction of Leip-Thorn. Our new quarteres were in front of Skepewjichytsche on a German farm. The farmer's wife, left alone with the Polish trash, was supposed to meet with the local party leader to trek away early next morning at a road junction. I advised her to load up her cart immediately and head to the west. She refused to butcher a pig since there was a death penalty for "black slaughter." So I ordered it done and also had ten chickens plucked, which the Polish women were unwilling to do.

On January 21, we marched toward Kulmsee in the vicinity of Kulm, and we were billeted in a navigation school. We were able to acquire about 100 liters of fuel. The next day, we moved to the settlement of Herrmansdorf. At the army supply depot, an accounts clerk was sitting on top of his wares and didn't want to hand out anything, although we were in great need of food. Finally, he agreed to hand out the following: 4,800 cigarettes, forty bottles of schnapps, three bags of sugar, three kegs of marmalade, one keg of sauerkraut, and one keg of gherkins.

The commander came back from army headquarters. He had waited in Riesenburg in vain for our gun crews after his request for new guns had been approved. So twenty-four brand-spanking-new Panzer IVs with L70 guns were left behind for Ivan in Allenstein, which, in addition to Deutsch-Eylau, has fallen. Twenty-six men were loaded onto a truck and transported to army headquarters, where the commander still wanted to get new guns.

On January 23, we were supposed to cross over to the other bank of the Weichsel at Graudenz. Endless columns up to ten kilometers long stood on the approaches to the bridge. We had to wait for eight hours; there was simply nothing else to do. Then I saw a railway bridge 200 meters upstream. The trains weren't running anymore, and the truck experts can go to hell—we crossed there instead. We were billeted in Neuenberg, where prim and proper "youth teacher for the eastern territories" had little idea about the situation.

On January 25, we had nice clean quarters in Klein-Milwen, about five kilometers northeast of Neuenberg, in a castle with First Lieutenant Schäfer and Dr. Cordes. The next day, I drove to Danzig with four trucks in order to collect fuel at Baltische und Amerikanische Petrol. I drove on to Zoppot for a sentimental reason. In the Cafe Astoria, I bought a cake and some coffee made out of beans. My honeymoon hotel, Zum Stolzenfels, was now housing troops. I went by foot from Langenfuhr to Neufahrwasser. There I ate with the navy. In the harbor were two new U-boats, *Hamburg* and *Deutschland*.

On January 27, north of Mewe on the Vistula near Klein-Grünhof, I received eight new guns for my 3rd Battery. Each had two machine guns, one coaxial and the other free with a 360-degree field of fire. We occupied positions on a dyke along the Vistula facing east. The brigade headquarters was housed in the mayor's residence, whose windows were blacked out so that the Russians couldn't see us from the right bank of the Vistula. Mewe had been almost completely abandoned by its population; only a shoemaker was still open. In vain, I tried to convince the owner that when the Russians came, he wouldn't be able to continue in his trade, but he only wanted to sell shoes against a requisition form. Lt. Adalbert Mueller from the 2nd Battery beat off a Russian attempt to cross the Vistula south of Mewe with pontoons and ferries. They were shot to pieces, and many Russians drowned in the river.

On January 29, the 251st Infantry Division received its marching orders to get to Schwetz. The Russians were pressing toward the north. In a raging snowstorm, we marched eighty kilometers. My VW had to be dug out and hooked up to a truck. In Dretz, we went into corps reserve (XLVI Panzer Corps) and awaited fuel.

At nine o'clock on January 31, I got orders for the 3rd Battery in person from General Heuke, commander of the 251st Infantry Division, at his headquarters in Dretz: counterattack with the 184th Grenadier Regiment at Buchenau in order to make a link-up with the remains of the 31st and 73rd Infantry Divisions. In high snow, I drove to Buchenau. The village was right in front of us. Staff Sergeant Glaumann rapidly accelerated to a frightening speed, and we were barely able to keep up. Two Russian tanks disappeared behind the barns toward the right of the village. No shots had been fired yet.

Then I took the point and drove toward the right along the high street. On the left, a smaller street branched off. I had barely passed it when a round from a tank or antitank gun exploded in a house right behind me. Now I knew where they were hiding! Therefore, I guided the following guns through the gardens on our right side in order to circumvent this danger. Soon I was standing thirty meters in front of a T-shaped crossroads where the main road ran from north to south. To our left, Russians were swarming behind the hedges of the gardens. We opened up with machine-gun fire. Suddenly, one of the infantrymen who are accompanying us jumped into my gun: "Lieutenant, sir, there in front to the left, around the corner, is a Russian tank!"

It was about thirty meters away. With my heart beating rapidly, I coldly evaluated the situation. I decided to wait because I concluded that whoever was driving that tank would eventually grow impatient and advance. In the meantime, I wanted to force the enemy infantry—which assuredly was accompanying the tank—to retreat and aim for the top of the roof with a high-explosive grenade. I hardly had time to aim when my driver, Corporal First Class Tischler, shouted: "He's coming!" My loader quickly pulled a high-explosive grenade out of the chamber (we would have been done had it jammed) and threw in an armor-piercing grenade.

The Russian tank only peeked around the corner of the house with his barrel—miserable driver! Apparently, he didn't spot us. He came out once more and drove toward us in a large curve. Before he had a chance to stop, our shell penetrated its side. We pumped three more rounds into the SU-85 assault gun. An Ivan crawled out of the turret hatch and disappeared on the other side of the gun. We were overjoyed and relieved. We withdrew toward the southeastern part of the village, where the guns took up ambush positions.

It grew dark and spooky. In order to provide security, we torched the house on the corner, right where the antitank gun had taken a pot shot at me. We needed food. In the cellar of the large house next to our gun, there was an elderly, very corpulent, and apparently very ill German woman, the mistress of the house. She was lying on a bed of straw, accompanied by Polish scum. She begged and pleaded for us to take her back. We couldn't do it; she wouldn't fit into the gun and would freeze to death on top of it. Besides, what were we supposed to do with her later? One of the Poles said there was a smoking room on the top floor of a neighboring house, and by candlelight, we opened the lock and watched out for Russian machine-gun fire that could strike through the roof tiles. We loaded up with two giant smoked hams and several poles dangling with smoked sausages. Why should we leave everything for the Russians?

We accomplished our mission and killed an SU-85, captured an antitank gun, and destroyed five more. By 11:00 P.M., we withdrew toward Dretz. General Heuke informed us of his appreciation. We held the right wing of the 251st Infantry Division and made possible the withdrawal of the 542nd Volksgrenadier Division as well as the link-up with the remains of the 31st and 73rd Infantry Divisions from Thorn.

At eight o'clock on February 1, we received orders from the 251st Infantry Division to beat off enemy tanks operating south of Dretz. Suddenly, Russian tanks, acompanied by infantry, showed up. Without infantry of our own, we were able to hold onto Dretz until noon, but then we were flanked and had to withdraw. At 7:00 P.M., we blew the bridge over the Schwarzwasser in Sauermühl. The guns of Lindner and Hehling were at the 251st Infantry Division's headquarters. Those of Lieutenant Geil, Sergeant First Class Schwarzbach, and Staff Sergeant Kampmann broke down. Together with Staff Sergeant Kampmann, Sergeant Pahlke, Sergeant Fröbel, and Sergeant Oschee, I was in Osiec with the brigade.

On February 2, we were organized into new and secure positions with Battalion Brüggeman near Sauermühl.

On February 3, all eight guns of my battery were ordered into action with the 448th Grenadier Regiment (under Major Schulze-Hagen) near Dretschmin. During the march, the adjutant, a first lieutenant, came up to meet us in a *kettenkrad*, showed us our positions on the map, and led us to them without a recce. Along the way, we were collected by General Heuke of the 251st Infantry Division in person. It seemed that our arrival was desperately needed. We were honored. The general pulled out a bottle of schnapps and an entire package of Juno cigarettes. "Gun commanders to the front!" We finished the bottle, which gave us enthusiasm. The cigarettes made their way back toward the guns, which each had been carrying ten paratroopers (from the 2nd Parachute Flak Battalion) with First Lieutenant Uhrmann and Lieutenant Braksch, the tank killer. They were armed to the teeth with carbines, machine pistols, hand grenades, and *panzerfausts.*

First, we took up positions in the village of "A," about 1.5 kilometers in front of our objectives, which were the estate of Belino and, behind it, Katsau. We were at the side of the village to take cover from enemy aircraft. I drove the *kettenkrad* to regimental headquarters, where the commander informed me about the situation and our objectives. Afterward, he drove back to "A" with me. Now I wanted to employ—for once— what I had learned at the assault gun school in Burg. I knew from my own sad experience how it was to sit in a gun without a clue and then drive somewhere without knowing the situation or objectives. To prevent that, I was eager to give everyone down to infantry squad leaders our orders. Although the regimental commander opposed it and wanted to make haste, I ran down the village street and shouted, "All gun commanders, platoon commanders, and squad leaders, come with me!"

Once the room filled up, I pinned a 1:25,000 map to the wall and briefed them: "Here we are in 'A.' In front is our main line of resistance. Over there in Belino is where the Russian is sitting. We'll attack him. Belino is the village everyone can see on the other side of the valley at a distance of about 1.5 kilometers. Take care, though; our own boys, who'll be attacking with us, are not very far from the leftmost houses of the estate. We'll attack frontally, starting at 1300 hours after a bombardment by the artillery, first taking Belino and then Katsau. It's clear to us that the Russian has lined the edge of the village with assault guns, antitank guns, and tanks. Therefore, we'll have to take it in a coup de main. The plan of attack is as follows: forming-up positions for the assault are to be taken up on the far slope of the valley, without showing anything to the Russians. After the artillery bombardment, Glaumann's platoon will drive upslope with four guns but stop as soon as its barrels peek across the edge of the slope. Then it will open as rapid a fire on the edge of the village as is possible. Underneath this covering fire and making use of the surprise of the Russians, I'll quickly advance with my platoon to the middle of the 300-meter long harvested field and open rapid fire. And now Glaumann's platoon will drive into the village under my covering fire. After that, I'll penetrate the village frontally. After that, we'll advance on Katsau on a broad front, again in an outflanking attack. Is everything clear? Questions? None? Right then. Take up the forming-up positions!"

It was clear to everyone what was going on, and there was no need of more talk. By 1:00 P.M., we were in our forming-up positions, which we had reached without being spotted by driving through the valley. Now and then, individual shells from a light field howitzer howled over us and exploded in Belino in the "schnapps factory." Then there was a pause. At 1:10, Sergeant Glaumann suddenly advanced with his three guns to the edge of the slope, and fire cracked from all barrels. At first, I though he went bonkers. Our attack was supposed to begin with a preparatory bombardment from the artillery. But there was little else to do now. Glaumann started the attack, and we had to join in. (It turned out that Glaumann was right: those meager six or eight shells had been the bombardment.)

Immediately, I drove to the middle of the harvested field with maximum speed, stopped, looked around, and . . . I realized that I was standing there alone as a target on the wide open field. The three other guns of my platoon simply remained in cover and did not follow. All alone, I stood on the plateau. My heart was beating a mad tattoo, and I felt like I was being strangled in my throat. I thought that I was certainly done for, that in a few seconds I'd be blown away by a barking antitank gun or tank. The courage of desperation took hold of me, and I stook up on top of the turret and waved with my arms. "Come forward, you bloody bastards!" I had the feeling that I had only a few seconds to live, but then two guns drove up, thank God. (I later learned that Sergeant K had some damage to his engine or tracks at the exact moment he was supposed to break cover.)

The crash of a Russian round and the shell's air pressure blasted past my head.

"Lieutenant, sir," Strohbach shouts, "I see their fire!"

This time, the shell passed even closer overhead.

I shouted, "You've got it?"

"Yes!"

"Fire!"

A Russian assault gun in the bushes on the edge of the village burst into flames. Soon we were in the village, with the Russians running around and our infantry penetrating from the left. We drove past the burning Russian gun onto the giant farm. Standing close together are sixty cows, with Russians squatting between them, using the animals for cover. I had to go straight through the cows; it was horrible. Everything happened in a flash. The Russians fled, but around the corner of the last barn was an Ivan who kept peeking out and firing with his machine pistol. "We'll get you, sonny!" I yelled, firing a high-explosive shell through the barn. The Russian was gone.

All the Russians were running in a panic. Past the barn was an SU-85, moving about and seeking cover. It didn't want to withdraw in the direction of Katsau since it would've been killed for sure. We fired a round, and the Russian vehicle exploded. We took Belino! I have killed two assault guns. The total score: five armored vehicles killed (three SU-85 assault guns, one T-34/85, and one Josef Stalin 122—the last killed by Glaumann), two 4.7cm antitank guns, thirty prisoners (including a captain). We suffered no losses. Everyone was pleased and wanted to rest. No one was thinking of Katsau. To get there, we had to cross 1.5 kilometers of rolling terrain. In the general chaos, I stood up on the turret and pointed with both hands in the direction of Katsau, showing everyone the direction of advance. I left two guns near Belino to cover our new advance. Looking toward Katsau, we could see only two houses and a few high trees, with a kilometer-long wood next to it, sloping down to the valley of the Schwarzwasser at Sauermühl.

Soon we were advancing on a broad front with the infantry and paratroopers, whose self-propelled, four-barreled antiaircraft guns provided covering fire on the edge of the woods. It was fantastic to see the four bands of tracer at the same time. Having advanced about halfway to Katsau without having run into resistance, I suddenly heard aircraft noises. Seven German Stukas were circling above us. We shouted with joy, "Now Ivan will be in deep!" But what's that? I saw two Stuka's dive down on us, their horrible siren growing louder and louder; from their wings, a large number of high-explosive bombs (five kilograms) fell and came toward us in close bunches. Horrified, I dove down into the gun and shouted to my three men, "They're dropping their bombs on us . . . we've had it . . . we're finished!" The bombs exploded, and then I thought of the flares. I fired all our white flares and then started firing the red ones. I then fired a tracer in the direction of the enemy in Katsau. The Stukas got the message and curved away. They didn't drop their bombs on Katsau but instead disappeared.

It was a miracle we survived. One paratrooper was killed, and many were wounded. Major Schulze-Haten was bleeding from his head, and after the general paralysis was overcome, he commanded another attack while his head was bandaged—what a fellow! Soon Katsau was in our hands, and our job was done. Nevertheless, I drove my gun down a road in the woods. It was spooky. I had no infantry with me. Finally, I heard tank noises in the sunken ground near Sauermühl near the blown-up bridge. I left First Sergeant K—whose broken engine has been repaired—with two other guns, to which we transferred our remaining ammunition, in Belino for the night to cover the infantry. The rest of us drove back to Laskowiecze to stock up on ammunition and fuel and to eat and sleep. In Laskowiecze, there were mountains of field post packets and letters from loved ones back home. Now they were sure to fall into Russian hands.

On February 5, we attacked again, this time at Lniano with seven assault guns plus another six assault guns from the assault gun company of the 227th Infantry Division and forty paratroops from the 2nd Anti-Aircraft Battalion. While we advanced over the rolling fields toward Lniano, I saw a burning

German assault gun behind a pinewood while two Russian tanks disappared quickly behind some houses. Under cover, we tried to advance to Lniano frontally over a broad slope. The village was spread out in front of us about 1,000 meters away. With a great deal of luck, I killed a JS-122 and SU-85 between the houses.

Since we weren't able to advance frontally, I drove around to the right of the road that led to Lniano and through a gully in order to reach the village. While I was doing that, I spotted several Russian tanks coming from our rear; they were heading toward Lniano. I prepared to shoot the first tank in order to stop the Russian column, but it disappeared behind a small hill, showing only its turret. I ordered my gunner, Sergeant Strohbach, to aim at the hill just underneath the turret and a little in front of the tank. The tracer of our armor-piercing shell curved over the hill and disappeared behind it. The T-34/85 exploded! The other tanks turned tail.

Now we penetrated the village from the right. A German described to us how he had to watch in the cellar under gunpoint as his wife and daughter were raped by a dozen Russians. Another woman, who had seven gunshot wounds in her body and had been picked up by the Russians in no-man's-land, was raped by eight Russians despite her wounds. We were supposed to pass on such reports, which are horrid and not new to us, to higher authorities. But now we had no time for that. We had killed three SU-85s, one JS-122, one T-34/85, and two T-34s. We took one 7.62cm antitank gun and one truck and destroyed three antitank guns. We suffered no losses.

On February 6, we stood by in Osché. We also met our commander, Captain Sewera, who, together with his adjudant, Lieutenant Schmitt, came up to award the four Iron Crosses, First Class, and the thirteen Iron Crosses, Second Class, that I had proposed for the 3rd Battery for their performance. At this point, our gun had eighteen white rings around its barrel. I also received three extra Hetzer tank destroyers. For the following two days, we were on standby in Klinger.

During the night of February 10, we were billeted in a forestry house north of Stenzlau in a massive pine forest in stand-by positions. We were on the southern edge of the Tucheler Heath, a massive forest. The Russians were penetrating the woods from the south. In the morning, we received orders for action.

On long, narrow forest tracks, we drove forward. The front was thundering. At headquarters, in the deep cellar of a farm building in Eibenhorst, Captain Golzen of the 2nd Battalion, 366th Grenadier Regiment, 227th Infantry Division, briefed me on the situation and gave me my orders: the enemy had to be thrown back. Without infantry, we drove with seven guns along the southern edge of the woods in an easterly direction. Sometimes, we had to drive over log roads in marshy ground— not good for assault guns. After a kilometer, I saw a hill in the woods overgrown with young pine trees taller than a man. We drove toward them.

From a distance of 400 meters, I saw the village of Stenzlau; entire columns of Russian infantry were passing through the village in order to penetrate the woods to the northwest. I drove about ten meters out of the pines and took position behind a very flat hill. My driver, Corporal First Class Tischler, shouted at me, "Sir, we can be spotted here. We've got to go back!"

Just then, I saw a Russian antitank gun being pulled by two horses in front of the houses. It looked like they had forgotten to establish flank protection or were just now building it up. I went down in the turret to direct the gun to the Russian target. Suddenly, there was a horrible explosion, and everything grew dark around me. When I regained consciousness, I realized that though I was alive, the next round would certainly kill me. I wanted to rise from my seat, but I wasn't able to—my left leg no longer obeyed me. I felt blood on my upper left thight, and my leather trousers were torn up. I grabbed my left leg, not knowing whether it was completely severed (the foot and toes were dangling backwards), and managed to get out of the turret on my right leg. I fell to the side of the gun and then crawled on my back.

My gunner, Corporal Wenck, jumped up to me and dragged me fifteen meters, pulling me by my armpits. Using braces from his winter trousers, we made a tourniquet to tie off my leg. Then three comrades from the second gun—which still stood in an open space amid the pines—came up, picked me up in a rain cape, loaded me onto their gun, and drove me back to battalion headquarters. Before leaving, I said that Seelbach or Kampmann had to continue the attack.

The Russians had the farm under very heavy artillery fire. Lying on the assault gun, I thought that at least here I'd be able to rest. The battalion doctor came out of his bunker and gave me an injection as well as my wound ticket. After what seemed like an eternity, a *panje* wagon arrived and transported me with two other wounded men. At every crossroads—where the Russians were concentrated their artillery fire—the driver whipped the horses to maximum speed, forcing me to hold my leg in pain. In front of the main dressing station, Sergeant Major Hufnagel came up to us in his machine-gun car. He was about to bring food up to the front. I shouted and waved, and he turned around. "Hufnagel, they can't use any food in the front line now. They're up to their necks in shit!" At this, Hufnagel said, "Lieutenant, what's happened to you?"

Inside the dressing station, which was a farmer's cottage, I was laid down on a wooden pig trough, and my rubber boots and leather trousers were cut away. My leg was badly broken in the upper thigh, and I had a giant flesh wound. Thank God the main nerves and blood vessels weren't hit. When I woke up later, I asked the wounded man lying next to me, "Is my leg still attached?" God be praised, it still was. However, my neighbor, who had been next to the operating table, had heard the doctors discussing whether to amputate the leg or not. To this day, I am still grateful to those doctors.

In Heiderode, I was loaded onto a cattle truck with straw. All officers of the staff came down to say good-bye to me. I think I must look pretty miserable lying down like this. Lieutenant Schmitt whispered into my ears that Captain Sewera put me up for the Knight's Cross.

On February 11, in Berent, a plaster cast was put on my thigh and leg. From there, I was transported to a field hospital in Schlawe on the Baltic coast. I was lying with twenty officers in a hall. A naval lieutenant with fifteen machine-pistol bullets in his body died. Next to me was a tank captain who was completely burned; only his eyes, nose, and mouth were visible through the bandages. Everyone laughed when I told them that the Russians were advancing thirty kilometers per day and that since I was wounded about 210 kilometers from here, they'd arrive here in seven days. After six days, however, there was a great cry. Russian tanks were in Pollnow, about twenty kilometers away.

We were than drive in wagons for twelve hours, with one empty tin to piss in. Two nurses accompanied us. We just managed to escape before the Russians closed the East Pomeranian pocket near Stolp. In Pasewalk, I was loaded into a fine hospital train, which on its way south was shunted around Berlin for two days while the Allied bombers attacked day and night. There was no safety anymore. At Kronach in Upper Franconia, I was hurriedly transferred with a few comrades because I had a high fever. I was laid down on a stage in a great hall; the walls shook during an air raid. I remained feverish for three months and endured four operations, but my leg remained attached.

My assault gun remained standing where it was killed. Both of my dead comrades, Tischler and Strohbach, remained with the destroyed gun, unable to be recovered. I didn't find that out until 1951, and I didn't learn until 1974 that I had won the Knight's Cross. In 1996, I found out that two young Poles from Lniano pulled our dead comrades from the assault gun and buried them. A cross marked their graves, but until then, they were unidentified.

A crew poses in front of its tank

Atop a vehicle.

Issuing orders.

A gun crew takes a break.

Regeniter receiving a commendation.

A gun crew.

A crew pauses for a picture.

A brief respite from combat.

A supply train.

Stocking up on ammunition.

A soldier stands next to his camouflaged vehicle.

These lucky men have supplemented their rations.

A moment of levity.

On the march.

An interesting find.

Pausing for a photograph.

A local girl dons a German uniform.

Another crew poses.

A gun on the frozen Eastern Front.

A supply train conveys more guns to the front.

A pause in operations allows time for pictures.

Tankers.

Looking for the latest reports.

Negotiating the rubble.

On the road.

Gerd Döhler.

CHAPTER 5

Combat Group Döhler at the Oder Bridgehead, 1945

Gerd Döhler and Hans Kamradek

GERD DÖHLER

A chance meeting put me in contact with Hans Wijers in Holland, who diligently and with great interest took it upon himself to edit and work out the details of the battles around Rogau in the beginning of January 1945.

During this work, he managed to get in touch with some survivors of the battle who showed themselves more than willing to support his work with their memories. Immediately after the war, in the summer of 1945, I wrote down my own wartime experiences from December 1939 to May 1945, and I was able to supply Mr. Wijers with my notes for January 1945. In this way, a report came about which vividly and authentically describes the situation on the German Oder front in 1945, without any pathos or hero worship. For this, I am especially grateful to Mr. Wijers, Mr. Ganserer, and Dr. Kamradek.

The following pages are an extract from my war memoirs, written down in 1945, starting with the second half on January 1945.

As commander of the 3rd Battery of the 1st Battalion, Flak Regiment 111 (motorized, all-terrain capable) during the winter of 1943–44, I took part in the defensive battles in the Dorpat-Narwa area. Equipped with protective gun shields and tracked prime movers, we became a flak assault battalion destined for fighting on the ground.

In April 1944, we were moved to Baranovichi airfield in the area of Army Group Center, where we were to be refreshed and serve as flak protection. The following month, we were told that we would be moved once again to act as "invasion reserve" near Paris, France. We were astonished when we unloaded in Cosel to provide flak cover for the large factories of Blechhammer and Odertal.

Along with two others, my battery was formed into a large battery in Rüdershagen. At the beginning of July, the 1st Battalion was transported to Kurland. I was ordered to the staff of the 11th Flak Division and detached to the Sagan training area in Silesia as training officer. My job there was to lead ground-combat training for a few days for the men of the three regiments that made up the 11th Flak Division (Regiment West in Heydebreck, Regiment East in Catowice, and Regiment South in Ratibor). These men would come in small groups to Sagan to take my course. In November 1944, I was told that I would become chief of a 10.5cm flak battery (the "Royal" class of flak guns). These guns were to take over the positions of the Home Defense Flak Battery Rogau. Other events overtook these plans. The Upper Silesian front collapsed, and as signals officer of the 11th Flak Division, I came to Catowice, and the 10.5cm guns were used in the defense of Breslau.

HANS KAMRADEK, AIR FORCE AUXILIARY YOUTH, FLAK BATTERY 244/IIIV

On January 2, 1945, I was enlisted in the home defense in Upper Silesia. Our unit was Flak Battery 244/IIIV in Blechhammer, near Heidebreck. We had to protect an industrial area that included the Upper Silesian synthetic fuel hydration factories of I. G. Farben, Leuna, and perhaps Schafkotsch (I am not sure of that name anymore). By late summer 1944, we were assembled into a large battery north of Blechhammer consisting of eighteen 8.8cm guns.

In December 1944, our guns had been taken over by Hungarian troops, and we were relocated to the western bank of the Oder. This was undoubtedly because the front was closing.

As the first flak battery in Upper Silesia, we were to be reequipped with the considerably more modern 8.8cm 1941 guns. Until the middle of January 1945, we remained in a small village ten kilometers west of Cosel.

The Russian offensive in January pressed the Eastern Front toward Upper Silesia. In the second half of January, we were ordered to immediately join our new battery in the village of Oderschlenke, close to the western bank of the Oder. There we met our new commander, First Lieutenant Döhler, for the first time. We were still standing in road columns and Döhler was still welcoming our unit (sixty flak auxiliaries and about thirty flak soldiers) when three Ju87s dropped their bombs a few hundred meters from us on the other bank of the Oder. We were at the front.

GERD DÖHLER

In Cosel, they were digging tank ditches with a will and had put 8.8cm guns in open terrain near the bridge. I could only shake my head at such foolishness. When I got to the positions near Rogau, I found a large number of strange soldiers. A sergeant major told me that they were sick members of the flak regiment.

My battery had been on the road since morning for ground operations on the Annaberg. I called the battalion and its commander, my friend Dr. Lutz Schneider, who told me that my men had been sent forward without any arms by mistake. They were to send trucks immediately to pick up my men. Once reunited with my men and the four 8.8cm guns, we were to move to Krappitz as a ground combat group. I was told to acquire infantry weapons by myself.

Late in the evening, the first truck returned, loaded with dead-tired men from my battery. I took this truck and drove it to the Neumann Barracks in Cosel, where the combat commander, Colonel Meyer, a harmless old grandfather, ruled. I gave him my request and received thirty carbines, five MG15s, five submachine guns, thirty *panzerfausts*, and 500 hand grenades. I also managed to obtain 20,000 small-arms rounds at various roadblocks and reception commands.

It was late at night by the time I returned to our positions. The next morning, I divided up the weapons, and in the afternoon, I drove down to visit the commander of Fighter Command Silesia, who was just in the process of loading up to move west. Lieutenant Göhlich and I managed to load up some sleds with weapons.

HANS KAMRADEK

Our new guns had reached the Cosel railway station, and from there, we were ordered to another sector of the front. All we found were six embankments that were meant to protect our guns. In front of the earthen walls stood old Russian 8.5cm guns that he been rebored to 8.8cm caliber in order to accommodate our shells. Of course, we had no training on these war-booty guns! A few minutes later, two or three trucks drove up, bringing us rifles and plenty of ammunition, three captured machine guns, and hand grenades. We could handle the rifles and grenades, but none of us had ever handled these machine guns.

We were billeted in the houses of the village along the bank of the Oder, usually in the attics. The Oder had frozen over and was no obstacle at all. Some Flak Auxiliary Youths remained with the guns and tried to make them ready for action. We were handicapped because we did not have any shells with contact fuses. We were using time fuses that worked like shrapnel. Furthermore, the guns were located outside the protective cover of the earthen berms. The village had been evacuated, and in the enxt days, we saw no German troops. Only some *Volkssturm* men passed by and mocked us: "You want to win the war?"

GERD DÖHLER

When we regained our position, which was located in Oderschlenke, Russian tracers fired from the other bank of the Oder and whizzed over our heads. The position resembled a disturbed ant heap. About 300 soldiers flooded in my direction; they were the sick and infirm. With cold sweat on their

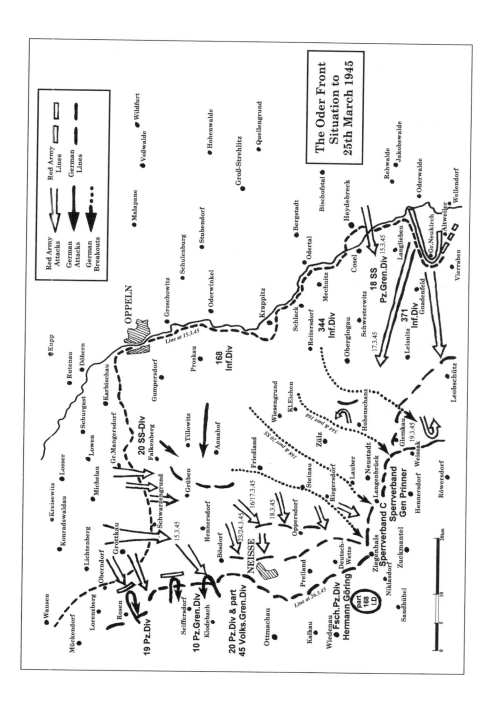

The Oder Front
Situation to
25th March 1945

brows and fixed stares, these people all of a sudden became bright and cheery as they hastened out of their positions. I walked to face this cowardly mob, drew my pistol, and threatened to shoot anybody who dared to take another step. "Back into your positions!" I shouted at the stunned mob. With the muzzle waving in their faces, they stopped.

In the meantime, Sergeant Major Gaudi had the infantry weapons dragged up and handed them out to the keen Air Force Auxiliary Youths, sending them to the Oder front line. I had an 8.8cm gun transported to the Oder, which was about 250 meters away, and had the three remaining 8.8cm guns manned. I made contact with both the battalion and the regiment. I picked out the best of the tired and sick soldiers and distributed them to the guns. The auxiliary youths took up positions in the houses along the Oder, and I formed the sixty lads into groups, which were commanded by sergeants or other NCOs. The machine guns were also commanded by experienced NCOs.

As dusk set in, my one-kilometer-wide defensive front along the Oder was in place. Joining it to the right was the *Volkssturm*. A platoon of *Volkssturm* was located in my sector as well, cowardly slinking around in the cellars. To the left, in Oderschlenke, was a *Volkssturm* company from Cosel. I had my men make camouflage clothing from bed sheets and cushion covers and showed them how to use infantry weapons. I face the coming days confidently.

Now I want to describe my position briefly. The three 8.8cm guns were sunk into the sand hollow, which to the north was lined by a three-meter-high slope. On this—100 meters away and dug into the earth—was a barracks next to the communications and radio direction-finding equipment. The command post had been established in the barracks since some communications equipment remained there. In a small hollow fifty centimeters to the right were about eight smaller barracks. The position was bordered in the east by the village of Rogau, which lay on the Oder; in the south by Cosel; and in the west, about 300 meters away, by an estate. To the north stretched an open plain for 500 meterse down to Oderschlenke. Most of the civilian population had fled. My superiors did not show themselves. I took supplied from the abandoned houses since nothing had arrived from the battalion. I established a first-aid post in an inn that had very strong walls. I had become my own combat commander.

At eight o'clock the next morning, while I was still busy preparing, a guard stormed into my barracks and shouted, "First lieutenant, the *Volkssturm* in Oderschlenke is bugging out. The Russians have crossed the ice to the north!" I ran out into the open and saw the problem. The *Volkssturm* men were running head over heels to the west, with Russian infantry in close pursuit. At the same moment, the two MGs of my strongpoint under Sergeant Radtke (an experienced veteran of World War I who was sadly killed a few weeks later during the breakout from the pokcet) on the northern edge of Rogau opened up and forced Iwan to take cover. In the blink of an eye, a furious firefight broke out, and after a few minutes, the first auxiliary youths came up huffing and wanted ammunition.

Since the *Volkssturm* in the estate to our left was bugging out as well, I walked with Sergeant Major Westphal, a keen soldier, with two MGs and six men to the estate, where I made the troops dig in in the attic. With one of the MGs, I opened up and sent 700 rounds at the Russians as they were dragging mortars and machine guns across the ice and positioning them along the border of Oderschlenke. Under heavy fire, I ran back to the command post in the deep snow and ordered Lieutenant Göhlich to open fire on Oderschlenke with the 8.8cm guns. He did this, and the shells howled over our heads, crashing with thunderous explosions into the houses on Oderschlenke. Göhlich directed the fire on all Russian resistance nests that could be made out. Though several shells hit the slop when the gunner aimed too deeply and a field latrine was hit, all went well.

In the afternoon, the Russians fired furious barrages with antitank guns and mortars at our positions as well as into

Rogau. Sadly, one auxiliary youth and one *Volkssturm* man were killed, and three auxiliary youths were wounded. This was a bitter blow. In the evening, it grew quiet, and I took advantage of the calm to check combat readiness among the men and improve the positions here and there. The battalion, regiment, and all superior commanders remained silent.

The next day brought increased fire from Soviet mortars, machine guns, and antitank guns. That night before, we heard how the Russians were digging in and bringing men and supplies to the Oder in trucks. All day, the firing went back and forth, increasing and decreasing. At Radtke's strongpoint, a machine-gun crew was severely wounded by a direct hit that demolished the building. From boats that had been frozen in place in the Oder, the Russians fired at anything that moved. We had to run, keep down, crawl, and stay on guard.

Meanwhile, Lieutenant Göhlich had managed to make contact with two large batteries of 10.5cm and 8.8cm guns. With these, he fired at Oderschlenke, the Oder crossings, and the Sturmwoods (the Russians' approach road). As soon as something moved over there, a few shells from each gun would scream over our heads. Our guns on the Oder also fired into the Sturmwoods. A lively firefight lasted all day.

We still could not make out the enemy's intentions, and after a quiet night—disturbed only by a scattering of rifle fire—the next morning dawned. The Russians showed frantic activity. Having occupied a small wood between Oderschlenke and the estate, they now tried to reinforce the position they had gained; groups of Russian infantry constantly ran into the first houses of the Schlenke and into the wood, dragging machine guns and mortars with them. They kept up their shelling, especially with their mortars, which increased more and more. One couldn't even lift one's head for a peek.

From everywhere, we heard reports from Russian reinforcements coming out of the Sturmwoods, across the ice, and into the Schlenke. With all available batteries, Lieutenant Göhlich shelled the Sturmwoods and Oderschlenke without pause and harassed the assembling forces everywhere they were visible. The three 8.8cm guns were shelled so furiously by Ivan with antitank guns and mortars that it soon became impossible to fire at all from these positions. The situation of my battle group became more and more threatened. Day and night, I kept at it without tiring, going from strongpoint to strongpoing, helping out where I could, praising and punishing. I knew neither rest nor quiet.

HANS KAMRADEK

I dug in with some comrades in the last house on the northern end of the village. In front of us was an open field about 400 meters wide. On the other side was another small village. The next morning, we found out that the Russians had advanced across the frozen Oder to the north of our positions. On the opposite bank of the Oder as well, Russian troops could be made out. They fired mortars at us, and we replied with our captured guns, using shells with an "elevated detonation" since we did not have any impact fuses. With our rifles and machine guns, we fired at everything that moved. I think we were all terrified. Only our National Socialist education kept us sixteen-year-olds from running away.

GERD DÖHLER

My group of Air Force Auxiliary Youths and other soldiers—all between sixteen and twenty-five years old—were tired and exhausted by exertions that they weren't used to. The Russians had not attacked yet, but their preparations clearly indicated that a major attack on Cosel from the north was imminent. I had little cause for optimism since, apart from my own battle group, there was no capable German unit to be found nearby.

In the afternoon, a sergeant major with a platoon of infantrymen came up, which the commander of Cosel had sent out to reinforce us. After a short discussion with my group leaders, I called up the regiment and report to Major Höck, telling him that I wanted to attack Oderschlenke at 8:30 P.M. that night. I requested artillery support from 8:00 to 8:30, and

I told the battalion infantry commander who was in charge of north of Oderschlenke what I intended to do so that he could also attack.

HANS KAMRADEK

I was in the northernmost house in the village. I do not remember what day it was. From the village café, where our first lieutenant had placed his headquarters, I was fetching some ammunition when I listened in on a telephone conversation. It was Döhler, who was saying, "I don't do battle with children, which is insanity." I don't know what made him change his mind, but the next day, he exhorted us to undertake an attack on the enemy bridgehead. We were ordered to attack the Russians—only with volunteers—and destroy the bridgehead to our north. I was part of these volunteers; as far as I can remember, everyone from my group volunteered.

GERD DÖHLER

By 5:30 P.M., Major König ambled up to our positions with two 2cm guns and a platoon of infantry. I put on of the guns at the estate and positioned the other right in front of the Soviets near Radtke's strongpoint. The attack was planned as follows: Between 8:00 and 8:25, four reinforced batteries of 8.8cm guns, as well as the guns from my combat group, would fire an interdiction barrage at Oderschlenke and the Sturmwoods. From 8:25 to 8:30, all batteries would fire a bombardment from all available tubes. During this period, both 2cm guns would open up on all the Russian field works that could be seen. The two platoons, commanded by the sergeant major, would close to within storming distance of Oderschlenke, while I would advance north along the Oder with twenty men.

HANS KAMRADEK

All day, we fired our guns on the village that we were to take by storm. During this time, all three of our guns were knocked out by shells that exploded in the tube. The enemy's mortar fire prevented us from using other guns. In the evening, two or three nearby flak batteries supported us for twenty or thirty minutes. Then it was time. With a cry of "Hurrah," we stormed toward the village, which was 300–400 meters away. After 100 meters, we stopped shouting because of the exertions of running through deep snow. Thank God, the Russians had evacuated the village while it was under fire, so we were able to take it without any opposition. I had not seen a single human being at any range closer than 200–300 meters.

GERD DÖHLER

We had been ready since before 8:00. I was now with my men at Strongpoint Radtke, waiting for the bombardment to begin. At exactly 8:00, rolling fire began as shells burst from the high strongpoints. It was a hurricane of fire. Fifty-seven heavy tubes fired everything they had. At 8:25, the fire increased to a deafening noise. Oderschlenke was completely submerged by flashes and powder smoke. At 8:30 on the dot, the flare signal from the two platoons went up, and the artillery fire immediately ceased.

Then we stormed forth, stumbling and crawling, shooting, and shouting amidst the rattling of MGs and the explosions of hand grenades. My men were hushed and ghostlike. Shouts for medics rang out. Our batteries again began firing on the Sturmwoods. We wildly rush from house to house among dead Germans and torn-apart Russians. Confusion reigned.

It lasted probably an hour, until we had Oderschlenke in our hands. The two platoons advanced farther north along the Oder and remained there. I had our dead deposited near a building and showed my men their positions in the buildings in order to establish a defense. Since I no longer believed the Russians would attack again, I returned to the command post and reported to Major Höck that Oderschlenke had been taken. When I had given the necessary instructions to Lieutenant Göhlich, I soon went forward again, where an ever-increasing firefight was in progress. Soon I ran into my men, who were shouting that the Russians were attacking in great numbers—the ice was literally black with Russians—and could not be thrown back because our men had run out of ammunition. From the direction of the Oder, I heard the hoarse shouts of the Russians.

HANS KAMRADEK

In the village that we have just taken, we are divided amongst various positions. At most, there were thirty of us, some of whom were soldiers. I was ordered to secure the village in the direction of the Oder. I was lying in the snow with a dead Russian as my cover. After a short while, intense Russian mortar fire started. After about two hours—for a long time, I had seen no one—several machine-gun salvoes rattled over my head. Trembling with fear (I was sixteen years and four weeks old!), I abandoned my post and ran into the village. Apart from a dead German and a few dead Russians, I saw no one and continued running toward the starting point of our attack. I was relieved when I heard someone say in harsh German, "Halt! Who goes there?" The Russians had retaken the bridgehead.

NSG EXTRA REPORT FROM UPPER SILESIA, JANUARY 30, 1945

Like breakwaters, the flak batteries of the Upper Silesian industrial area are stuck into the mounting Soviet flood that ran into them from the north and east. Almost overnight, the heavy and very-heavy flak guns—which had been mounted to fire at aerial targets—had become the main line of defense. Their positions were on heights and in dense forests and were therefore less suitable for ground combat. The guns were manned by young Air Force Auxiliary Youths and personnel that was not fit for the front lines anymore.

In six months, they and their regiment had shot down ninety four-engine bombers and a mass of fighters from the Allied squadrons that were coming in from the south. This had made them one of the most successful flak regiments. Now the commander had to organize his resistance with his officers in a matter of hours. The Air Force Auxiliary Youths reported enthusiastically to the flak combat groups and to the tank-hunting commandos.

So they motored into enemy-held territory in courageous bands in small cars, hid their vehicles, and set up ambushes in woods and bushes. One of the groups with three men ventured out into Groß-Strelitz and saw a Russian tank hidden behind a wall. As the rattling steel colossus noisily approached to within eight meters, Lieutenant Kröger from Neumunster fired his *panzerfaust*, and the T-34 disintegrated on the spot. The confidence from this success passed on to the other young men, who were waiting with hearts beating heavily to hurl their *panzerfausts* against the monstrous tanks. Air Force Auxiliary Youth Metzger was the first of them to wear the tank destroyer badge on his uniform. There were many who sought to emulate his example.

When a call went out to form a reconnaissance party, many hands flew up. These lads would storm into danger, possessed by the thought of destroying the enemy. They did not ask how many divisions or armies were opposing them. They grew more silent and pressed their lips together tightly when a comrade was wounded or killed. These young auxiliaries and the tank hunters destroyed twenty tanks in five days. They distinguished themselves with brave deeds.

For example, at Loben, the flak combat group of First Lieutenant Schenk waited for the Russians at dusk; the enemy announced his arrival with the rattle of tracks and the roar of engines. It was too dark to spot him in the distance. Cold-bloodedly, Schenk's men waited at the sights of their 8.8cm guns with thumping hearts until they saw the bulky outlines of the leading T-34. Hoarsely, someone ordered them to fire. Fractions of a second later, flames spouted from the hit tank, which provided enough illumination to kill the next three T-34s with direct hits.

Near Rudershagen, the wrecks of eight Soviet tanks stood in front of two destroyed flak guns. Lieutenant Primes was in command here. Only when the entire group of tanks was within his grasp did he attack. The gunlayer of the leftmost gun fell out. Lieutenant Primes took his place and shot up five tanks while lying in the dense hail of shells from the enemy. A sergeant killed three T-34s with the other gun until the barrel of his 8.8cm gun was destroyed by an enemy shell. A gun commander of a neighboring combat group reported this determined act by men who died completing it.

Sergeant Jürgens from Schleswig-Holstein waited as a forward observer in a house on the road to Mittelbrück north of the Adolf Hitler Canal. He saw a battery of heavy Soviet antitank guns starting to take up positions about twenty meters from him—a very small distance indeed. Jürgens stared at the antitank guns and called in fire from his battery. He waited for some minutes, knowing how feverishly his comrades were dragging shells to the 8.8cm guns to his rear, and then the shells howled in. The first salvoes landed between the antitank guns. In wild chaos, the Soviets bolted to their rear. One shell took the roof of the house in which Jürgens was positioned. He remained there quietly until he finished his work; then he slunk back.

Hundreds of Soviet infantrymen poured out of the woods on the right bank of the river, running across the ice to establish bridgeheads on the western bank. At the salt ferry north of Cosel, Heavy Flak Battery Rogau struck. Twice, the Soviets flooded up from their assembly areas in the Sturmwoods to the right of the Oder, and twice, the flak beat them back. First Lieutenant Döhler directed the fire of his battery with great calm, although he noticed the great danger, for at this time, his battery had insufficient infantry weapons. The heavy guns had to win the unequal battle, and they did. The thrown-back Bolsheviks left 170 dead, including a battalion commander who fell in front of the flak positions on the snowy banks of the Oder.

At an Oder ferry north of Cosel in the last days, a soldier and a boy held out to the last round against the Soviet infantry storm. Here the private first class and sixteen-year-old Auxiliary Youth First Class Schulz experienced the exciting moment when enemy infantry stormed toward them in a tight mass.

They retained the heart to stand up to the Soviet storm. Mechanically, they aimed, fired, loaded, and looked for new targets. Until their ammunition pouches were empty, they kept firing. Their comrades rescued them.

Even if the two men slowed down the enemy for a few hours, the Soviets needed those hours to complete their grand plan of advancing through Silesia and across the Oder. Many times, however, he was stopped by the anger of German *Volkssturm* men as well as the bold, low-level attacks of German Air Force pilots and fighters who know only that the front faced east; they held on without being moved. So time was won.

The trains with tanks, heavy weapons, and combat-ready units rolled up, and the resistance got tougher. The flak castles in Upper Silesia lowered their barrels and fought the defensive war against waves of Soviet tanks and infantry with the same intensity. They were the cornerstone against an enemy who took for granted his superiority in men and materiel. Every man on the flak guns in Upper Silesia knew that this colossus could be beaten back if the individual German soldier wielded his weapons boldly to the last.

GERD DÖHLER

With tears of anger and empty ammunition pouches, we returned to our starting positions. Lieutenant Göhlich directed the fire of the five batteries and both 2cm guns onto the Russians. The Russians remained lying down and then retreated into Oderschlenke. Then, on both sides, exhaustion set in.

While my men sank down and slept as if dead, there was no quiet for me. Now it was time to send out combat reports and interrogate prisoners. We had used 1,500 rounds of 8.8cm and 10.5cm ammunition, 800 2cm rounds, and 3,000 rounds of rifle ammunition. The prisoners revealed that opposite us was a cavalry regiment with about 800 men, armed with antitank guns and mortars. Their commander was a Major Antoschkin, and they had orders to take Cosel in a storming attack from the north. Thrown back by the resistance in Rogau and the flak fire, the entire regiment had been thrown into the battle and was to attack at dawn, but my combat group's attack preempted them. They had suffered great casualties and lost two thirds of their regimental strength. They were completely worn down and longed for relief. Antoschkin had been killed, and a captain took over command.

The next day, it was quiet, and only a few barrages from both sides ensured that we did not forget that there was a war on. The next morning, an infantry company arrived with orders to attack Oderschlenke. My warning that it was sheer madness to attack by daylight across an open field with flanking fire was dismissed grandly by the company commander. I let it pass. The company began its attack and was completely shot up by the Russians; barely half of them returned. The Russians fired into my position and wounded two Air Force Auxiliary Youths. On the other bank of the Oder, two T-34s drove up and shot up my "Oder" 8.8cm. Three were severely and two slightly wounded. Cursing this shit, I let the company commander and his remaining men move off. Now I was alone again. I had the 2cm gun from Strongpoint Radtke moved to the estate since the positions over there seemed too weak to me.

The following morning, a lively shelling took place, which was unpleasantly disturbing. In the afternoon, four squads of infantry came to reinforce us; I positioned them by the banks of the Oder to relieve the completely exhausted Auxiliary Youths. Two squads were also located on the farm estate. Furthermore, Colonel Meyer directed one company of *Volkssturm* to Rogau. I finally felt that the load of responsibility had been lifted from my shoulders. In multiple telephone conversations, I requested the relief of my worn-out soldiers, and I was assured this would happen. The next day brought relief. First Lieutenant Großmann and First Lieutenant Mauska came into our position with 100 men, armed with French rifles and a ton of machine guns, in a cautious and timid manner—as if they feared that a Russian could appear from behind every corner. I was expected to hand over the entire armament of my combat group to the relieving force, and I had to remain in Rogau for one more week to show them their positions. That was too much for me and resulted in a fearful argument. I ordered my men to march off and drove to see Colonel Meyer with First Lieutenant Großmann. Meyer gave me new weapons for my men; he understood my argument.

HANS KAMRADEK

Over the next two or three weeks, we were in constant contact with the enemy. I have seen six or seven dead (covered by blankets) in the battery. They had been killed by a rapid-firing gun from the other bank while attempting to bring a gun into position; one of our guns later took out the Russian gun. We were supposed to have five or six wounded Auxiliary Youths. I saw only one of them and helped him myself. I heard the name Battle Group Döhler for the first time after the breakout, which took place undramatically. I know nothing of hero's deeds. Three or four Russian mortars were said to have been destroyed by our guns.

After about three weeks, we were replaced by some infantrymen. We left our battery overnight, and west of Cosel, we were taken up into a village and pampered by the civilians. After our breakout, being a combat-proven group, we were equipped with assault rifles that we could use in our role as a "fire department" in threatened sectors.

The volunteers for the counterattack were reported to the Luftgau for the award of the Iron Cross, 2nd Class. Here I found out that Battle Group Döhler had been mentioned in dispatches from the front. One more time, we were brought to the front by night. Our trucks were shot up; we could not advance any farther and had to retire. We did not get into anymore operations and the award of the Iron Crosses never took place because we were discharged in order to be drafted into the army in March 1945.

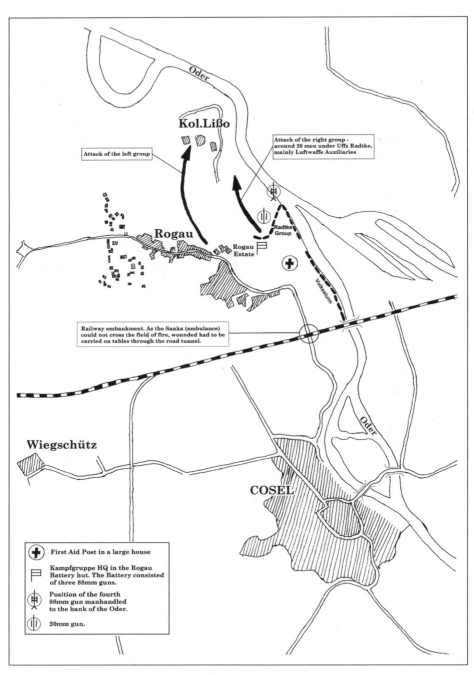

Situation near Rogau and Cosel.

GERD DÖHLER

When we returned to our positions in Rogau, we ran straight into the attempt of about fifty Russians to take out a strongpoing in the farm building. The Russians ran straight into the fire of the 2cm gun and were shot down completely. Eighteen dead remained in front of our positions. The next morning, dead tired and very weary, I drove to the assembly area of our prime movers in Gnadenfeld. Here I finally heard what had been taking place in the sector of the 11th Flak Division in Upper Silesia while we had been in Rogau preventing the taking of Cosel by a Russian cavalry regiment. The reinforced flak batteries east of the Oder had collapsed.

Without having spotted an enemy, Reinforced Battery Rudershagen, commanded by Captain Wurm, sent 3,000 shells in an easterly direction and then blew up the guns, after which 300 combat-capable soldiers hurriedly abandoned their positions. The officers went first in a car and abandoned their men, who scattered in all directions and were assembled only weeks later, far to the rear in Riesengebirge. Captain Wurm and his officers were arrested in Sudetenland.

The reinforced 10.5cm battery in Bischofstal was defended by a sergeant while First Lieutenant Ditt and his officers bolted for Subgroup Blechhammer and Captain Schneefuss; they reported that the battery had been overrun and the Russians were on their heels. On hearing this, the battalion staff also ran, fleeing toward the Oder. In this manner, one reinforced battery after another failed, only because the officers had no front experience and fled. Only Battery Oderwalde remained brave and steady.

By order of the flak regiment, my battery was declared a flak-assault company and equipped with Mp 44 assault rifles. In early February 1945, all Auxiliary Youths were drafted into the army, and with that, my assault company was disbanded. Then I took over command of a flak combat group that consisted of 8.8cm and partially motorized 2cm guns. After ground combat north of Cosel, we withdrew toward the Sudetenland with the receding front line. At Deutsch-Rasselwitz, we managed to break out of Russian encirclement with SS Division Horst Wessel, though we lost all our vehicles and guns.

We continued to move backwards, fighting in the Sudetenland; we had meanwhile been reequipped with 8.8cm guns. Finally, we participated in the general retreat toward the west as part of Army Group Schörner. In May 1945 we were on the Moldau south of Tabor, where we had to halt. American Sherman tanks had blocked the bridge across the Moldau, and we were ordered to await developments. The American troops were supposed to advance and save us from the Russians, but at dawn, no Americans came. Instead, Russian motorized infantry showed up, deploying to the right and left and declaring us prisoners. In the general confusion, Captain Schneider and I broke through the Russian blockade, jumped into the Moldau, and managed to get through to the Upper Pfalz.

In Kötzting, we met up with the German 11th Panzer Division, which had been interned by the Americans and whose members were being discharged. So by late May 1945, I was standing with my American discharge papers in front of my parents' home in Duisburg, where I was greeted with disbelief by my intact family, who believed that a miracle had brought me home.

REPORT BY HERMANN GANSERER

I was born on July 27, 1928, in Hermannsberg in the vicinity of Sulzbach-Rosenberg (Opf.). Together with my classmates, I was drafted at Regensburg as an Air Force Auxiliary Youth with the 3rd Battery of the 484th Heavy Flak Battalion. Our battery was equipped with six captured Russian guns, which had been re-bored to 8.8cm.

When the entire aircraft industry in Regensburg had been flattened by bombs, the Air Force Auxiliaries were posted to the 6th Battery of the 232nd Heavy Flak Battalion in Stettfeld, between Bamberg and Schweinfurt, on March 14, 1944. In order to protect a ball-bearing factory in Eltmann am Main, a battery with six 8.8cm guns was raised. The battery commander was First Lieutenant Braun. One night, the neighboring village was plastered with a bombing carpet that also hit parts of our battery. The civilian population suffered twelve dead and many wounded. When the ball-bearing factory itself was bombed, we were not allowed to open fire.

After the factory had been destroyed, the entire battery was loaded onto wagons with an unknown destination. Finally, we ended up in Poppitz in Upper Silesia. The village was located about ten kilometers north of Cosel. Our battery was established in a potato field to protect the Upper Silesian Artificial Fuel Works. On August 8, 1944, our guns were taken away for use at the front, and within the Cosel area, we were transferred to the 8th Flak Battery (10715, "For Special Purposes") in Rudershagen. Our battery commander was First Lieutenant Döhler. Since not enough soldiers were available, the Air Force Auxiliaries had to do full duty. For example, I did duty as a loader (K-3).

On September 10, 1944, we were transferred to the 6th Heavy Flak Battery (658/0) in Wolfswiesen. Here a reinforced battery of eighteen 8.8cm guns was created. Increasingly, the gun crews consisted solely of Air Force Auxiliary Youths. We remained in Wolfswiesen until the Russians came. I had just returned from a short leave, and on the night of January 15–16, 1945, I had to perform guard duty right away. In the north, we heard a loud engine noise. At dawn, we were informed that the Russians had broken through in the direction of Breslau. The female Air Force Auxiliaries and our Russian prisoneres were moved off, and we slighted our earthen gun berms and prepared for ground combat. The first Russian tank spearheads were met by an assault party of our reinforced battery consisting of seventy men with two moveable Russian 8.8cm guns, commanded by First Lieutenant Sauckel from Amberg. This group was surprised by the Russians and was almost completely destroyed; only ten men returned.

Contacts with the enemy grew stronger by the day. Three Air Force Auxiliaries were shot by Russians while getting milk in Wolfswiesen. We beat off an attack by Cossack cavalrymen using time-delay fuses. People were killed on both sides. We had to fire throughout both day and night. Nearby was an approach route the Russians used; we constantly covered it with fire. Our ammunition was slowly running out. Before the Russians arrived, we received a large number of armor-piercing shells that did not, however, fit our guns.

After the last round had been fired on the night of January 24–25, 1945, Captain Thermer ordered that the position was to be abandoned. We removed the firing pins from the guns and destroyed the other instruments. Of the crews, only 10 soldiers and about 100 Air Force Auxiliaries remained. We had two MG42s and about ten carbines. We tried to make it through to Cosel by moving through the woods. We succeeded.

In front of Cosel, the bridge across the Oder had been prepared for demolition, and not far from it stood a heavy flak gun. We marched down to a barracks and were housed in huts. We were so tired that some fell asleep standing up and toppled over. In the morning, we had to stand to. We were informed that the Russians had already crossed the Oder and built a bridgehead. In order to clear it, all remaining soldiers from our battery and the fifteen Auxiliary Youths should be handed over. The fourteen kids who were stationed in the Bavarian café Villa Sorgenfrei in Wolfswiesen volunteered.

Soon we were transported to the site of the action in trucks, and since we did not know the area, we were given a short briefing. We received French and Belgian long carbines, ammunition, and egg hand grenades. We were in the middle of the front line, where there was constant firing back and forth. We fired at everything that moved and especially at a building 400 or 500 meters toward the Oder. A Russian mortar round detonated smack in the middle of a group of soldiers and Air Force Auxiliaries, many of whom received fearful neck and head wounds.

At the edge of the village was a 2cm gun that was firing constantly. At 4:00 P.M., I was given the task of forward observer on the western edge of the village. I was lying in a ditch by the side of the road. It was cold, and it started to snow as it grew dark. I didn't have a good view of anything in the distance.

The firing continued as before, but now tracers were used. I felt ill at ease. I was to be relieved at 6:00 P.M., but nobody came. I was freezing and, at 7:30, returend to the village. At 8:00, we were to assemble in a machine hall, which I assume was part of the estate. We did not know the place and did not know we were in Rogau, a suburb of Cosel. At this time, I didn't know that Flak Battery Döhler was in our immediate vicinity between the estate and the Oder.

All of a sudden, there was hissing, roaring, and whistling overhead. We heard firing and impacts of shells. I had never before experienced such an inferno. Our squad leader, a sergeant major, informed us that this was the the firing of the nearby flak batteries, which were preparing the objective of our attack, the bridgehead. The barrage lasted about thirty minutes; the time spent waiting was horrible. When it got quiet again, our squad leader gave the order to attack, and we were to storm the buildings on the slope of Oderschlenke from the left. A second group was to come in from the right. First, we advanced over open terrain in deep snow for about 100 meters. Then we descended two or three meters through the reeds to the frozen bank of a river—a loop in the Oder that had been isolated from the main river by its canalization.

After the bombardment by the flak batteries, it remained relatively quiet. But when we climbed the embankment on the other side, an incomprehensibly intense fire suddenly opened up on us. We immediately hurtled ourselves to the ground and returned fire. Rounds howled overhead, and the snow burst up again and again. The terrain was overgrwon with bushes, behind which we tried to take cover. We directed our first toward the buildings. Slowly, we crawled forward, jumped, lay down, and fired again. Next to me, Sgt. Friedl Rausch caught a round when he tried to stand and collapsed backwards. The fire was still quite fierce, and we managed to advance only slowly. By now, the houses were in range, and we aimed at the windows and doors and everything that moved. After the fire in our vicinity slowed down a bit, we gingerly closed in on the buildings. We threw grenades through all windows, doors, and other openings. After we had cleared the buildings, we assembled behind them toward the Oder.

The Oder was about 100 meters away. It was rather quiet; hardly a shot was fired. Our squad leader fired a flare to signal the other assault group to come in from the night, but we saw nothing of them. We awaited a Russian counterattack. All of a sudden, in the dark, snow-lit landscape, someone saw waves of Russians coming out of the woods on the other side of the Oder. We laid ourselves down in a chain in the snow. The squad leader passed an order to let the Russians get close; we were to open fire only on his order. We waited, and in the faint light, we saw the Russians approaching. Thank God, nothing happened, and the tension ebbed away.

My school friend and I—we were an inseparable combat team—went down to the Oder and set ourselves down in the snow on the river bank. Without thinking, my friend lit a cigarette. Immediately, tracers were fired at us from the woods. We ran for our lives. Again and again, tracers came for us, and we were sure we were done for. But the rounds landed in the snow several meters behind us.

When we closed with the houses, I suddenly caught my foot in a wire. Terrified, I waited for a mine to explode any second. But nothing happened. I lifted the wire, which led to a Russian who was lying in the snow in a white fur coat and hat. He had a telephone box in front of his chest and was apparently making a call. My friend tried to tear the receiver out of his hand by pulling on the wire. It didn't work, and the Russian continued his call. We then ordered him to surrender, but he still continued his call. We had no choice but to put him out of action. Then we returned to our squad in the starting position. My carbine had its butt plate show away, and I had four bullet holes in my great coat.

In the village, I met First Lieutenant Döhler. He praised our spirit and will. He wanted to carry out other actions with us, but we were extremely tired and were moved off later that day. With the thunder of the front to our backs, we marched out. In another village, I met up with First Lieutenant Braun, our former battery commander. After a hearty greeting and a report from me, he informed me that he had the commissary leadership for the unit and wanted to discharge us on the basis of a Luftwaffe convention concerning the prohibition of the use of flak auxiliaries in the operational area. The Russians treated any Air Force Auxiliary Youths like partisans. We received our discharge papers, which were handwritten on a page that had been torn out of a pocket diary.

Gratefully, we said goodbye to Braun and were taken away by a truck full of empty ammunition cases. When we drove through Lessnitz, in which there was much military activity and refugee columns, we sang, "We travel to Bavaria, the beautiful homeland." The joy did not last long as Russian low-level aircraft strafed our truck. We had to leg it again. First Lieutenant Braun had advised us to travel to Troppau since it was possible that trains still departed there. After some day and night marches, we reached Troppau. At the station, there was a train with wounded men. The train driver thought that since the direct way to the west was blocked, the only opportunity was to drive east, turn around, and come out at Prague. In any event, we got on the train, and despite being fired on constantly, we managed to get out intact.

On February 9, 1945, I finally arrived home. Shortly after six in the morning, I rang the doorbell. My mother opened the door carefully and at the same time let out a great cry as she believed she saw a Russian prisoner and immediately shut the door again. (Russian prisoners were used in the ironworks in our town.) But when I rang the door bell again and identified myself, the surprise and the joy were great. My parents had not received any sign of life from me for more than two months. But they had heard reports about the actions of Air Force Auxiliaries in Upper Silesia on the radio, and after my brother had been killed in Russia in 1942, they were very worried. As I had not washed myself for two months, I took a long bath and tried, as far as as possible, to clean myself of lice, fleas, and ticks. The war was not over yet. The draft into the RAD followed. But that is a separate chapter.

After the war, I was busy with school, studying, and professional training, and the war faded into the background. But starting in 1980, I met up with a small group of former Luftwaffe Auxiliaries from Uffenheim, Schwandorf, and Sulzbach-Rosenberg, and we relived the wartime experiences. We regularly organized meetings of former Luftwaffe Auxiliaries. The urge to visit the old operational sites in Upper Silesia grew ever stronger. I went there and saw the remains of the bunkers and earthen gun berms of our three battery positions. Sadly, I did not find the place of the action on the Oder.

In 1997, I went to Upper Silesia again and met up with Air Force Auxiliaries from the Sauerland who had been stationed in Mittenbrück with 10.5cm flak. I had gotten ahold of maps and studied them deeply. I managed to find the Rogau estate on the map, and my wife and I drove to Rogau. We talked with some elderly people in a pensioner's home near Rogau and the Oder. As I described my wartime experiences, one man called for an old woman who was supposed to have lived in the village in 1945 and witnessed everything. A woman of seventy-five appeared, and she really did know the details about everything.

We drove to Rogau with her and found the ditch by the street in which I had lain in the snow as a forward observer. From the village, we could see Oderschlenke. We drove along the wall of the estate toward the Oder, where the Russians had crossed the frozen river for the first time. Here was the slope on the Oder where my friend and I had sat in the snow. The woman told us that Oderschlenke had changed hands several times after our attack and that the ground was littered with dead Russians and Germans. She also showed us the locations of two mass graves on the Oder, where the killed were temporarily buried before being reinterred in cemeteries.

The next night, my wife and I drove once again toward Oderschlenke to have a quiet look at everything. We also talked to the people who lived there but knew nothing of the wartime events. They told us that the houses that had been shot up in the war had been demolished and rebuilt. Because of the high water, the quiet loops of the Oder were filled with water up to the edge. It was a beautiful, peaceful evening. The setting sun was mirrored in the water, and we sat down on the slope of the Oder and watched the water flow silently past. On the other side of the Oder was the Sturmwood.

For me, it was a special feeling to be there once more. The front of the Cosel area had held on until late March or early April of 1945, according to an old lady from Wolfswiesen whom the Russians had drafted for digging trenches and who had returned home only in early April 1945.

Loading an antiaircraft gun.

A gun crew.

Waiting for supplies.

Another gun crew poses.

Defending a river bank.

Keeping watch.

Lying in wait.

Manning the trenches.

Looking out over the vast front.

On patrol.

Ready to be towed.

The aftermath of combat.

After a battle.

Günther Meyer.

CHAPTER 6

Surviving the Russian Offensive at the Seelöwer Heights, April 1945

Günther Meyer

In March 1945, I was an *oberjäger* (*unteroffizier*). I had received the EK 2, the Infantry Assault Badge, the Parachute Jump Badge, the Wound Badge in Gold, and the Close-Combat Bar in Bronze. I was a member of the 1st Battalion of the 25th Fallschirmjäger Regiment of the 9th Fallschirmjäger Division, which was brought to Grünberg (Mecklenburg-Vorpommern), a small village east of Prenzlau, near the railroad that leads from Pasewalk to Locknitz to Tangermünde.

We found places for ourselves in the large sheep stables of the manor. Because of the bad weather, we received very brief terrain training. It was insufficient, and we didn't get the important training in sharpshooting. The newcomers that we had received as replacements hardly had a chance to survive. The *jäger* companies had only a few battle-hardened men, NCOs, and officers; the rest were newcomers from schools, the Luftwaffe, or the navy. As one of the veterans in the battalion, I had to present lessons on "Knowing the Enemy's Weapons by Their Sounds" and "How to Behave and Defend Oneself as a Jäger."

Finally, at the end of March 1945, we received new orders. We were going to the front at Stettin, where we were supposed to defend the Stettiner Haff. I called my men together and told them about our new orders. When I heard how we were

going to go to Stettin, I didn't think we would ever get there—
by train in broad daylight. This was a suicide mission since it
was extremely dangerous to travel by train during the day; the
Russians took to the air everyday, and our own air support was
almost nonexistent.

Suprisingly, we arrived in the afternoon without any air
attacks. My platoon was in the last wagon. At the railroad station, we learned that our orders had changed. The Russians
had already taken the Stettiner Haff on March 30. The whole
German bridgehead had to retreat before the storming Russians. Our new orders had us going back immediately in the
direction of Wrietzen, again by train—another suicide mission!

Incidentally, our wagon was parked next to a train wagon
of the Waffen-SS, which was loaded with tons of supplies for
the troops but never reached them. It had been abandoned by
the Waffen-SS and was now guarded by old *Volkssturm* men. By
playing some tricks behind the backs of these poor old men,
we "liberated" some of the food, and our men at least had a
decent meal. We knew that it could very well be our last.

Somewhere along the railroad track, the train had hidden
itself in a wooded area. It was beautiful weather, with blue sky,
and Russian planes were over us all the time. We were going to
stay concealed until it got dark. We were close to the front line,
though I really wouldn't call it that anymore, since the Russians had broken through it in several places like a sharp knife
through a small piece of butter. When it got dark, we again
moved to the area of Wrietzen (Oderbuch), where the unit
was unloaded in a small village, which I believe was called
Letschin oder Zechin. This was shortly before April 13, 1945.

On April 14, our regimental commander, an SS officer,
and some other officers celebrated the promotion of the regimental doctor. I was invited to the party, where I played the
piano in a family house just outside the little village. The party
ended with a big argument among the officers, with their pistol cases lying open on one of the tables. I kept playing "In der
Roten Laterne von Sankt Pauli." It looked like all the men
were more or less convinced that their end was near—that the

Russians would attack. None wanted to end up in a Russian POW camp. Awaiting this end played with the nerves of these officers, and so the party ended in this fight. Some of the attendees had to be treated by the newly promoted doctor. I had to carry my company commander back to his quarters.

The next morning, April 15, 1945, my company commander brought me and my platoon to the front line (HKL: *Hauptkampflinie*, or main line of resistance). It was a trench, about 1,100 meters long, that was dug out by locals who were convinced that it would stop the Russians. Where were the men who occupied it before us? It seemed that they retreated to a second defense line somewhere behind us. Why? Did they think we were "supermen," that we could stop the Russians and that they could catch the ones that made it through our line? I felt that we were now on our own and that all hopes were built on us.

When we entered the trench, I gave my men orders to fire without pause on the Russian troops who were supposed to be 60–100 meters behind the wall. Our positions were in the Oderbuch; in front of us was the Old River Oder; and a few miles behind us was Letschin. The trench was filled knee-deep with water. I deployed my fourteen men along this new defense line. The whole time, a Russian airplane (*Nähmaschine*, or "sewing machine," because it made a hell of a noise and was very slow) circled over us, watching us. The Russians would get the impression that the defense line was occupied and heavily defended with all means. Now I knew we were going to be sacrificed!

Twice on our right, we saw a *Huckepack* flying in the direction of Küstrin, below 1,000 meters. It was directed to the streets where the Russians moved their men and equipment in preparation for their big attack. Shortly after, we heard a huge explosion. Late in the afternoon, the Russians tried to overrun us. In a fruit orchard in front of our trench, about thirty or forty Russian soldiers were trying to get close to us. They were crawling in our direction, to the right side of my defense line. At that moment, I was all alone there and had to secure the area. One of my men came to warn me, and because I had given an order not to shoot before I gave the order, these Russians felt secure and unseen and came very close to our positions. When they were about fifty meters away, I gave the order to open fire with all machine guns. None of the Russians came out alive. The trees were too small for them to hide behind. We had no losses, but we knew this wouldn't be the only attempt.

Early on the morning of April 16, 1945, it seemed like the end of the world. Later that day, we received the long-expected Russian bombardment. The earth was shaking all around us. We tried to find cover in any ditch we could find. I didn't think any of us would come out alive. We just waited for what would come next. It was Armageddon!

A dark fog spread over us, and it was getting dark from the smoke of a small village about 500 meters to our left, which had been hit and was burning. We had not seen this village as we tried to get out, and if we had seen it, maybe we would have tried to find a hiding place there. If we had, we would probably be dead now. As I looked at the burning houses, I suddenly could see Russian tanks moving across the field. The silhouettes sharply contrasted against the yellow-orange sea of flames.

We had landed right in the middle of the Russian offensive against Berlin! We and the Russians were moving in the same direction, but the area around us was not very useful for tanks. On the route we took, the enemy tanks would be stuck in the moor, so no enemy tanks followed us. No Russian tanks means no Russian infantry, and no Russian infantry means no Russian tanks. You could say we were secure on our way back.

In the early-morning hours, we found our way back to our unit. None of my men was wounded—a miracle! I was responsible for them, and I was the one who sent them on this suicide mission, so I had to get them back out of the old line of resistance. I did. When I reported back to my commander, he was just flabbergasted to see us back here alive. We didn't get a minute of rest; we were thrown into the new defense line, which was on a little hill. I still can remember that position very well: a steep valley in front of us, with bushes and small fir trees.

Just as we got into position, we received a new order that our regiment had to move back to a new defense line. Our way back led us across an open field that was under constant artillery fire by the Russians; the fire was directed by the damned Russian sewing machines. Left and right of us, civilians were fleeing the battlefield with their few belongings. Not long after that, we found civilians dead on the roads and in fields. The Russians had no mercy on them. We later learned that they fired directly on the civilians with their 76mm guns. The Russian artillery also took its toll among the retreating men of our regiment.

As we moved farther back, we saw a small fortress on a little hill, with a completely camouflaged 88mm battery. In front of it was a large formation of enemy tanks, moving toward the fortress. We had to act fast. I went to the positions and found the lieutenant who commanded the 88mm unit. I asked him if he was staying and trying to stop the enemy tanks. He said that if I stayed, he would, too. So I instructed my men to take up positions near the 88s and stay out of sight of the enmy.

The 88 battery still had full ammunition, and we—forty paratroopers—would give them fire support with everything we had. I checked in with each man in the unit and told him that it was going to be a "hot corner" here, for us and the enemy. When the 88 commander gave the order to fire, we were to fire on escaping tank crews and infantry. That's how it played out. The Russian tanks came in a battle formation. The first row consisted of five T-34 tanks that were 400 to 500 meters away from us. They rolled in at walking tempo in our direction. Behind every row of tanks walked enemy infantry— perhaps a company's worth. Behind them was another row of tanks, followed by yet more infantry. How many rows would be behind them?

So far, not a single shot had been fired. The sound of the heavy engines of those moving fortresses was frightening; most of my men had never seen such a group of armor. I knew that the new men would be scared, so I kept an eye on them to make sure they didn't run. As the Russians moved in our direction, the rest of our parachute regiment was trying to get out of this inferno and received a great number of casualties from Russian artillery.

Behind our little hill was the "field of death," which was full of gravely wounded soldiers, bodies torn apart by direct artillery hits, soldiers who couldn't bear it anymore and walked around as living dead. It was a chaos of dying human beings, a field covered by bodies everywhere you looked. I can still hear their horrible screaming.

In the meantime, the Russian T-34s were closing in on our still-uncovered position. After a few minutes, they were within 100–150 meters of the little hill. We were dead quiet since we didn't want to give away this opportunity to strike back. Whenever the smoke cleared enough to give us a view of the battlefield, we stared at the location where we expected the enemy tanks to show up. Then all hell broke loose. The 88 battery commander gave the order to fire. The first three T-34 tanks were burning and then exploded. Then three more tanks were knocked out, burning and exploding the same way as the other three. At that same moment, we opened fire on the Russian soldiers who were trying to find cover in the open field. I think we had six MG42s with us, which fired until their barrels were smoking from the heat of firing. It was complete chaos in front of us. Every tank that had exploded took its toll on the infantry behind it, and we took care of the ones trying to get away.

For two hours, the Russians tried to break through our little fortress without success. The 88 guns kept on firing, and our group fired and fired on every enemy soldier we could see. Suddenly, they retreated. They left behind their dead and wounded. The field was littered with burning wrecks of T-34s and at least four companies of dead enemy soldiers.

The 88 battery had used all its ammunition. We had to try to get out of here because it wouldn't take long for the Russians to come again, surround us, or just bypass us. I looked at my men. None of them was wounded. I talked with the 88 battery commander. We wished each other good luck and tried to get out our own way.

I called my men together and said, "Let's get out of this damned area!" But even now, we had to pay attention as we moved out to avoid becoming a target. We didn't want to end up like those men on the field behind us. So we moved out one by one, our bodies bent as far as we could. Below the field was a little stream, and as we reached it, we used it to get out of the area. We managed to get out of this hell with no further casualties.

I had survived!

Stackpole Military History Series

Real battles. Real soldiers. Real stories.

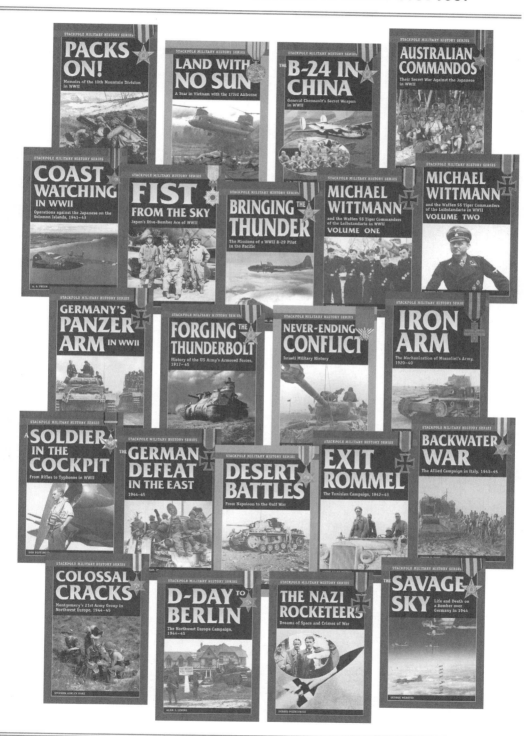

Stackpole Military History Series

Real battles. Real soldiers. Real stories.

Stackpole Military History Series

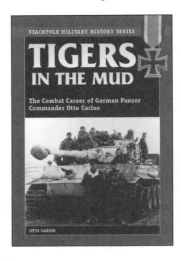

TIGERS IN THE MUD
THE COMBAT CAREER OF GERMAN PANZER
COMMANDER OTTO CARIUS

Otto Carius,
translated by Robert J. Edwards

World War II began with a metallic roar as the
German Blitzkrieg raced across Europe, spearheaded
by the most dreadful weapon of the twentieth century:
the Panzer. Tank commander Otto Carius thrusts the
reader into the thick of battle, replete with the
blood, smoke, mud, and gunpowder so common
to the elite German fighting units.

$19.95 • Paperback • 6 x 9 • 368 pages
51 photos • 48 illustrations • 3 maps

WWW.STACKPOLEBOOKS.COM
1-800-732-3669

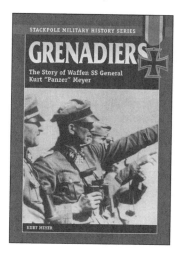

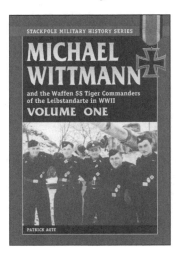

Stackpole Military History Series

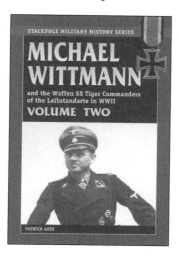

MICHAEL WITTMANN AND THE WAFFEN SS TIGER COMMANDERS OF THE LEIBSTANDARTE IN WORLD WAR II

VOLUME TWO

Patrick Agte

Barely two months after leaving the Eastern Front,
Michael Wittmann and the Leibstandarte found themselves in
Normandy facing the Allied invasion in June 1944. A week after D-Day,
Wittmann achieved his greatest success, single-handedly destroying
more than a dozen British tanks and preventing an enemy
breakthrough near Villers Bocage. He was killed several months later
while leading a Tiger battalion against an Allied assault. The
Leibstandarte went on to fight at the Battle of the Bulge and in
Hungary and Austria before surrendering in May 1945.

$19.95 • Paperback • 6 x 9 • 400 pages • 287 photos • 15 maps • 7 charts

WWW.STACKPOLEBOOKS.COM
1-800-732-3669

Stackpole Military History Series

ARMOR BATTLES
OF THE WAFFEN-SS
1943–45

Will Fey, translated by Henri Henschler

The Waffen-SS were considered the elite of the
German armed forces in the Second World War and
were involved in almost continuous combat. From
the sweeping tank battle of Kursk on the Russian
front to the bitter fighting among the hedgerows
of Normandy and the offensive in the Ardennes,
these men and their tanks made history.

$19.95 • Paperback • 6 x 9 • 384 pages
32 photos • 15 drawings • 4 maps

WWW.STACKPOLEBOOKS.COM
1-800-732-3669

Stackpole Military History Series

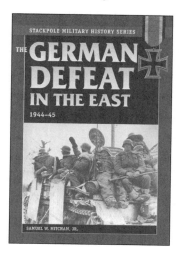

THE GERMAN DEFEAT IN THE EAST
1944–45
Samuel W. Mitcham, Jr.

The last place a German soldier wanted to be in 1944 was the Eastern Front. That summer, Stalin hurled millions of men and thousands of tanks and planes against German forces across a broad front. In a series of massive, devastating battles, the Red Army decimated Hitler's Army Group Center in Belorussia, annihilated Army Group South in the Ukraine, and inflicted crushing casualties while taking Rumania and Hungary. By the time Budapest fell to the Soviets in February 1945, the German Army had been slaughtered—and the Third Reich was in its death throes.

$19.95 • Paperback • 6 x 9 • 336 pages • 35 photos • 21 maps

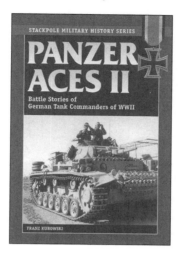

Stackpole Military History Series

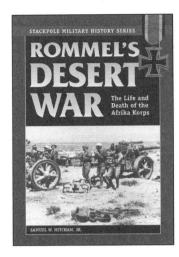

ROMMEL'S DESERT WAR
THE LIFE AND DEATH OF THE AFRIKA KORPS
Samuel W. Mitcham, Jr.

In a series of battles marked by daring raids and quick
armored thrusts, Erwin Rommel and his Afrika Korps
waged one of World War II's toughest campaigns in
the North African desert in 1942. In June the Desert
Fox recaptured Tobruk, a triumph that earned him a
field marshal's baton and seemed to put all of North
Africa within his grasp. By fall, however, after setbacks
at Alam Halfa and the battles of El Alamein, the Afrika
Korps teetered on the brink of destruction.

$16.95 • Paperback • 6 x 9 • 272 pages • 19 b/w photos, 13 maps

Stackpole Military History Series

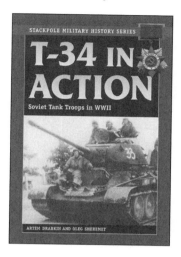

T-34 IN ACTION
SOVIET TANK TROOPS IN WORLD WAR II
Artem Drabkin and Oleg Sheremet

Regarded by many as the best tank of World War II, the Soviet T-34 was fast, well-armored, and heavily gunned—more than a match for the German panzers. From Moscow to Kiev, Leningrad to Stalingrad, Kursk to Berlin, T-34s rumbled through the dust, mud, and snow of the Eastern Front and propelled the Red Army to victory. These firsthand accounts from Soviet tankmen evoke the harrowing conditions they faced: the dirt and grime of battlefield life, the claustrophobia inside a tank, the thick smoke and deafening blasts of combat, and the bloody aftermath.

$16.95 • Paperback • 6 x 9 • 208 pages • 40 photos, 5 maps

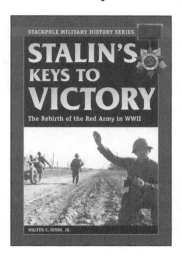

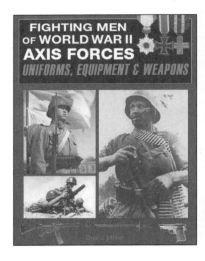
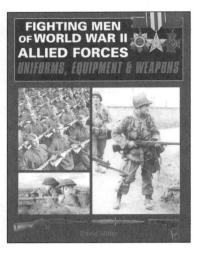